GW00976041

DARE WE TRUST THEM?

A New Vision for Europe

DARE WE TRUST THEM?

A New Vision for Europe

John Macdonald
with
Sir Andrew Bowden

The Book Guild Ltd
Sussex, England

First published in Great Britain in 2005 by
The Book Guild Ltd
25 High Street
Lewes, East Sussex
BN7 2LU

Copyright © John Macdonald and Sir Andrew Bowden 2005

The right of John Macdonald and Sir Andrew Bowden to be
identified as the authors of this work has been asserted by them
in accordance with the Copyright, Designs and Patents Act 1988.

All rights reserved. No part of this publication may be
reproduced, transmitted, or stored in a retrieval system, in any
form or by any means, without permission in writing from the
publisher, nor be otherwise circulated in any form of binding
or cover other than that in which it is published and without a
similar condition being imposed on the subsequent purchaser.

Typesetting in Times by
Keyboard Services, Luton, Bedfordshire

Printed in Great Britain by
CPI Bath

A catalogue record for this book is available from
The British Library

ISBN 1 85776 980 5

This book is dedicated to the town of Winchelsea and its warm and hospitable people.

The authors chose Winchelsea as their writing base for its charm and tranquillity.

We little realised at that time that it was once the base for Simon de Montfort who led an early rebellion against 'foreign influences on our constitution'.

Contents

Europe is currently in chaos, without direction or a sensible set of priorities for its future. Strong diversity of opinion between individual state governments and between governments and their people threaten a concerted European ideal. The lack of vision or political and organisational principles that can be shared by all is at the heart of this chaos. Part One examines the present state of Europe and the elements of division.

This chapter traces the roots of the European movement, following the devastating shock of the First World War.

Two treaties too far? This chapter examines the political acceptance of lost direction, the fudging and compromise of principle and the lost opportunities. The growth of the doctrine of inevitability.

An examination of the differing objectives and attitudes of France, Germany, Italy, Britain and others. Hidden agendas and political manipulation of the community's institutions have bedevilled Europe and are potentially dangerous for the future.

The authors have argued that the man from Whitehall does not always know best. They view the growing power of the Commission and other European institutions with a similar horror. This chapter examines the creeping paralysis and corruption emanating from Brussels.

The divergence of economic objectives and methods between the UK and the combination of France and Germany endangers the future of the European Union. The blind race to some form of single state before this divergence is resolved is economic madness.

The mindless haste with which the Single Currency has been introduced is dividing Europe to no purpose. This chapter examines the tensions and distortions of economic common sense that may be catastrophic.

PART TWO: FUTURE UNCERTAINTIES 181

Part One made clear that a purposeful fog surrounds the future of Europe. To disperse the fog the authors contend that three key issues need to be brought out into the open, debated and resolved.

PART THREE – A NEW VISION 243

The authors present their own vision of the future. They are convinced that the present state of the European Union is far from that vision and fear that it may be drifting onto the rocks. They explain their commitment to evolution rather than revolution. They are convinced that all the issues of a thousand years of history cannot be resolved in a couple of decades. There is time for a re-think.

Foreword

My views on the European Community have always been straightforward and clear.

In what some political historians might see as a Conservative tradition, I am a pragmatist about the European Union. When I was Prime Minister that led the more extreme protagonists in the European debate to argue that I had no views on the issue, since I did not agree with them: that is not, and never was, so. I believe it is in our economic interests to be a member of the EU. I welcome sensible co-operation with our European neighbours. I have no hang-ups about Germany. I fully accept that being one of a Community of nation states means that sometimes we have to reach a consensus that is not entirely to our taste.

Those views do not make me a Europhile, committed to the vision of a federal Europe. Britain must retain a significant level of independence in line with her historical role in Europe. Similarly, this does not make me a destructive Eurosceptic, always ready to condemn everything that emanates from Brussels.

During my premiership I had to endure continuing disputes about European policy that made the management of a small Parliamentary majority particularly difficult. At my first European Council meeting I was shocked to discover that Margaret Thatcher's strength of will had united most of the other members of the Community against Britain. As a result

I was keen to rebuild shattered fences, to prevent Britain from being seen forever as the odd one out, to be excluded from the private consultations that so often foreshadowed new policies in Europe. In this, I was only partially successful, for I soon saw the wholly different approach to the European Union that so often left Britain isolated.

In this book the authors describe themselves as Eurosceptics, but with a positive attitude that I easily accept. They seek the right answer rather than the fashionable one which echoes my own pragmatic approach to the European Union.

The authors' final chapters on a new vision for Europe contain some intriguing reforms for the organisation of the Union. I do not agree with them all, but they do inspire serious thought about how Europe should develop its future.

The Rt. Hon. John Major CH

Preface

This book has been written by John Macdonald and the term 'author' refers to John, but the contents represent the shared experiences, research and strongly argued opinions of both the writer and Andrew Bowden. In that sense both are authors of the book.

The authors' friendship dates back to the late 1940s. Both intended a political career and were active in the Young Conservative movement. Andrew became National Chairman of the YCs and John an elected Westminster City Councillor. They were both Parliamentary Candidates when they led a Conservative Party delegation to the Council of Europe in Strasbourg in 1962. Andrew had already moved the motion for Britain to sign the Treaty of Rome at the 1961 Conservative Party Conference. In other words they shared an active interest in Europe from an early stage.

Andrew went on to political success as a Member of Parliament, which included ten years as a member of the Parliamentary Assembly of the Council of Europe. John settled for an international business career that led to his success as a writer. His interest in Europe was maintained by his business involvement in Eastern Europe and a continuing social association with Provence.

The authors' friendship and collaboration has survived this ordeal. They still learn and argue, but happily somehow more often reach decisions rather than compromises.

Andrew Bowden, John Macdonald, Summer 2004

Acknowledgements

The authors did not create this book isolated in a closed room. Writing on such a wide subject, over a long period, is a culmination of shared experiences and relationships with many people. This motley band of family, friends and colleagues provided continual stimuli and constructive criticism. Many of them have read the manuscript at varying stages of its development. We view them all as collaborators, though, we release all of them from responsibility for the final result.

Clearly, acknowledgements are specific to either John or Andrew, but a large number are shared. Rather than detail the specific contribution of each we have listed them all below, in alphabetical order. However, we do wish to make special mention of a few, without whom we would probably not have completed the book:

- First, our wives, Anne and Benita, who were not only tolerant of our absences and tantrums but provided continuous positive support.
- Mary Hodge, Andrew's long suffering PA, who typed several versions of the original manuscript from John's illegible handwriting.
- Nigel Jones and Joanna Bentley our excellent editors.
- Three journalists who have been writing about the same subject throughout our six-year collaboration.

Without knowing it they have continually stimulated us with their writing; they are Andrew Alexander, Christopher Booker and Andrew Neill.

Our thanks for their help to David Atkinson MP, Sir Richard Body, Wing Commander David Bourne, David Callam, Ivor Caplin MP, Sir Sydney Chapman MP, Tom Cox MP, Michael Fabricant MP, Helen Farmer, the Rt Hon Frank Field MP, Roger Gale MP, Professor Al Gini (USA), Joan Hall CBE, John Haynes, Narinda Haynes, Dr Nigel Knight, Wayne Kost (USA), Bob Lapin (USA), Ruth Lea, Brian Long, Ian Matthews, George McGowan, Dr John Price, Joy Robilliard, Roy Smith, Sheila Stevenson (USA), Adam Trimingham, Linda Vincze (USA) and a special thank you to the Rt Hon John Major for his Foreword.

Introduction

The European Union is drifting on the stormy seas of global political and economic change without a chart or a compass. To make matters worse national politicians and bureaucratic interests have combined to shroud the whole journey in a purposeful fog. Since the early visionary days preceding the Treaty of Rome there has been little informed debate and certainly no democratic decision about the future nature and shape of the Union. The peoples of great nation states have been manipulated, step by step, from the original concept of a community of countries collaborating for their security and economic progress (*Europ des patries*) towards the growing likelihood of an autocratic super state. This is wrong and flies in the face of history. It is also highly dangerous for the British people and should be unacceptable to millions of other European citizens.

The Euro establishment have been preaching the doctrine of historical inevitability as their rationale for the inexorable march to federalism. The disparate peoples of Europe have been down this route many times before, to their cost. In the 20th century the *inevitable path* argument was used to support the advent and growth of Communism, Fascism, Socialism and even genocide. Between them these ideologies brought untold misery to the people of Europe. History has proved that there was nothing inevitable in the success of these now rejected answers to the social and economic ills of Europe.

1

Some leaders of the establishment have seen the European movement as an opportunity to bring back an elitist 'right to decide for all' through the back door. Their task has been made easier as the majority of the British people (and a substantial proportion of the continental electorate) have little knowledge of how the European institutions operate and until recently did not care. Powerful factions have used all the organs of state propaganda and the European Commission to cloud the issues by stealth. Perhaps the most pernicious example of this activity has been the campaign waged through the state school systems to influence future generations to accept the inevitability of the Federal state of Europe in the 21st century.

The process is being driven by the human weakness of wanting to see all the results of one's work in one's lifetime. All problems and philosophical issues that could delay decisions must be solved instantly. A pause for thought or debate is anathema and must be avoided at all costs. Politicians and ambitious academics are particularly prone to this weakness. Thus they want to constrain all thought and debate within one political term. When this becomes difficult, new answers are quickly invented and then proclaimed as faith, which all must accept. This quick fix approach leaves little time for analysis and even stifles debate. But there is no imperative for all the issues that arise from a thousand years of history to be solved in one generation. Europe needs evolution not revolution.

The present state of the EU provides a perfect example of an ever-present tendency in large-scale political management. As year by year the problems within the community and its institutions have become more complex and thus demand more time, there is a tendency to delegate or devolve them to permanent and non-elected officials or bureaucrats. Civil servants are masters at accruing power and revel in producing thousands of detailed directives, which are often incomprehensible to those they affect. Unbridled bureaucratic power always leads to that other deadly cancer: corruption. The European Commission has become too big, too powerful and too bureaucratic. That position was only slightly tempered by the scandals of 1999 that brought about the resignation of the Commissioners as a result of a resolution of the European Parliament.

Modern technology has encouraged a pernicious element in political organisation. The growth of the political soundbite culture and the methods employed to ensure unified communication of the authorised credo is one such element. The idea of serious political debate to arrive at the right decision is outside the comprehension of the modern political party *apparatchik*. There can be no shades of opinion; the individual position must be clearly labelled in black and white. All are now defined as Europhile, Eurosceptic or Don't Know and if the latter they obviously haven't turned on their pager. For most of this decade the Europhile has dominated the action without submitting to debate. They have managed to create an environment in which the Eurosceptic is the subject of contemptuous abuse. This whole approach is a patent nonsense and an abrogation of democracy.

In this context the term Eurosceptic is interesting. The future of Europe is not *divinely inspired* and so is not an article of *faith*. A doubting Thomas should be encouraged to ask searching questions *now* before irrevocable decisions are made.

There is now a growing scepticism in Britain about the current state of the EU and its future direction, and the British are not alone. *Dare We Trust Them?* The title of this book is a phrase that might well be heard in the capitals of most of the member states of the community. It is easy to forget how narrowly the referenda on Maastricht and the single currency were carried in France and Germany. Nor should we forget that it was General de Gaulle (often portrayed as an arch foe of Britain) who uttered the most powerful warnings about how the ideologists in the Commission might take Europe into a federal super state. De Gaulle and Thatcher had much in common – Europe misses their like.

In fairness to the reader the authors must here declare an interest. They are both active members of the Conservative Party and have no desire to change that allegiance. Both have also been involved in the European movement since the 1950s. But neither of them now believes that the present state and apparent future course of the European Union fits their original vision.

Within that context the authors recognise that there are strong and valid arguments for and against a single currency. There are strong and valid arguments for and against a federal Europe. There are many arguments about the European Constitution, the Common Agricultural Policy and the many other issues surrounding the future direction of the community. What they will not accept is that the federal state is inevitable and therefore that argument is a waste of time.

The authors therefore declare that this book was influenced by their common feeling for the destiny of the British people that has been forged over a thousand years of history. We humbly believe that there are many others in the European community of nations who have similar aspirations.

As a result the purpose of this book is threefold:

- To examine the current state of the European Union with objectivity and common sense.
- To consider the conflicting arguments over the future of the Union.
- To propose our own vision for the future of the Union and British involvement.

PART ONE

EUROPE IN CHAOS

Europe is currently in chaos, without direction or a sensible set of priorities for its future. Strong differences of opinion between individual state governments and between governments and their people threaten a concerted European ideal. The lack of vision or political and organisational principles that can be shared by all is at the heart of this chaos.

Chapter One

March From War

'The cankers of a calm world and a long peace.'

William Shakespeare, *Henry IV Part One*

You do not have to be anti-German or anti-French to be against the domination of Europe by either or both countries. You are just a citizen of an adjacent sovereign state exercising its historical role. You are not being 'extreme' or unleashing the 'forces of conservatism' to fear the possible subjugation by the alternative of a supranational state. This is particularly so if that alternative has never been openly debated. You are only being reasonable in the light of history. But in the soundbite language of today's politics you must be labelled 'Eurosceptic'.

The point about terms such as 'extremist', Europhile and Eurosceptic is that they are not used to promote debate and the sharing of ideas but to quote Andrew Alexander from his *Daily Mail* column, 'to end discussion by labelling rivals, or people one does not like, as in some way sinister or untrustworthy'. The authors admit to being Eurosceptic but not as an article of faith. Scepticism to them is really a questioning attitude to conventional or fashionable wisdom based on a desire to reach a truth that they can accept.

This questioning attitude has never been easy for political parties to accept. Throughout history politicians have been

7

jealous of the perceived power of Archbishops and Popes to declare their thoughts as divinely inspired and thus not open to question. Political leaders hanker after a world in which their speeches and statements are accepted as articles of faith to be proclaimed and obeyed by the faithful. In today's world the modern party political conference fulfils the role of the 'sermon on the mount' and spin doctors are substitutes for the apostles. In that context it is amusing to reflect on Prime Minister Blair's reaction to the 'heretic' Ken Livingstone whom he had 'excommunicated' but was unable to silence. The suspicion remains that, at the time, Blair would have liked to have had the power to burn Livingstone at the stake. Now to his chagrin he has had to welcome the heretic back into the fold. In truth political parties have a major advantage over churches in that they are not divinely inspired and defending the faith. They are allowed to welcome a doubting Thomas rather than reject him as 'ye of little faith'. In fact Thomas, the sceptic, provides an opportunity for reflection before rushing headlong toward an unknown objective. In view of their history this would seem to be a natural and sensible attitude for the British to adopt.

Historically the idea of a single Europe is not a new concept. Several Roman Emperors and a few Popes toyed with idea. Charlemagne, Charles V, Napoleon and Hitler, amongst a host of would-be Führer, brought a coerced unity for short periods but all collapsed, some, like the last, in devastating violence. But these were all false unities depending on conquest and the power to subjugate nation states. In the history of Europe each attempt to create empires or supra-national entities has sowed the seeds of its own destruction because it ignored an essential truth. The conglomeration of nations called Europe does not have common interests, a common culture or even a common language. The glory of Europe is its diversity not its unity. Short-lived conquest or

8

when its diverse interests coincided because of external threats, real or perceived has only achieved rare and short-lived periods of European unity.

A central argument of this book is that though we do not wish to repeat history, we ignore its lessons at our peril. Our long history has demonstrated that the diverse interests and cultures represented by the European national states are not mere tradition but are real and usually strongly supported by indigenous populations. From time to time, and sometimes over long periods, the interests of individual sovereign states converge and alliances are formed. It is also true that outside influences such as fear for survival can greatly broaden common interests. Logically we must also accept that outside opportunities, such as the global economy, could have a similar effect. However, it is essential to remain aware that the powerful diversity of interests in Europe is as relevant today as it was in the past. The recent wars in the Balkans and the Austrian conflict with Brussels only serve to underline this truth. Whether imposed or entered into voluntarily, any attempt to build a *new Europe*, which ignores this self-evident truth, is doomed to failure.

The judgment that we are seeking to make in this book is whether the future development of Europe can be channelled into a path that encompasses what Sir Richard Body in his book has called 'a Europe of many circles' or is on the road to ruin culminating in a federal Europe. Whether driven by a fear of survival or chasing the false gods of global opportunity, the authors believe that the latter course will lead to a new world megastate of subjugated national states, cultures and peoples. We do not believe that the British people are automatically hostile to the concept of a united Europe and are ready to leave the European Union. However, we do believe that they are as instinctively suspicious of the 'man from Brussels' as they have always been of the 'man from Whitehall'. Currently the British are even more suspicious of the Euro and where it may lead, but they are not prepared to jump on a fanatical anti-Euro bandwagon. Like Thomas, the British people have not yet made up their minds and would like more evidence. That is not weakness but evidence of a strong inner conviction that would prefer the right decision to the quick decision.

For most of its long and evolving history the entity of Europe was maintained by the concept of the balance of power. Allegiances were formed to ensure that no one national state or group of states could organise their political, economic and military power to dominate Europe for their own ends. As new threats or opportunities arose, individual nations or groups of nations would enter into new alliances and treaties to maintain the balance. Some of these alliances used war to protect a common interest. Others ensured peace for long periods. It is worth noting that the balance of power produced longer periods of peace and stability than is generally recognised.

The system of shifting national interests and alliances reached its epoch with the Concert of Nations in 1815, which concluded the Napoleonic era and brought about a period of more than fifty years of peace, stability and economic progress for Europe. Over the following fifty years a combination of old and new enmities threatened the balance and Europe was plagued with revolution, rampant nationalism and competitive imperialism that culminated in the First World War. The ensuing four years of conflict dramatically changed the relationship between states and ended the very existence of many. Above all, the sheer futility and horror of the war led Europeans and others to turn their backs on the previous order and to seek solace in new ideologies such as Communism, Socialism and Fascism. These all-encompassing utopias hypnotised many, and the remainder were so shell shocked that they readily put their faith in new solutions such as the League of Nations.

10

The League was established to rid the world of the pestilence of war. This ephemeral supranational authority fostered the Kellog-Briand pact that outlawed war and was signed by 64 nation states. Without any power to support its decisions or pacts the League relied on admonishment to urge states to settle their grievance by debate or arbitration. Aggressive nations around the world sensed that the reality of the balance of power was waning. Germany, Japan, Russia and even Italy in Abyssinia seized their chance and soon the world was once again plunged into another global war. In recoiling from the monstrous reality of twelve million dead in the First World War the nations of Europe ignored historical precedent and plunged the world into the Second World War and a further forty million victims who were witnesses to the failure of false dreams. Supranational ideologies and authorities had proved to be even less successful than the old concept of the balance of power.

The importance of the balance of power to the arguments in this book is twofold. First that England and its later incarnations as Great Britain and the United Kingdom has relied on the concept, throughout its history, to preserve its own national interests and independence. The second element is that at Maastricht in February 1992, the then twelve member states of the EU signed a treaty which proclaimed in Title V that a *'common, foreign and security policy is hereby established'*. In other words that the UK had now abrogated its historical role to a supranational collective; a massive surrender of our traditional and proven national rights and sovereignty.

For centuries, maintaining the balance of power in Europe was the principal driver in English diplomacy. As an island and a maritime European state its survival and economic growth depended on free trade with Europe and *the rest of the world*. This need demanded free access to ports and freedom for its unarmed merchant vessels to sail worldwide

11

shipping lanes at will. England's policy naturally competed with the other European maritime states of Spain, France, Holland and the city states of Italy. In the interests of England none of these competitors could be allowed to become too powerful and dominate the sea-lanes of the world or the coastline of Europe. As a result England was involved in constantly changing alliances to maintain a balance of power. Perhaps this manipulative history accounts for the deeply felt suspicion that other Europeans have for 'Perfidious Albion'.

Of course it must be admitted that Britain's historical role has always been to ensure the division rather than the unity of Europe. However, it can also be said that the interests of these small islands have often coincided with the interests of a wider Europe. In opposing tyrannical opponents to its own interests, such as Philip II of Spain, Louis XIV, Napoleon, Kaiser Wilhelm II and Hitler, Britain could truly have been judged as also supporting the interests of the majority of European states. Britain's strength in each of those periods was its uncomplicated focus on the real issue.

For a long time Spain, Holland and France were the natural enemies of England. Prussia and the central European nations posed no direct threat and so became allies or parties to discrete alliances of mutual interest. Portugal, though also a maritime state, became Britain's oldest ally. She needed England's protection to ensure her independence from her more powerful neighbours and was also able to provide strategic ports for the English Navy. It was only the egotistical decision of Kaiser Wilhelm II to challenge England head on and start the construction of a German High Seas Fleet that disrupted this traditional pattern of a European balance of power.

But the natural element in these enmities also contained a shared mutual respect for competing interests. Their competitive interests arose primarily from economic motives in contrast with the racial or ethnic rivalry so common in Southern European states. This love-hate relationship is important in that it provided a relatively easy transition to a new balance. As the newly unified Germany began to flex her muscles and seeks its own *Lebensraum* the traditional enemies, Britain and France were able to establish another alliance, the *entente cordiale* in 1904 to protect new common interests.

As an aside, but relevant to this complex mosaic of attitudes that are germane to the argument, the author has never forgotten his first visit to the French Naval Museum in Toulon. The museum is imaginatively laid out and uses beautiful models of French warships to illustrate the dramatic history of the French Navy. Viewing the exhibits was a traumatic experience for two impressionable Englishmen. With few exceptions every description of a great ship was concluded with the phrase, sunk by, burned by or captured by the English. An easy triumphal attitude was quickly tempered by later exhibits and references to the more recent engagement at Mers-el-Kebir (the tragic episode in July 1940, still bitterly resented by France, when Churchill ordered the Royal Navy to attack the French Fleet to ensure that it did not fall into German hands). The realisation that so many of the citizens of Toulon had been sacrificed to our joint histories was added to similar feelings on visiting the battlefields of the Somme, Verdun and the horrifying mountain battles of the Izonzo between Italy and Austria-Hungary. Those attitudes have served to maintain the dream of a Europe united in a partnership of interest to avoid a senseless repetition of a terrible shared history.

Despite or perhaps because of these strong human emotions, it is vital to remember that all these horrors were perpetrated in the name of national interests. The temptation is to claim that all these national interests are now so obviously evil or outdated that they can be consigned to the back pages of history: filed under the apologetic title of an 'Imperialist Past'. The authors are not so sure and find this view too simplistic. But from the perspective of this chapter we need answers to the following two questions:

- What is Europe?
- When and why did the present proclaimed need for a *single* Europe emerge?

What is Europe?

At any stage of history an attempt to define Europe in terms of nations sharing an identity of culture or common purpose would be difficult. In such a vast area comprising so many sovereign national entities, the accident of geography alone divides interests and popular will. Additionally entrenched ethnic and religious beliefs born of history divide many countries from their neighbours. The whole concept of Europe is built on the shifting sands of national attitudes. However, geography naturally groups the nations into distinct areas of interest that can be loosely defined as the ocean or maritime states; the landlocked or central states; the southern states; and the eastern prairie states. Each group has some unity of culture, forged in history but the intrinsic interests of each will fluctuate depending on the current power potential of the group and its neighbours. Over history, the converging interests of these broad groups have served to define Europe.

One question has always bedevilled a complete definition of Europe. Is Russia part of Europe? The Russians themselves have been divided over the question, arguing between a strong western or European bias, a separate Slavic one, or even Orientals. This question is particularly important today as we witness a massive re-alliance of interests in the southern and eastern states following the collapse of communism and the Soviet Union. These new alliances have been welcomed by the ocean states where they are seen as a counterbalance to the newly unified Germany and as a token security in seemingly pushing the boundary of Europe further to the East. But suppose a new Russia under a new strong leader was able to harness market forces to match the real potential of Russia's resources and her people? Would this create a new centre of gravity or economic interest for countries such as Ukraine, Belarus, Rumania or Poland? The problem lies in that vast hinterland to the east of the Urals, but if we consider Russia part of Europe then in the future the EU could be the second Union in the world that stretches from the Atlantic to the Pacific.

This change of perspective has already provided one major jolt to the EU and France in particular. Chancellor Helmut Kohl's rapid re-unification of Germany took Europe by surprise and was accepted with little or no debate in the EU, yet it took the EU boundaries deep into the east and created a host of new problems. As one French politician said 'he liked Germany so much that he was glad that there were two of them'. The move has re-awakened French fear of Germany and has motivated her to push for faster and deeper integration to 'lock Germany' into the new Europe.

The original co-signatories of the Treaty of Rome were only prepared to accept six nations whom they considered had enough common interests to form the original European Economic Community. The initial success of the EEC and, to some extent, perceived economic and political threats from outside, have led another nineteen nations to join the now renamed European Union.

Since the collapse of the Soviet Union many other states have now joined the Union but the EU still only represents about half of the nation states that consider themselves as part of Europe. The total number of nations that see themselves as European is 38, give or take the odd principality. In addition there are peripheral states such as Israel, Turkey and Lebanon and to a lesser extent the North African nations who have a closer affinity with Europe than with Africa or Asia. The United Nations body, the Economic Commission for Europe, OECD and the Council of Europe are the only organisations that can truly claim to represent the interest of most European countries.

The question 'what is Europe?' raises many issues beyond which countries we include in a definition of Europe. We have noted the cultural diversity of the nations that currently form the EU. As culture really represents the attitudes and aspirations of nation states it is a vital issue in considering the future of the EU. Reflect for a moment on the difficulties the EU has faced in satisfying the cultures of Germany, France and the UK. Now envisage a meeting of the Council of Ministers that included the Ukraine, Turkey, Poland, Cyprus and Slovenia. Cultural diversity could become a fish too big to swallow. In the next chapter we will concentrate on these cultural diversities. In Part Three we will discuss and make proposals for an EU organisation that could bring the benefits of free trade and community collaboration to the mutual benefit of all. The real challenge is to achieve this common purpose without the dangers inherent in trying to force all countries to comply with the common interests of a small core. Europe is a much greater concept than merely solving the historic problems between France and Germany.

The need for a single Europe?

The long drawn out Versailles Peace Conference following the defeat of the Central Powers in 1918 planted the seeds that would take nearly forty years to bloom. The arguments were dominated by a total abhorrence of war, but were strongly divided over how to achieve a peaceful Europe.

Broadly these arguments could be summarised as the reconciliation route (President Wilson) versus the victor's route, which was to crush Germany and her ability to make war. The final Treaty of Versailles adopted the victor's route but at the same time spawned the League of Nations that represented the other side of the argument.

The League espoused worthy ideals that all nations could support in the abstract but did not support in practice. It sought to settle disputes by arbitration and to use collective force against aggressors. It was the forerunner of the United Nations to whom it transferred its remaining operations in 1946. The League was unable to practice its peace-keeping role because the key powerful nations who might have made it effective did not really participate. Of the European powers only France fully participated due to the influence of the pacific Premier Aristide Briand. The USA returned to isolationism. Great Britain, Germany and Russia did not sign the Geneva Protocol of 1924 on the settlement of disputes. So the great nations drifted, without clear-cut objectives and workable alliances, towards the Second World War.

Throughout the twenties two men dominated the forward *thinking* for Europe. Both had formerly led their countries. Both now served as foreign ministers and played a formidable part in the League of Nations. They were Gustav Stresemann, ex-Chancellor of Germany, and Aristide Briand, ten times Premier of France. In 1925 Stresemann obtained Germany's return as an accepted member of Europe and the League of Nations in the Locarno Pact. Briand supported Franco-German reconciliation, and was a close collaborator with Stresemann on the Locarno Pact. He then turned his attention to the Kellog-Briand pact for the renunciation of war and his concept for *European union*.

Briand's proposals for European union were first raised in a speech to the Assembly of the League of Nations on 5th September 1929.

17

'I think that among peoples constituting geographical groups, like the people of Europe, there should be some kind of federal bond..., obviously, this association will be primarily economic, for that is the most urgent aspect of the question ... still, I am convinced that this federal link might do useful work politically and socially, and without affecting the sovereignty of any of the nations belonging to the association...'

(quoted from Norman Davies, *A History of Europe*).

This is an outline for European union that most people in Britain would find acceptable today. Indeed, many current Eurosceptics would say that Briand's description fits the union they thought they were joining in 1972. Briand later chaired a sub-committee of the League set up to examine his proposals that were developed further in a detailed Memorandum published in May 1930. It called upon the 27 European members of the League to study a range of issues including finance, labour, trade and inter-parliamentary relations with a view to setting up a European Union. It is interesting that among all the national responses to the Memorandum only the Dutch noted that such a union involved a reduction of sovereignty. But events overtook Briand and diverted the attention of Europe's leaders. The Wall Street crash of 1929 brought the economic depression to Europe. Stresemann died in 1929 and Briand died in 1932. At his death his contribution to Europe was widely recognised. British statesman Austen Chamberlain noted that 'There is no one of his stature left' but his ideas were put on the backburner for more than a decade.

Jean Monnet has been called the 'father of the European movement' and if that is so his fellow countryman Briand could be considered the grandfather. The connection is apposite because Monnet first came to international attention as Deputy Secretary General of the League during the 1930s and is credited with giving Winston Churchill the idea for a Franco-British Union in 1940.

Stresemann, Briand and Monnet represented a strong strand of thought which dominated the twenties as politicians recoiled from the Great War. But the striving for peace and co-operation was steadily submerged during the thirties as the same politicians wrestled with the problems of economic depression and the rise of new nihilist doctrines such as Nazism and Stalinism. Booming populations arising from industrialisation had been exacerbating the sense of injustice throughout the 19th century. To this potent mixture was added the hopeless futility of war fought on an industrial scale, which finally destroyed the faith and cohesion of the old order. The ideologies of Communism, its softer variant Socialism and Fascism provided new Platonic utopias and fell on fertile ground. These new political forces were seemingly implacable foes and yet in practice exhibited similar totalitarian tendencies. Europe first and then the rest of the world were soon embroiled in a conflict which was to exceed even the horror of the First World War.

This is not the place to dwell on the Second World War other than to note some aspects of European unity that arose on both sides of the conflict. The totalitarian nations each in their way had a vision of a unified Europe, though they intended, as in the past, to accomplish their ends through subversion, coercion or conquest. Italy's fascist dictator Mussolini had ludicrous dreams of rebuilding the Roman Empire but his armies in Abyssinia and Albania hardly emulated Caesar's legions. Russia's Communist boss Stalin used his opportunities in defeating Hitler's Germany to subvert or coerce most of the nations of eastern and central Europe. For a short time it seemed possible that communism might capture Italy and France. But Russia was never able to breach President Truman's line of containment in the west. Norman Davies in his *History of Europe* reminds us that Nazi Germany was looking for more than *Lebensraum*, had ideas for a racially united Europe, and published a journal called *Nation Europa*.

No one could possibly accuse modern Germany of Nazi racial aspirations but there are many in Europe who are concerned that there is still an element of Himmler's phrase *It is natural, that the German nation, as the largest and the strongest, must assume a leading role'*. Recent evidence that this arrogance lingers is seen in Chancellor Gerhard Schroeder's initial horrified reaction to Vodafone's bid for the German company Mannesmann. It seemed that it was natural for German firms such as BMW to take over British car-makers Rover but a totally different matter for a British telecommunications company to take over the leading German company in the field.

The democratic nations also gave some thought to unity and a supranational approach to issues during the Second World War. At first these ideas stemmed from the need for survival but later, as victory seemed assured, attention turned to looking forward to the post-war peace.

The most startling idea of all was proposed by Jean Monnet in June 1940. He suggested a Franco-British union and persuaded both Churchill and de Gaulle to accept his plan to prevent the French government surrendering to the Germans. In that sense the idea was a failure, but it has some intriguing aspects. The proposals amounted to the merger of the French and British peoples into one nation. In view of the nationalistic beliefs of Churchill and de Gaulle and the current arguments about national sovereignty, it is staggering that such a concept should ever have seen the light of day. Perhaps it was a case of the old adage 'the fact that you are to be hanged tomorrow tends to concentrate the mind today'.

Jean Monnet who had collaborated with Aristide Briand's schemes for European union in the early thirties was later to become the real architect of what was to become the EU. Both these Frenchmen were internationalists, but Monnet in particular had close working relations with the British. He spent the First World War working in London on financial planning before moving to the League of Nations. During the Second World War he worked in Washington as a 'British' official. In 1944 he returned to France and was charged with designing France's economic recovery. He was to be the leading light in the moves to European integration and was the direct link from the thinking of Stresemann and Briand to the present day.

In 1940 with France and her other continental allies defeated and occupied by Germany, Britain had to turn to America for help. Winston Churchill was steeped in European history and had written an acclaimed biography of his great ancestor John Churchill, Duke of Marlborough, who in his time had been master of the European battlefields. But Churchill's mother Jenny had been an American, which gave him a romantic attachment to the USA and the idea of a concert of the English speaking peoples. This dichotomy of allegiances is still a live factor in the arguments over Britain's future in Europe. Churchill built a strong relationship with President F. D. Roosevelt well before the Japanese attack on Pearl Harbor brought the USA into the war in December 1941. In August 1941 they had signed the Atlantic Charter that established principles for the later United Nations Charter. These principles included *'the countries seek no aggrandisement, territorial or other ... to respect the rights of all people to choose the form of government under which they will live ... and the abandonment of the use of force'*. The Atlantic Charter was a powerful unifier. It led to the Washington Pact of January 1942 in which twenty-six Allied nations undertook not to sign a separate peace with any of the Axis Powers. The continuing discussion between those states was to lead directly to the replacement of the League of Nations by the United Nations.

The Second World War was won in 1945, but was not really over. Its consequences and the diverse attitudes it engendered amongst both victors and vanquished would permeate European deliberations for a very long time to come. Now a devastated, exhausted and, practically bankrupt Europe had to pick up the pieces and concentrate on managing the peace. The immediate issue was what to do with the defeated Germany, once Europe's most powerful economy. Its cities lay in ruins and much of its industry was destroyed or was being dismantled by the victors. Apart from the Germans there were millions of displaced Europeans. Many were survivors of the slave labour system and the concentration camps, lost in Germany and in search of family and homes. A series of questions dominated this period and their eventual answers would help shape the future of Europe:

- Who was going to feed and care for these millions of displaced persons and how was it to be done?
- How was the pestilence of Nazi ideology to be eliminated from Germany and indeed the whole of Europe?
- Who was to be responsible for reviving viable and self-sufficient economies throughout Europe and how was it to be achieved?

In answering these questions other issues would arise which would become crucial to the future unity of Europe.

- How would the continent be organised to make competitive war in Europe unthinkable?
- How would the European nations with an imperial past adapt to the 'winds of change' of decolonisation?
- How would Europe relate to the new super-powers, the USSR and the USA, who had emerged from the Second World War?

Few of these questions were spelled out to the peoples of Europe as the basis for specific policies, but all influenced the political and economic thinking of international decision makers. Each of the questions would justify a whole book to examine their ramifications but in this book we can only give a cursory examination of the issues relevant to our general thesis.

The Marshall Plan

In 1947 General George Marshall, President Truman's Secretary of State and wartime US Army Chief of Staff, announced the European Recovery Program that was to bear his name as the Marshall Plan. Though the Plan had elements of U.S. self-interest, it was unique in all history as an act of incredible generosity. The Plan distributed a total of $12,500 million until the end of 1951 between sixteen participating European nations. Though Britain and France were the major beneficiaries, some nonetheless went to allies, neutrals and ex-enemies. The Plan was overseen by the organisation that later became the OECD.

Russia ordered her East European satellite countries not to accept any Marshall aid and branded the USA as the new imperialists. Yet in truth the Plan insisted that the funds were only available to nations that would dismantle trade barriers and take action to increase production and hasten their own recovery. The Marshall Plan set Western Europe on the road to recovery and prosperity and together with NATO, signalled that there was to be no return by the USA to the isolationism that followed the First World War.

De-Nazification

There was initial enthusiasm among the occupying powers (shocked by the awful reality of the liberated concentration camps) to de-Nazify Germany and bring war criminals to justice, but this soon abated. The British Foreign Office and the US State Department had other priorities and ignored or obfuscated orders to hunt down and prosecute the perpetrators of the greatest crimes in history. Tom Bower, in his book, *Blind Eye to Murder*, has produced incontrovertible evidence that both bureaucracies ensured that thousands of guilty Germans were simply reinstated in the professional elite of European society.

Of approximately 150,000 known individuals identified for immediate arrest in 1945, only 30,000 had been brought to justice by the early 1960s, and the vast majority of those were in Eastern Europe. Expediency, as a reaction to a growing Communist threat, capitalist competition for industrial and military technology and a sickening old boy network of elitism allowed criminal backgrounds to be 'lost' and terrible guilt to be forgotten or absolved.

Some current Eurosceptics argue that this same hidden network of international mandarins, industrialists, lawyers and financiers lies behind an inexorable movement towards a single European state. A clandestine elitist euro club that believes that it knows what is best (for them) and uses their power to make it happen. (See Appendix: The Bilderberg Group.)

The emergence of the European movement

As early as 1946 Winston Churchill, in his famous speech at Fulton, Missouri, warned that 'an iron curtain was descending across the continent'. His speech, together with a growing awareness of the Soviet subversion of the eastern European states behind the Iron Curtain, changed the perspectives of both Europeans and Americans. Fearful of the growing Russian menace, five countries (Belgium, Britain, France, Holland and Luxembourg) formed an alliance providing for economic and military co-operation. The Brussels Treaty of 1948 was to lead to the Western European Union and to the North Atlantic Treaty Organisation. Both organisations were to have a major influence on the future of Europe.

The Soviets misread the growing awareness and collaboration between the west Europeans and the United States. In 1948 seeing what they thought was a weak and divided alliance they attempted to throw the Western allies out of Berlin. By closing all rail and road links to Berlin (which lay deep within the Soviet sector of occupied Germany) against all international agreements they established a blockade which they assumed would lead to the withdrawal of allied forces. They were thwarted by the dramatic success of the 'Berlin airlift' that for over a year supplied and fed not only the allied occupation forces but also the German population of West Berlin. Very few recognise the debt the West owes to the American General Turner, who commanded the airlift and achieved a logistical victory unsurpassed in history.

The USA had attempted to build bridges with the Russians by including the east Europeans in Marshall Aid, but Stalin was having none of it and continued on his own path to European union as part of the Soviet Communist empire. In response, the USA under the strong leadership of President Harry Truman, developed the policy of containment. In time the confrontation between the East and West became known as the 'Cold War'. Europe was in the front line of this new war.

In 1949 the North Atlantic Treaty was signed to establish an international organisation (NATO) to 'safeguard the freedom, common heritage and civilisation of its peoples, founded on the principles of democracy, individual liberty and law'. The primary purpose of NATO was the military defence of Western Europe, but its wider objectives were in tune with new political aspirations emerging in Europe. From the outset NATO included a much wider spectrum of Europe than the initial EEC. In time it was to expand its associates into the Eastern Bloc following the collapse of the Soviet Empire.

The success of NATO provided the spur for European political and economic collaboration, but it also provided an essential lesson for all those concerned with the future of supranational organisations. NATO is an international organisation of sovereign national states with a wide divergence of cultures and special interests. Yet they all collaborate in immense day-to-day actions and expenditures without sacrificing their independence and with little rancour. It is not necessarily structures such as federalism that guarantee success, but rather a *clear purpose*, openly agreed and supported by a continuing focus on the need for actions arising from the purpose.

Throughout this post-war period the merging European movement was active. A European Union of Federalists was formed in Montreux in 1947 and strands of British support were evident in the activities of the Moral Rearmament movement. Following his 'Iron Curtain' speech Winston Churchill returned to the subject at Zurich in September 1946 and called for 'a kind of United States of Europe'. He used the threat of the atomic bomb to press for early action and said that the first step was to be a partnership between France and Germany if 'we are to form a United States of Europe'. During this period Churchill frequently returned to and developed his theme for 'a fraternal association' of three interlocking circles made up of the British Commonwealth, the European Union and the United States. He envisaged that the British should act 'as the vital link between them all'. He may have defined the three-pronged stance of Britain toward Europe but this was all too much for the ruling Labour Party in Britain that stressed that 'no iota of British sovereignty was negotiable'.

But others were listening to Churchill and he was invited

to chair the Congress of Europe, a private conference held in The Hague in May 1948. A West German delegation attended, led by the future Chancellor Konrad Adenauer. This was a strong indication that Germany was once again emerging as a European nation.

Churchill told the Congress:

'We must proclaim the mission and design of a United Europe whose moral conception will win the respect and gratitude of mankind, and whose physical strength will be such that none will dare molest her tranquil way ... I hope to see a Europe where men and women of every country will think of being European as of belonging to their native land, and wherever we go in this wide domain we will truly feel "Here I am at home".'

The Congress closed by calling for the creation of a European Assembly and a European Court of Human Rights and established a liaison committee to keep the aims of the Congress alive. This Congress can rightly claim to being the birthplace of the modern European movement. The power and influence of its deliberations can be gauged from the fact that its honorary Presidents were statesmen of the calibre of Winston Churchill, Robert Schuman, Alcide De Gasperi and Paul Henri Spaak.

End of Empire

Europe was clearly in transition, but for some European nations there was another transition that was to absorb their attention and resources for some time to come. Within Western Europe were grouped the centres of great colonial empires which had largely survived the war. It soon became clear that Britain, Holland, France, Belgium and Portugal

27

would not be able to resist the winds of change and maintain their empires. France, Belgium and to a lesser extent Holland tried to resist the change with traumatic effects on their domestic politics. These traumas later led those nations to concentrate their minds on the developing EEC. The British Empire, the largest of them all moved fairly smoothly to its dissolution. The renamed British Commonwealth of Nations, which the UK used to assuage imperial pride and to help the peaceful transition from Empire, was to provide a diversion of focus. Britain, or at least Churchill, were initial leaders in the European movement but the end of the Empire and the need to support the Commonwealth provided some explanation for Britain's isolation from the founders of the new Europe.

As Norman Davies points out, nothing better reveals the divide between Eastern and Western Europe at this stage. 'At the very time that the Soviet Union was extending and consolidating its empire over the people of Eastern Europe, the imperial governments of Western Europe were desperately seeking to dismantle theirs'. Yet at that time few would have envisaged such a short life for the 'evil empire' of Soviet Russia.

At the heart of Europe

The 1948 Berlin blockade was a catalyst for the formation of the West German Republic. Though many West German leaders wanted to wait and battle for a united Germany, the blockade hastened the decision and the new constitution was passed in the very week that the blockade was lifted. The *Bundesrepublik* was formed with its capital in Bonn and a newly elected Chancellor, Konrad Adenauer, at the helm. The Soviets reacted quickly and formed the German Democratic Republic (DDR) in 1949 with its capital in East Berlin. The new republic was firmly under Communist control led by Walter Ulbricht. Two new European states had been established and now Germany, albeit divided, was back at the heart of Europe.

For the next forty years the two Germanys and the divided city of Berlin were to provide a unique controlled experiment into the efficacy of the opposing Capitalist and Communist systems. The two new republics formed from the same peoples, the same culture, the same language and the same shared history, were now to prove whether Soviet style communism or democratic capitalism were the better system for human development. It didn't need forty years. A little more than a decade later in 1961 the DDR erected the Berlin Wall that was soon extended to all its boundaries with West Germany. For the first time in history a nation was building a wall to keep its own people imprisoned rather than to keep enemies out. This highly visible experiment at the heart of Europe was to play a significant part in the final collapse of the Soviet Empire.

Historically always at the heart of Europe, France had ended the Second World War included with the victors. She took part in the occupation of Germany and was one of the 'Big Five' in the newly formed United Nations. However, this did little for French pride and national unity. The divisive experience of defeat, occupation and the hidden truths of collaboration were soon followed by the corrosive traumas of a collapsing empire. General de Gaulle had returned as 'liberator' and became the first President of the Fourth Republic but soon resigned in disgust at the divisive policies of the Communists and the *'Ponjadiste'* right wing. During the ill-fated Fourth Republic France was condemned to a new Prime Minister and a new government about once every six months. This destructive period was to last until the recall of de Gaulle in 1958 and the formation of the Fifth Republic. This decade of ineffective government and frustration led a large number of French politicians into active involvement with the alternative of a supranational European federal body and with a strong executive, prepared to resist the 'nonsense of democracy'.

The author has never forgotten an experience on his first visit to Paris in 1948. He watched a window cleaner tackling the display windows of the Galleries Lafayette department store. But he was only cleaning the windows as far as his hands could reach from his standing position on the pavement. The rest of the windows were left as he had found them – encrusted with years of grime. This visible image of a nation that had lost its pride and no longer cared was recalled to the author's mind during the 'winter of discontent' in Britain in 1978–79.

The European movement was growing apace but Britain declined to take the lead and place herself at the heart of Europe. The result of the Second World War had made Britain the natural leader of Europe and indeed Churchill, though in opposition, showed early enthusiasm for the concept of European unity. But diverted by the issues of Commonwealth and her 'special relationship' with the United States, Britain missed a great opportunity to define the future of Europe and has never returned to a central position. As a result the leadership of Europe in the fifties and sixties went by default to France. In July 1948 Vincent Auriol, the outgoing French Foreign Minister, made a strong speech in support of a European unification. This opened the door for his French colleagues Monnet, Schuman and Plevin to take the lead in the European movement.

Jean Monnet, as we have seen, was a fervent apostle of European union and was now heading the French National Economic Plan. He argued for *functionalism* or the steady transfer of national functions to supranational control. Robert Schuman, a long time supporter of Monnet, was now in a key position as Foreign Minister and he was joined by Rene Plevin, who had twice been Prime Minister. The importance of the friendships built at the Congress of Europe and its liaison committee now came to the fore. Schuman was now able to bring in Paul Henri Spaak, Alcide De Gasperi and had established a relationship with Konrad Adenauer. Spaak had been Foreign Minister, Finance Minister and Prime Minister of Belgium, and was the first President of the United Nations General Assembly. De Gasperi was Prime Minister of Italy and Adenauer was now Chancellor of the fledgling West Germany. A powerful and influential new euro club was now driving Europe forward.

The Council of Europe

The Council of Europe was formed in 1949 to promote European unity and was based in Strasbourg. Perhaps because of its situation it is often confused with the European Parliament or the European Council but it has no connection whatsoever with the European Union. Its original membership of ten countries soon expanded to eighteen members and included Britain from the outset. Britain was thus able to ensure that the Council had no supranational executive powers. For most Eurosceptics the Council of Europe represents the model for European cooperation that they wanted from the beginning. It has few executive powers and consults rather than determines. It produces no laws or directives and must convince council member governments by debate and research papers to amend their national legislation. However, it has produced the European Convention on Human Rights, the European Charter and other declarations, some of which have been adopted by the EU.

The Council has steadily lost authority as a forum for European issues though it has seen a resurgence in its potential influence as it now has representation from 44 states including former members of the Eastern Bloc and pivotal countries such as Turkey. Since the collapse of the USSR the Council has regained some influence as a point of contact between parliamentarians of the East and the West for countries such as Estonia, Latvia, Lithuania and others. Membership of the Council of Europe is also regarded as a staging post to membership of the European Union by countries such as Turkey. However, it now seems highly unlikely that the Council of Europe could offer any alternative to the EU.

An early shared experience of the authors in 1962 in many ways represented the then British attitudes to Europe. As callow Parliamentary Candidates we were members of a Conservative Party delegation to the Council of Europe in Strasbourg. At that time our party, in power, with more important issues on its mind, sent junior level delegates whilst the party in opposition, with little to do, sent their most senior members. Our opposite number was George Brown, from the Labour Party. We were able to return to our constituencies and inform them that we had 'reached a wide measure of agreement' with the leaders of Europe and had made clear to General de Gaulle the 'views of Britain'. For us it was a great learning experience but our visit and those of many others made not an iota of difference.

Twenty-five years later, in 1987, Andrew Bowden was appointed by Margaret Thatcher to be one of the British representatives to the Parliamentary Assembly of the Council of Europe in Strasbourg and to the Western European Union based in Paris. For ten years he was 'at the heart of Europe' and has mixed views and recollections of this period in relation to both the usefulness of his role and to the activities of the Council.

Andrew notes that, on the day that Prime Minister, Margaret Thatcher, ' "invited" me to be one of Britain's representatives to the Council of Europe I admit that I only had a sketchy knowledge of its role and activities. I spent my first year

32

finding my feet and serving on a number of interesting committees. Towards the end of my second year I seriously thought of leaving the Council, as it was not much more than a talking shop. But I did find the social and political contacts with other democratically elected parliamentarians stimulating and worthwhile. The whole experience broadened my understanding of Europe and the views of countries as diverse as Finland and Portugal.'

Andrew continues: 'Then the Berlin Wall came down and there was a major change in the role of the Council. Older member countries gave encouragement and active support to the new fledgling democracies. Their representatives were eager to learn from us and to compare democratic institutions and methods. At this stage the Council was able to exert some influence on the EU and Europe as a whole. I remained on the Council until 1997.'

The Schuman Plan

The euro club had little time for the emasculated and powerless version of European unity represented by the Council of Europe. However, to be successful in its long-term aims it had to be wary of the Western alliance against the Communist threat. The USA and its closest ally Britain dominated the alliance. In essence the euro club produced a brilliant marketing plan. On the strategic level they produced far-reaching innovative visions for a future Europe. On the tactical level they concentrated on detailed plans to meet current economic and social problems. At the higher level they demanded the maximum but were prepared to settle for much less and were probably surprised by the level of agreement they achieved. At the lower level there was little opposition and the process of inevitability was born. The British and other independent minded European states are now paying a terrible price for British inactivity in the key formative period of the European movement between 1947 and 1951. This period provides some credibility for the argument that the UK must be at the heart of Europe.

The Schuman Plan of 1950 was the strategic element of the euro club's direction for Europe. It proposed a wide spectrum of economic, political and military supranational bodies. It called for an organisation managing key industries and the establishment of a European army. Taken together the Schuman Plan was nothing short of a blueprint for a United States of Europe. The Plan contained elements that were to divide Britain and the USA but (perhaps vitally) unified continental Europe. In the presentation and in the detail the Schuman Plan appealed to Franco-German reconciliation. Two European democratic Catholics (Schuman and Adenauer) with similar visions had apparently laid to rest the cancer of Europe in disunity. The confrontation between Germany and France appeared to be over. Who could resist that milestone? The strategic direction was accepted at a much higher level than the proponents expected.

The European Coal and Steel Community, set up in 1951, can be seen as the tactical element of the Schuman Plan. It was represented in the Plan as an approach to prevent the re-emergence of separate national military-industrial complexes and as such received widespread support. In the context of the times this was a highly emotional issue as the part played by Krupps, IG Farben and other industrial complexes in the Nazi regime became clear. It did not have the same impact in a Britain that had already nationalised the coal and steel industries. In retrospect the problems of these same industries that were to erupt in the 1980s in Britain might have been avoided by British participation in this community. France, in particular, noted this example of British coolness to the European movement. But the most important element of the Commission for our story is that this treaty brought together the original 'six member states' of the EEC in an active political participation.

There were elements of the Schuman Plan which ran into difficulty, in particular the military proposals which in some respects ran counter to deeper relations with NATO and other collaborative defence agreements. The Western European Union, formed in 1955, provided an annual review body but prevented further expansion in the military directions envisaged in the Schuman Plan. But no problem; the euro club now changed tack and concentrated on the economic elements of its strategy. It maintained its momentum and at the Messina Conference in 1955 it opened the drive for an economic community as the strategic priority. Before we consider the success of this approach and the Treaty of Rome, there are two other events that were to dominate European history for decades and influence its eventual direction. These were the German *Wirtschaftswunder* (economic miracle) and the return of General de Gaulle.

The Wirtschaftswunder

The image of a defeated Germany in 1945 was etched on the mind of history. The total destruction of German cities, her industry and millions of displaced people made such an impact that the energy of her recovery in such a short period seemed hardly possible and took the world by surprise. The *wunder* has remained to this day and undoubtedly enhanced German influence and her part in the growing union of Europe. Yet in reality the extent of this miracle was a myth. Germany had not surpassed her European colleagues by the end of the fifties or even by the end of the sixties. More accurately it should have been called the 'European Economic Miracle'. In fact the Italian *miracolo* was even more dramatic and she retained the highest GNP in Europe until the end of the sixties. By 1959 France,

Germany and Britain were very close in economic performance. Throughout the sixties France and Germany were close together playing catch up with the Italians, but the British lost their way and ended the period well behind the three leading European nations.

The initial phase of the widespread European recovery was undoubtedly due to the Marshall Plan. American aid had saved Europe and, to use the later economic term, 'primed the pump' and helped to re-establish industry and point investment in the right direction. A comparison with the progress over the same period of the eastern European nations is evidence enough of the dramatic impact of the Marshall Plan. But after 1951 Europe was on her own so national issues returned to the fore in attempting to evaluate what was happening. It is perhaps an oversimplification, but Britain seemed lost in trying to find its new role after Empire, to the extent that a torpor fell over its leaders and its people, which reached its nadir in the 'winter of discontent' of 1978/1979. On the continent, on the other hand, a new energy was galvanising nations. Monnet and Schuman had provided a fresh vision. We will never know what would have been the shape of the EU and what would have happened to Britain if the British leaders of the late fifties and sixties had enthusiastically followed Churchill's early lead and become deeply involved at the heart of Europe.

What we do know is that the euro club seized the moment with the message that has united central Europe for a long period: 'if we can do this individually, just look at what we can do together'. Economic success had now spawned European economic euphoria. It seemed, at the time, that the European Economic Community (EEC) would shortly rival and even surpass the United States. In their wildest dreams some believed that Europe was about to bestride the world like a colossus. Monnet and Schuman, had triumphed and their message was widely accepted and, to an extent, still is. This is the moment when the Europhile was born and its arch exponent, Edward Heath, began to influence the Conservative Party of Great Britain.

Chapter Two

Roads to Ruin: Rome, Maastricht and Amsterdam

'The destination will only reveal itself little by little.'

Jean Monnet

As the standard of living across Europe improved, the new collaborative message made sense. Let's bury the old historical enmities (and just to be on the safe side let's totally involve Germany so that we have none of that old nonsense about *Lebensraum*) and concentrate on the positive aspects of each nation, and so contribute to the common good. It was a seductive song that appealed to the predominantly Catholic Christian Democratic leadership of much of Europe. Of course it raised a whole series of political, ethnic and cultural issues. But for the moment they must remain unanswered as the economic argument holds the stage.

Unfortunately, Britain was not really involved in this debate but even if it had been it is not certain that they would have raised the essential question. 'Our current economic success has been achieved by individual sovereign national states managing their own economies, so what evidence do we have that by centralising those decisions in one supranational state it will produce an even greater success?' But, of course, that was not quite how the proposition

39

was put at the time of the Treaty of Rome or the British Referendum on joining the EEC.

The Return of the Prodigal

After Churchill the most towering personality on the post-war European stage was General de Gaulle. Churchill epitomised the 'British Bulldog' determination never to succumb to the Nazi hordes and in a similar vein de Gaulle represented the elusive *'gloire des Français'*. In 1958 he returned as the first President of the Fifth Republic, ostensibly to solve the Algerian problem. To the amazement of the world and some of his own right-wing supporters, the General exercised a complete *volte-face* in granting Algerian independence. Now that Algeria was 'out of the way' de Gaulle turned his attention to the wider issues of Europe.

The General, throughout the Second World War, had been a prickly ally of both the British and the Americans. There was never any doubt about his determination to protect the glory and the interests of France. During his involvement with the ill-fated Fourth Republic, General de Gaulle's opinions were clear and could be summed up as anti-American, anti-British, anti-German and certainly opposed to any idea of a federalist Europe. But his long reflective wilderness years in his home village of Columbey-les-Deux Eglises had changed the old warrior.

Back in power the General emerged as a passionate believer in Franco-German reconciliation and in collaboration to put their two nations at the centre of the new Europe. He toured Germany (as he was later to do in Poland and Canada with similar effect) and brought them back into the community of nations. It is difficult in hindsight to explain the influence of de Gaulle's personality on this period but at that time it was formidable. The Germans regained their political confidence to add to their economic muscle and returned to be a major player on the European scene. Britain, a little lost but still playing her traditional divide and rule role, had not taken part in the crucial discussions over the formation of the European Coal and Steel Community and so was excluded from the drafting of the Treaty of Rome and the formation of the European Economic Community (EEC). Watching this powerful new alliance emerging in the centre of Europe the UK desperately tried to form competing alliances of other nations excluded from the 'Six'. The European Free Trade Association (EFTA) was now formed by the seven leading European nations that had not been parties to the Treaty of Rome. EFTA never had the charisma and more important, the political and economic clout of the EEC. So Britain, the leader of EFTA, eventually decided to apply for entry to the EEC under the leadership of Premier Harold Macmillan.

France, but more specifically her leader, de Gaulle, vetoed British entry to the EEC. The General, perhaps correctly, saw Britain as giving only half-hearted allegiance to the European movement while developing her close special relationship with the USA. In his view the United Kingdom was intending to play Europe against America for its own ends. Rightly or wrongly the UK was not to join the EEC until after the death of General de Gaulle.

The Treaty of Rome

In March 1957 the Six signed the Treaty of Rome that established the European Economic Community (EEC). It is worth noting that from the outset in the UK, the EEC was usually referred to as the Common Market. To some extent that title obscured what was really happening, but it was a more comfortable idea for the British than envisaging a new supranational power in Europe. Now France, Germany, Italy and the Benelux countries were in a position to create and develop the short and long-term strategies and above all the operating cultures of the EEC. It would be fifteen years before Britain or any other nation would sit at the decision-making table. In essence, with the euro club leading, France, Italy and Germany were to shape progress at the centre of Europe.

Britain was in no position to object. She had dropped out of the original negotiations preceding the Treaty, concerned over sovereignty issues. In 1962 she changed her mind, but was then amazed when her application to join the EEC was defeated by the de Gaulle veto. As a first reaction to the federalist-leaning EEC, the UK took the lead in forming the European Free Trade Association (EFTA). The aim of EFTA was to establish a free trade area in Europe (a similar aim to that of the EEC) but without establishing supranational authority or uniform external tariffs. Britain was joined by Austria, Denmark, Norway, Portugal, Sweden and Switzerland (the Seven as opposed to the Six) and they were later joined by Finland, Iceland and Liechtenstein. But within eighteen months Prime Minister Harold Macmillan was applying for British membership of the EEC, only to be rebuffed by the French veto. Britain's lack of real commitment to EFTA had been clearly demonstrated. Eventually Britain and Denmark left EFTA to join the EEC, to be followed by Portugal, Austria, Finland and Sweden. Britain's first response to the loss of sovereignty to the EEC, by forming outside alliances, had dramatically failed. Now the UK had to achieve its aims from within the EEC and to sign the Treaty of Rome.

It is fashionable today for Europhiles and Eurosceptics to engage in pedantic arguments about whether the issue of loss of sovereignty and aims for a federal Europe are explicit in the Treaty of Rome. Certainly the Treaty is often regarded as the federalist bible but like the Bible it is open to many interpretations. In fact the Treaty is a moveable feast as it is constantly updated to reflect new Treaties. These alterations create a maze since documents are referred to Articles that now have different numbers. We should forget all this pedantic nonsense and allow common sense to prevail. The development of the Treaty of Rome from the Congress of Europe, the Schuman Plan and the European Coal and Steel Community are all logical steps in implementing the ideas of Jean Monnet and his apostles. The key elements of the Treaty were to remove all tariffs, to build a *common* external trade policy, to *harmonise* transportation, agriculture and *taxation.* But to harmonise taxation, for example, across fifteen nations, is a federal act. The terms federal or loss of sovereignty may not be specifically mentioned, but how could anybody conversant with the ideas of Monnet and Schuman come to any other conclusion about the purpose of the Treaty of Rome? In retrospect this is all clear now, but it was not so clear at the time. A purposeful fog has been created by the obfuscation and downright lies of leaders (the latest release of secret cabinet papers surely indict Edward Heath as a party to this deception) at each stage of the development of the EEC into the EU.

The signatories to the Treaty of Rome now settled down to melding their relationships within the EEC and concentrated on economic development. For the next twenty years the wisdom of the original decision seemed self-evident as their economies grew and their people prospered. The 'economic miracle' was well under way.

British Economic Decline

In Britain the picture was very different. She now entered into a long period of decline that was not to end until the 'Thatcher revolution' in the 1980s. The decline was evident in most facets of British life and culture and was much wider than mere economic performance. A tired nation had 'lost its role' and seemed to have no energy or spirit for the fight. In the 1960s, as the 'Profumo Affair' and the 'Poulson Case' unravelled, it seemed that the whole moral fibre of the nation was collapsing into hedonism and corruption. There is a lot of nostalgic nonsense talked in recalling the 'sixties'. For the majority of the British people it was a very difficult period. Not for nothing was Britain referred to as 'the sick man of Europe' towards the end of this decade.

On the British economic front the malaise went deep and was to make the eventual recovery painful. The nationalised industries had institutionalised bureaucracy and ludicrous management and union practices. As lame ducks they were subsidised by governments that created an environment, which led private industry down the same ruinous road. Continual strikes and inflationary settlements turned industry into a battlefield in which competitiveness and quality were sacrificed. It is worth recalling that during this period Britain lost its motor-cycle and bicycle industries, its radio and television manufacturing capacity, much of its car industry and most of its shipbuilding. Steel and coal were also in real trouble. At the same time Britain lost her traditional position as a leader in world trade and shipping. Management and union intransigence destroyed the competitiveness of British ports until finally the great Port of London was destroyed and the centre of sea trade moved to Rotterdam. The results of this economic decline were soon to follow with the collapse of Sterling and finally, in virtual bankruptcy, as Britain pleaded for help from the International Monetary Fund in 1976.

Neither of the British political parties covered themselves with glory during the sixties and seventies. The Conservative Party which took over from Clement Attlee's Labour administration in 1951 did make a start in deregulation and freeing the economy, but it did not have the courage to push back the socialist revolution and fully release the potential of the people. At heart it seemed to accept Labour Party rhetoric and was a little guilty about the 'class-ridden thirties' and so in a One Nation middle way strategy settled for running a semi-socialist state more efficiently than the Labour Party. Led by the slippery but slick Harold Wilson, Labour returned in 1964 to lead Britain into the 'white heat of the technological revolution'. The country soon found that this meant pouring billions of pounds into every failing industry or new scientific pet project. Trade Unions became a fifth estate of the realm, settling major industrial strikes over beer and sandwiches at 10 Downing Street.

Enlarging the EEC

In 1969 the governments of the Six met in The Hague and decided to enlarge the EEC to include those countries that would accept the terms of the Treaty of Rome. In 1970 the Six specifically invited four nations, Britain, Eire, Denmark and Norway, to open negotiations to join them. Harold Wilson's Labour Government accepted and began discussions around such issues as implementing the Common Fisheries Policy.

At this time most politicians were largely in favour of the UK joining the Common Market, if only as an escape from the nation's economic ills. Some emerged as dedicated Europhiles, arguing for the UK to take its place at the 'heart of Europe'. They included Roy Jenkins of the Labour Party, but the most prominent was Edward Heath, who had led the British application for membership that was thwarted by General de Gaulle during Harold Macmillan's premiership. Heath succeeded Sir Alec Douglas-Home as leader of the

Conservative Party in 1965 and became Prime Minister after his surprise victory in the 1970 General Election.

Heath had been a dedicated Europhile since the Second World War and in spirit was a member of the euro club. He now enthusiastically continued the negotiations started by Wilson, soon agreed terms, and in Brussels in 1972 he signed the Treaty of Accession to the Treaty of Rome. At the time there was considerable disquiet over the terms that Heath had negotiated and the impact they would have on the Commonwealth and the British fishing industry. Norway also found the fishing terms too onerous and eventually after a referendum withdrew from membership. But Britain, Denmark and Eire all became members of the EEC in 1973.

Edward Heath then became embroiled in a conflict with the trade unions and in particular with the National Union of Mineworkers, which finally led him to call an election in February 1974 with the theme 'who runs the country?' The country didn't believe that Heath could, and once again returned the Labour Party under Harold Wilson.

The new government was not happy with the terms under which Britain had entered the EEC and attempted to renegotiate them. But it was too late, and so Wilson called for a National Referendum (the first in Britain's history) to confirm or reject membership of the Common Market. Much of the argument centred on the 'betrayal of the Commonwealth' and the intricacies of the EEC Common Fisheries Policies. Heath and other Europhiles from both political parties were, to say the least, disingenuous with their pledge that the UK would 'never turn her back' on the Commonwealth having just agreed to the Common Agricultural Policy. In a similar manner the claim that there would be no reduction in British sovereignty was quite contrary to the views of government legal advisors, who pointed out the supremacy of Community Law in the Treaty of Rome. However, in 1975, the Referendum, by a two to one majority, confirmed Britain's membership

of the EEC. Britain had taken a seemingly irrevocable step on the road to ruin.

Andrew Bowden recalls how from 1972 to 1975 he had felt torn over the issue of Europe. 'My heart said, "keep out of Europe. I cannot forget the War and I do not trust the Germans, nor for that matter the French, although as a practising Christian I am trying to forgive." But then my head said, "wait a moment: Britain needs a large home market and 250 million is very different from 50 million to export its goods and services to. During difficult world economic times we will be isolated and vulnerable. Just as important economic integration would ensure that never again would there be another Western European war."' Andrew concludes, 'My head won and with considerable reluctance I voted accordingly'.

The EEC without Britain

This chapter has so far observed the EEC from the outside, but the seventeen years of the Common Market before Britain joined were not without incident. The period preceding its ratification and the Treaty of Rome were dominated by the euro club of dedicated federalists who planned to move step by step in that direction. But they had reckoned without General de Gaulle who was recalled to power in 1958. He was no federalist and had very strong views that the EEC was to be '*l'Europe des Patres*', or a community of nation states. He continually thundered about France's sovereign rights. It was therefore not surprising that he clashed consistently with the first president of the European Commission, Walter Hallstein, a German and a self-proclaimed federalist.

De Gaulle first clashed with Hallstein over the Fouchet Plan. Fouchet was a French diplomat who had been ordered by de Gaulle to prepare a plan for de Gaulle's vision of the future of Europe. The Plan was in effect a rejection of the terms of the Treaty of Rome. Fouchet called for the reorganisation of the Community, turning it into a voluntary union of independent states with wide national veto powers. This entailed reducing the European Commission's powers and moving it from Brussels to Paris, and at the same time putting power into the hands of national politicians. The other five EEC members resisted the General, so he went further in trying to weaken the Council of Ministers and ending the supremacy of Community law enshrined in the Treaty of Rome.

In the midst of his long-running battle with Commissioner Hallstein over the power of the Commission, de Gaulle turned his attention to his other objective; restricting the influence of what he called the Anglo-Saxons in Europe. From his wartime experiences and his recognition of tough competition to France, the General was determined to keep Britain and its 'American partner' out of Europe. His strategy was to form an 'indissoluble' pact between France and Germany. In 1963 de Gaulle vetoed Britain's entry into the Common Market and signed the Treaty of Elysee with Konrad Adenauer, Chancellor of West Germany. This was an astonishing act for two reasons. Firstly, Adenauer was a supporter of Hallstein. Secondly, in practical terms the pact has endured to the present day despite some fierce differences between Germany and France.

This Franco-German alliance is a crucial factor in considering Britain's future policy toward European Union and we will return to its implications in more detail in Chapter Three – *Differing Objectives and Hidden Agendas.* Suffice to say now that any British Prime Minister who claims that he will take the UK into 'the heart of Europe' must first overcome the strength of the Elysee Pact which has so far effectively ring fenced that heart.

Empty Chair Crisis

In the next stage of the conflict between the French President and the Commission President over the power of the Commission, Hallstein now took one step too far and enraged de Gaulle. He proposed to make the Community financially self-sufficient by extending the budgetary powers of the European Parliament over national Parliaments and to revise the finances of the Common Agricultural Policy. In addition, there was to be a transition period for the universal power of the veto established in the Treaty of Rome and its replacement by qualified majority voting in a number of areas. In July 1965 President de Gaulle ordered a French boycott of the EEC Council of Ministers, withdrew French representation at the Community and instructed Gaullist Members to absent themselves from the European Parliament. The impasse lasted for six months and was not resolved until the Luxembourg compromise in January 1966. This difficult period in the development of the EEC was called the 'empty chair crisis'.

The empty chair crisis had paralysed the Community as neither protagonist was prepared to climb down. Hallstein stood firm on the Treaty of Rome and indeed was determined to push forward along the euro club strategy. President de Gaulle was horrified by the advance of bureaucratic supranationalism and the intended introduction of qualified majority voting. To quote Rodney Leach in his *Concise Encyclopaedia of the European Union*, 'President de Gaulle took the line that the Treaty of Rome was ambiguous or flawed and that it was unthinkable that France should be outvoted by foreigners'. The Luxembourg Compromise of 1966 provided the way out of the impasse but only to a limited extent. The Compromise stated that any decision that affected 'a very important national interest' would be deferred until a unanimously acceptable solution could be found. If de Gaulle thought that the Treaty of Rome was ambiguous the compromise took ambiguity to its limit. The Luxembourg Compromise was never accepted by the Commission or given legal status but it effectively froze progress in the EEC until the General retired in 1969.

National Sovereignty

The early history of the EEC makes clear that the question of national sovereignty is not a recent issue or some peculiarity of English Conservatives. The France of Mitterrand and Chirac bears no relation to the France of de Gaulle in terms of pride and national direction. In similar terms the Britain of Heath and Blair bears no resemblance to the Britain that Margaret Thatcher or Winston Churchill represented. There is no guarantee that a future Chancellor of Germany or Prime Minister of Italy will not, in certain circumstances, feel equally strongly that their country's very existence is being submerged by an undemocratic supranational bureaucracy. In other words national sovereignty is a legitimate issue that has not been nullified by joining the EU.

The euro club would have us believe that the treaties of Rome, Maastricht and Amsterdam were inevitable steps that can never be retraced, and that it would be almost treasonable to attempt to question them. The political bigots of the Commission are there to 'defend the faith', along with their Europhile adherents in every country. De Gaulle and Margaret Thatcher were unable to halt completely the remorseless march of the committed. However, the fact remains that the Commission is still haunted by the possibility of a new Fouchet Plan emerging, or some leader who has the power and the courage to retrace some steps. The plea to be 'in Europe but not run by Europe' is not to fly in the face of the inevitable. The new mega state of Europe is only inevitable to those who knowingly commit themselves to it, or to those who do not have the courage to proclaim that it is not.

Margaret Thatcher

In 1975 a defeated Conservative Parliamentary Party decided to dump the Europhile Edward Heath, and in his place chose Margaret Thatcher as their new leader. Four years later Britain, disillusioned by the performance of Jim Callaghan's Labour government, turned back to the Conservatives and elected Thatcher as Prime Minister.

Anglo-European relations were about to change dramatically. Since Harold Macmillan's attempt to join the EEC was vetoed by General de Gaulle, Britain had become a supplicant nation and still acted that way even now that she was a member. This attitude was anathema to Margaret Thatcher. She immediately focused on Britain's disproportionate contribution to the EC budget and started her strident but successful call to 'give us our money back', which so shocked other European leaders. They were more used to the behind the doors diplomacy of the coalitions that dominated continental politics.

In many ways Margaret Thatcher and Charles de Gaulle were similar in their view of Europe. Like him, she was a powerful personality who dominated her colleagues. Like him, she was deeply committed to a vision of her country's place in history and its future independence. The General resisted any attempt to limit the sovereignty of France and in a like manner Thatcher was horrified at any idea of surrendering British sovereignty to some amorphous body. Both had contempt for obstructive bureaucrats and those of the Commission in particular. Both also had the advantage in their initial periods in power of the fear of the alternative.

51

In de Gaulle's case it was the turmoil of the Algerian war and in Thatcher's case a return to the chaotic 'winter of discontent'. Finally both also faced obdurate opponents in the President of the Commission. General de Gaulle was never able to fully overcome Walter Hallstein and Margaret Thatcher never defeated Jacques Delors. Neither of them was able to shift the Community or the euro club from its long march towards a European super state.

However, in practice the differences between the two were more important than the similarities. Margaret Thatcher was an active exponent of the Anglo-Saxon connection of which General de Gaulle had been so contemptuous. Her close working relationship with US President Ronald Reagan was a major factor in the defeat of Communism and its impact on Europe. She was able to continue that influence in the early period of the first Bush presidency ('George, this is no time to throw a wobbly' – one somehow cannot envisage Tony Blair talking to the second Bush in those terms). Again she was deeply suspicious of de Gaulle's creation of the Franco-German alliance that appeared to control EC politics.

Clearly, Thatcher was against the concept of a federal Europe. It is therefore puzzling to understand how she signed up to the Single European Act of 1986, which provided the impetus that led to the Maastricht Treaty. The answer lies in two aspects of the Thatcher premiership. First, she actually had a positive attitude to the development of a strong and wider common market for economic reasons. This was an area that the Act was trying to address. Secondly, she was surrounded by overt or closet Europhiles in her cabinet and the Conservative Party hierarchy. Her anguished cry that some colleagues were 'not one of us' was heartfelt.

Thatcher's uncompromising use of power caught the British establishment by surprise. Following the debacle of Edward Heath, her straightforward approach was, at first, refreshing to the Conservative Party establishment. Then came the realisation that they, and the mandarins of the Treasury and the Foreign Office, were not going to be able to *manage* her. She really did intend to reverse decades of appeasement and compromise. For Mrs Thatcher the current version of compromise was the quasi-liberal *One Nation* Tory philosophy to which so many of her colleagues proclaimed allegiance. At varying times her cabinets included philosophical opponents who also tended to be Europhiles, such as Kenneth Clarke, Ian Gilmour, Michael Heseltine, Geoffrey Howe, Jim Prior, Norman St John Stevas and Peter Walker. Of course, most supported her publicly from loyalty or ambition, but they did act as constraints on her actions and played a part in her final defeat. In particular Geoffrey Howe, in the pivotal role as Foreign Secretary, played a large part in signing up to the Single European Act. It is perhaps no coincidence that it was Howe who unsheathed the Brutus dagger that brought an end to Margaret Thatcher's Premiership in 1990.

With the exception of Winston Churchill, Margaret Thatcher was the strongest and most effective Prime Minister of the United Kingdom in the twentieth century. In a relatively short time she reversed the steady decline of Britain in terms of both economic performance and international influence. In doing so, she established economic and political principles that continue to strengthen the British economy in comparison with her European neighbours to the present day. She recognised the importance of the Anglo-American alliance but by no stretch of the imagination could she ever be described as an American poodle!

The Single European Act

The Single European Act of February 1986 was the first major revision of the Treaty of Rome and paved the way for the Treaty of European Unity better known as the

Maastricht Treaty. The Community had grown from six to twelve members and a series of disagreements made some revision or reform of the operation of the common market essential. The Commission, then led by Jacques Delors, had identified some three hundred actions that were needed to remove obstacles such as regulations and rules that hindered the development of the single market. But to achieve this the Commission proposed an extension of qualified majority voting and a strengthening of the European Parliament. As an approach to eliminating the logjam of obstacles to the internal market, the package appeared reasonable, but in reality this was the thin end of the wedge as far as the national veto was concerned. The Act addressed wider areas in social dimensions of the EC, but its primary significance is that it ended a long period of stagnation, extended qualified majority voting, launched Jacques Delors and revitalised the European movement.

The Collapse of Communism

The downfall of the Soviet empire has had a major impact on the European Union and its future. There are many philosophical, political and economic issues that arose from this dramatic change, but for the purposes of this book they can be summarised as follows:

- The vast expansion of the boundaries of the European Union to the east and the south will change the political balance within the Union.
- The number of new nations joining the Union raised or exacerbated conflict about the structure, distributive economics and the battlefield of national vetoes.
- The absorption of a nation of seventeen million people into the Union without real debate, through the back

door of German re-unification, once again brought to the fore the fear of German dominance.

- The porous frontiers of the new Europe raise new fears of a massive economic migration from the east that could disrupt the liberal social programmes of the Union.

Many of these issues are peripheral to this chapter other than noting that the road to ruin is becoming more complex. We shall return to all these issues in Chapter Seven – *Widening or Deepening*.

On the Move Again

The euro club celebrated the Single European Act (SEA) with the cry 'on the move' and once again moved enthusiastically down the road to integration, which had become the Eurospeak word for federalism. A new wave of initiatives swept the community for further financial, social, legal and political integration. At the same time the Commission, led by the vocal Delors, began implementing a flood of directives that went far beyond what most of the signatories of the SEA had envisaged.

Margaret Thatcher became alarmed at what was happening and was by now uncomfortable about her acceptance of the SEA. In a speech to the College of Europe in Bruges n September 1988 she voiced her concern over the moves to a 'European super-state' and an 'identikit European personality'. She restated her belief in a 'Europe of Nations' (echoes of de Gaulle) and strongly criticised the unaccountability of the Community's undemocratic supranational institutions. The issues were now clearly in the open and a new 'Bruges Group' of anti-federalists was formed. But Mrs Thatcher's increasingly strident tones over Europe were creating strong opposition from the Europhiles in her own party and two years later she was out of power. That same year, 1990, at the Madrid Community Summit Jacques Delors declared that an 'embryo European government would be in place within five years'.

Maastricht

The twelve leaders of the European Community met at Maastricht in February 1992 to consider a Treaty on European Union prepared by the Commission. The new British Prime Minister, John Major, unlike his predecessor had a reputation as a good negotiator and initially this appeared to be borne out by the results. The word 'federal' was now replaced by the doctrine of 'subsidiarity' (which meant different things to different people). He refused to sign the 'social chapter', obtained an opt-out clause on monetary policy, and persuaded the other leaders to reconfirm the role of NATO. The Treaty was agreed and the EC became the European Union. John Major returned to Britain claiming a great victory from the UK point of view.

As understanding grew of the detailed content of the Treaty it became clear that Maastricht was actually a triumph for the Commission and Jacques Delors. It represented a giant step forward for the Monnet concept of *functionalism* and the overall objectives of the euro club. The citizens of individual states reflected the sense of unease, and the Treaty came near to disaster as it moved to ratification. It was initially rejected by the Danish people in a referendum in 1992, accepted by the narrowest of margins in a French referendum in the same year and only just passed in Britain's House of Commons after unprecedented pressure by the government whips. The feeling persisted that the Treaty was a stitch-up, using obscure phraseology and much obfuscation to hide its real intent.

The intent was in the detail. With the benefit of hindsight it now seems incomprehensible that a British Prime Minister could have accepted most of the provisions of the Maastricht Treaty. The verdict of history must surely be that the cricketing John Major took his eye off the ball while concentrating on peripheral arguments with the umpire. He and the other leaders initialled agreements to the following provisions:

- Citizenship of the Union would be given to citizens of member states. (*As the new EU passports make clear we are now citizens of the European Community first, and citizens of the United Kingdom of Great Britain and Northern Ireland second.*)
- Member states should follow a common economic policy. (*We can now see that the Thatcherite economic policy of Britain is better fitted to the global economy than the flawed corporate state economies of Germany and France. Strength lies in the diversity of European economies not a Commission dominated universality.*)
- European Monetary Union and a European Central Bank were to be achieved by 1999. (*Britain negotiated an opt-out and though it may be too early to make a judgement on the single currency, the supporters of the euro are distinctly uncomfortable. French and German citizens remain uncertain about the advantages gained from the demise of the Franc and the Deutschmark.*)
- The European parliament should be given powers of co-decision with the Council of Ministers. (*In practice more power to the Commission which it is intended will become the government of Europe.*)
- An advisory Committee of the Regions to be established. (*A back door approach to subverting the central governments of nation states. Brussels can now directly approach the 'regions of the community'. Not many*

citizens of England realise that their country has now disappeared from the Brussels map of Europe. Scotland and Wales still exist as regions but England is divided into nine separate regions with direct funding relationships with the Community.)

- Common foreign and security policies to be pursued. (*Only a supranational federal state would in reality carry out this policy for Europe. Experience in the Balkans leads to some scepticism in this area and perhaps we should ask whether Britain would have been able to resist aggression in the Falkland Islands under this provision?*)

- Subsidiarity should leave Community action 'to Member States'. (*Major argued that subsidiarity had protected British sovereignty and was a replacement for the federal ideal. Nonsense; in the mind of the Commission it means that Britain may be allowed to implement the decisions of the Community – not overrule them.*)

- Other chapters outlined community integration in policies on education, culture, health, energy, justice, immigration and crime. (*Most of these areas hove been the cause of much conflict and/or disgruntlement ever since.*)

The discussions at Maastricht and the provisions of the Treaty dealt in depth with Economic and Monetary Union (EMU), the future of the Exchange Rate Mechanism (ERM) and the introduction of the euro as the single currency. Rather than tackling this subject twice, it will be discussed in detail in Chapter Six – *A Divisive Single Currency.*

Treaty of Amsterdam

In the light of the long-running controversy over the intent and meaning of the Treaty of Maastricht, the 1997 Treaty of Amsterdam was generally viewed by both Europhiles and Eurosceptics as a 'damp squib'. It was intended as a sequel to Maastricht concentrating in more detail on democratic rights and actions needed to ease enlargement to the Community.

The Treaty adds countless amendments to previous treaties that with a whole new series of reference numbers adds to the confusion. Tracing the purport of amendments to sections, parts, titles, articles or chapters through a series of treaties is now a gargantuan task. It is difficult to escape the conclusion that this represents a deliberate intention of the bureaucrats. The apparatchiks of Soviet Russia used the same techniques to ensure that the Party was always the arbiter in every decision and remained in control. In the EU for Party read Commission.

Unravelling all the clauses makes it clear that Amsterdam determined that Community Law takes precedence over national sovereign laws and that subsidiarity is no solace to Eurosceptics. Majority voting in the Council of Ministers was extended but defence was excluded. Other provisions strengthen the position of the Commission and to a lesser extent the European Parliament. In general it represents a further step forward for the euro club.

However, the Treaty's principal step forward was to recognise the concept of the two-speed Europe. It accepted that some states would move faster toward integration. Handled with guile and perception, this could actually provide a 'Trojan Horse' for national Eurosceptics. On the other hand, the Treaty permitted the European Council to suspend the voting rights of a member state considered to be guilty of contravention of 'liberty, democracy, respect for human rights and fundamental freedoms'. This was a real move against the sovereign rights of nations. Though ostensibly intended to safeguard against a *coup d'état* in a member state, it caused a shock when used against Austria after the election of a far right government in 1990.

A Debate at Last

The European issue has remained at the forefront of British politics since Maastricht. Though not the main reason for the defeat of the Conservative Government in 1997, the Eurosceptic rebellion was a divisive element within the Conservative Party. Additionally, a one-issue party calling for withdrawal from Europe, the Referendum Party, was formed to fight the election and resulted in the loss of a number of Conservative seats.

The new Labour Government led by Tony Blair quickly demonstrated its Europhile intentions by accepting the Social Chapter and declaring its aim to be 'at the heart of Europe'. But by 2000 it was beginning to realise that the heart is reserved for the French and the Germans. The leader of the Conservative Party, William Hague, nailed the party's flag to the mast with Churchill's old slogan 'in Europe but not run by Europe'. This was highly successful in the European Parliament Elections in 2000 but carried little weight in the 2001 General Election. The electorate were happy to wait for a referendum on that issue. But that also accounted for the British public's argument for a referendum on the proposed European Constitution that was finally accepted by Blair. The old labels are no longer sufficient and though Tony Blair may use the terms 'extremist' and 'Eurosceptic' in the House of Commons he and his Cabinet are modifying their own original uncompromising Europhile stance. The new leader of the Conservative Party, Michael Howard, has read the current mood and modified his own strong Eurosceptic position.

There are also subtle changes in the attitudes of the other members of the Union. The euro club is no longer speaking with the same certainty, and British influence in both the Council of Ministers and the Commission is increasing. In the next chapter we will look more closely at these changing attitudes in the diverse community that is Europe.

Chapter Three

Differing Objectives and Hidden Agendas

'We must recollect what it is we have at stake, what is it we contend for. It is for our prosperity, it is for our liberty, it is for our independence, nay, for our existence as a nation; it is for our character, and it is for our very name as Englishmen. It is for everything clear and valuable to man on this side of the grave.'

William Pitt the Elder, 1708–1778

'Smile at us, pay us, pass us; but do not quite forget. For we are the people of England, that never have spoken yet.'

G.K. Chesterton, 1874–1936

In June 2000 the German *Reichstag* Parliament in Berlin (recently restored in the fashionable neo-global glasswork by a British architect) played host to a landmark oration by the French president Jacques Chirac, the first foreign leader to address the *Bundestag* of the re-united Germany. His speech, coupled with one by Joschka Fischer, the German foreign minister, a few weeks earlier, brought out into the open a wide diversity of opinion about integration and the future of the Union.

Chirac called for a Franco-German axis to lead a 'pioneering group' of European states to accelerate 'farther and faster' towards greater integration. He envisaged a new 'inner core' of states drawn from those that have accepted the single currency. 'One country must not be able to block the progress of others' and 'those countries that want to proceed further with integration must be allowed to do so without being held back'. He went further and declared that the inner core would need 'its own secretariat to ensure coherence' and discussed the need for a written constitution to be drawn up allowing a 'two tier Europe' to take shape. In essence he was extending the Amsterdam Treaty.

In his speech Fischer had gone further and called for 'the transition from a union of states to full parliamentarianism as a European Federation'. Fischer noted that this meant 'nothing less than a European government which really does exercise legislative and executive power within the federation' and he also argued for a directly elected European President. The idea of retreat and handing back *any* power to nation states was rejected and he welcomed the progress being made in removing the 'sovereign rights of individual states'.

In fairness to Chirac he had been careful to add 'Neither you nor we envisage the creation of a European super state which would substitute for our nations and mark the end of our existence as players in international life'. But many of his listeners both within and without the *Reichstag* did envisage exactly that: the creation of a European super state.

The reaction to Chirac's and Fischer's lead was mixed and in some instances vehement. The German response was generally supportive, perhaps not surprising in view of the fact that the German Christian Democrats had proposed 'an inner core Europe' as long ago as 1994. However, the owner of *Der Spiegel* magazine, Rudolf Augstein, castigated Fischer for 'juggling with the catchword Federation' which he stated 'was like a red rag to a bull for many EU members' and continued 'old skeletons are being dragged out of the cupboard which suggest that Germany will dominate because of its size and act purely in its own interests'. French opinion was generally supportive of Chirac though carefully modified by Lionel Jospin, the Socialist leader and the French foreign minister, Hubert Vedrine, who stated that the 'president's idea was not an *official* French proposal' (the Quai d'Orsay can be as ambivalent and duplicitous as the British Foreign Office). But the majority of those nations presumably confined to the 'outer circle', were critical and certainly those nations waiting in the wings to join the EU were most unhappy at being cast as members of a second class Europe.

The Spanish foreign minister, Joseph Pique, made his country's opposition very clear, 'enhanced co-operation must under no circumstances mean the existence of a hard core of states moving faster than the others'. Spain believed that she had recently come in out of the cold and was not about to be hurled back to the periphery of Europe. Denmark and Austria were hostile to the proposals. Poul Rasmussen, the Danish prime minister, challenged Chirac, saying 'I see no need for a federal Europe. I see the need for closer co-operation on the basis of our current agreements'. The Austrian foreign minister, Benita Ferrer-Waldner (already smarting about the sanctions imposed on Vienna against her party) said 'We can't have a Franco-German core Europe that relegates other countries to a second class'.

The strongest opposition came from the ten Central and East European states who were concerned that the proposals would cause more delay to their accession to the EU. They sensed that they were already relegated to a second division of the EU. 'There are some worried that we will be accepted but again Europe will be divided' said Borivo Hnizdo, professor of political science at Prague University. Vaclav Klaus, president of the Czech parliament, said 'It was unacceptable for a Franco-German directorate to start dictating

European policy'. His remarks were echoed by Janz Drnovsek, the former Slovenian prime minister, who said that this country's experience as part of the former Yugoslav Federation 'had made it wary of giving up too much sovereignty'.

In Poland, Adam Michnik, an adviser to the government, said that he 'wanted to remain a citizen of an independent Poland until I die' while Bronislaw Geremek, the Polish foreign minister, articulated the concerns of most of his countrymen and other former communist states that as a citizen of a country 'that had only recently regained its sovereignty' he was not prepared to support the idea of Poland being 'subsumed by a fully federated Europe'.

There was even sympathy for Eastern Europe from within the European Commission in their reaction to the idea of second tier members. Chris Patten, the European Commissioner for External Relations asked: 'What is the message to countries that want to become part of the EU, if we say, "You're going to become part of a club in which you'll be allowed to stay below stairs, you can eat in the butler's pantry, but all the Georgian silver and the best napery is going to be used upstairs by some of the older members?"' (A woman politician remembering her experience of London clubs on reading Patten's question said forcibly, 'Tell me about it!')

The British Prime Minister, Tony Blair, was left blinking in the headlights as his pledge to put the UK at the heart of Europe seemed to be disappearing, but he reacted diplomatically and merely noted that Chirac's statement was 'interesting'. However, the British media were almost unanimous in the use of emotive adjectives in describing the impact of Chirac's proposals on the UK. They took the line that France and Germany were now committed on a fast track to integration or as one put it to a 'super state dream'. Their headlines declared that Britain was left behind, isolated or condemned to the slow lane. In other words not only were Chirac's proposals bad news, but by implication the government must take action to prevent it happening or alternatively join the French and Germans in the fast lane. Irrespective of the destination it seemed that for most of the media the race was the thing and national pride demanded that Britain should be up with the leaders.

In truth the Eurosceptics should have been cheering Chirac's speech from the rooftops. The federal debate was now out in the open. Here, for the first time the leaders of the euro club were admitting that the current, let alone future, nations of the EU had widely divergent priorities. But, even more, those at the centre were declaring that these divergences were legitimate and could be encompassed within a multi-speed Union. Chirac had opened a Pandora's box. Logically, permission to go faster must also mean permission to move at a different pace or even stop. Chirac had said that those who wanted further integration 'must be allowed to do so'. It therefore followed that those who did not wish to move deeper into the European super state must also be allowed to hold back and at the same time remain in the Union. Or to put it another way, the Conservative Party's policy of 'Britain in Europe, but not run by Europe' is acceptable to the leaders of the EU, if not to Tony Blair and the UK Europhiles.

Jacques Chirac also introduced the concept of two secretariats or commissions to manage a multi-speed Europe. This must have come as a shock to the Commission President Romano Prodi and his Commissioners as the impact of Chirac's proposals emerged. At a stroke the single purpose source of the Commission's almost dictatorial powers was put at risk. The establishment of a fast lane secretariat, probably based in either Berlin or Paris, could lead to a re-examination of all previous major directives of the Commission to consider their relevance to the slow or the fast lane. The steady progress of functionalism for all was now in question and for the first time since the Fouchet Plan of de Gaulle, Chirac had raised the possibility of determined nations calling for the revision of existing treaties. To the hidden mandarins of the euro club Chirac had made a massive strategic error. In effect he had opened the gates of fortress Brussels and invited the Eurosceptic Trojan Horse to decamp in the centre of the Grande Place.

The European Union is not yet a federal supranational state but a dangerous fiction has evolved that the EU already is a union of like minded national states. Chirac, Fischer and the multitude of national reactions have destroyed that illusion to the long-term benefit of the Union. It is now clear that these 25 nations represent a wide diversity of national interests, cultures and political attitudes that go to the heart of our national liberties. For a long period this diversity has been obscured by a purposeful fog and sublimated to the activities involved in a flurry of treaties, the launch of the new currency and major political change in Britain, Germany and Italy. This period of instability and adapting to change has tended to hand the stage to the Europhiles, while the majority were hypnotised by the concept of inevitability or the 'wait and see' argument. Now that the euro has lost its novelty and is being judged on performance, and new political regimes are well past the honeymoon period, natural national traits and concerns are again emerging.

Time will tell whether or not President Chirac's speech in Berlin really did mark a watershed in the evolving history of the EU. But in the light of the success of the European movement for more than fifty years there has to be a question mark. Monnet and his successors always knew that their dream of the European super state would never see the light of day if spelled out in plain terms. Since the Congress of Europe in 1948 their strategy has been based on two elements; fear and activity. Interestingly these same two elements have always been the drivers for idealists and were clearly essential to both Communism and Fascism.

Fear

The horrors endured in the last century have meant that the fear of another war is deep in the psyche of most Europeans. In fairness, the founders and the followers of the European Movement have been genuinely motivated by this fear and see a supranational integration as the only answer. Eurosceptics are not certain that a thousand years of national history has to be sacrificed to sort out the German problem. Yet the Eurosceptics have not provided a coherent alternative that wholly allays that fear. Certainly the fear of war has been used to maintain the case for integration, but it waxes and wanes as events take precedence. Since German re-unification the fear has again waxed, and France, in particular, has become far more focused on the integration of Germany into Europe. When this fear wanes, another fear is paraded which has less validity but can appear plausible. That is fear for economic survival.

Even with the help of the Marshall Plan it took a long time for the European nations to recover from the devastating economic cost of the Second World War. Some states also had to adapt to the debilitating loss of empire and thus international influence. At the same time they witnessed the growth of the new superpowers that appeared to dwarf their own significance in the world. But as they began to recover their self-confidence as nations the economic front was devastated by the onslaught of the Japanese. This nation of geisha girls and cherry blossom had caught both the Europeans and the Americans by surprise and were flooding their markets with products that were eagerly sought after by their citizens. This experience led to the second great fear, which at times overshadowed even the fear of war. The fear of economic survival in the new global economy. Again and again the Europhiles have re-iterated this fear and warned that Britain cannot afford not to be in Europe.

It is now surely time to put this particular fear on the backburner. When one considers the economic success of nations like Taiwan and South Korea it is difficult to accept that the world's third, fourth and fifth economies need to relinquish their sovereignty for economic survival. In whatever economic order one puts Germany, Britain and France they are all strong economies in their own right. For Britain, this growing economic power strengthens the opportunity that it has practised throughout history to make economic and political alliances of its choice. Some of these alliances may entail some loss of sovereignty for the advantage of itself and a number of like-minded nations. The European Union is one such alliance. Fear should not be an element in that choice. The fundamental issue for Britain is the degree to which it can exercise this choice in the future.

Activity

Continuous activity has been a feature of the Commission's control of affairs from the early days of the European Economic Community through to today's European Union. Every treaty, every summit of the heads of state and every meeting of the various Councils of Ministers has been used as an opportunity to formulate or agree the Commission's directives. Each individual directive is then amended and implemented by national civil servants, often with more rigour or detail than originally intended by the Commission. Again each individual directive causes a change, minor or major, in the way the national government previously operated. In other words each directive reduced national sovereignty if only to a minute degree. But the devil lies in the detail, as the devisors of *functionalism* well knew. There have been thousands of such directives and they have already profoundly changed the ability of fifteen sovereign states to control their destinies. It has to be said that from the point of the euro club this strategy has been an unqualified success to date.

Growing Debate

The dual strategies of fear and activity have continued almost unchecked for some thirty years and in the mind of the Commission will continue at an increasing pace. But the debate is opening and there is growing evidence that leaders of opinion in many countries are prepared to call a halt to all this mindless change. As more feel free to express their hidden feelings, every facet of the EU will come into focus and be exposed to the best of argument. Though most Europhiles will find it hard to accept, the opportunity for Thomas to express his doubts may eventually strengthen rather than weaken the EU.

The strongly independent Danes have been (to their credit) the most likely to embrace the role of Thomas, but a small example in 2000 showed that the placid British were finally ready to take a stand. A minor directive over weights and measures provided the straw that broke the camel's back. Eurocratic inspectors (disguised as British civil servants) were using the punitive weight of European law on defenceless market traders. They were impounding their scales and other tools of their trade and threatening them with fines or even loss of liberty because they had defied a Brussels directive that fruit and vegetables (indeed all food) must be sold in metric measure rather than the customer desire for pounds and ounces. Elements of the media protested but the Eurocrats remained supreme (as they always had done) until a giant corporate power (Tesco) had the courage to stand on its declared principle that the customer was right, and rejected the Brussels directive. Corporate lawyers were now ordered to question the legality of this directive. This may seem a minor incident but this or a similar small episode could represent the withdrawal of the finger from the dyke.

Diversity

Diversity within Europe is wider, more complex and subtle than an easy characterisation of the difference between individual national states. There are elements in that diversity that favours a federal solution, but the strength of the other elements make the success of a super state problematical. The elements of diversity that will be touched on in this chapter are as follows:

- National diversity
- Ethnic issues and extremist groups
- Regionalisation
- Corporate groupings

National Diversity

In his book *Europe of Many Circles*, Sir Richard Body poses the question whether the circles of interest are best represented by concentric circles or a series of interlocking circles like a jumbled-up Olympic Games symbol. Both are valid, depending upon the emphasis given to different interests. He rightly makes the point that no nation can afford to be outside any circle, but the allocation of nations within the concentric circles is open to argument. The Eurosceptic view tends to portray France and Germany forming the inner core surrounded in the next circles by the other members of

Euroland or the single currency area. Presumably the outer circle is for 'difficult' or errant members and potential new entrants.

The authors see a rather different classification of the concentric circles. There is certainly an inner core, but Italy should be included on the basis that it is probably more difficult for Germany and France to impose their viewpoint without the support of Italy. However, the two outer circles cannot be simply defined by membership of Euroland or otherwise as that condition is not the basis upon which the other nations argue the issues of integration. We define the two outer circles as the dependent circle and the independent circle. Clearly a number of nations are, on the basis of their size or their economic circumstances, dependent on the EU for their well-being. Another group of nations, because of their economic strength or their history and culture, are fiercely independent and are thus capable of forming other associations, as for example with the United States.

The dependent circles include Austria, Belgium, Eire, Greece, Luxembourg and possibly the Netherlands. (The latter probably included with this group because of its close identification with the Benelux Group.)

The independent circle includes those nations that have to date shown an independent streak in relations with the Commission and the concept of Europe. Britain, Denmark and Sweden are natural leaders of the group, but Spain and Portugal could well feel affinity with the group. Finland's natural desire would be to join this circle but her size and economic circumstances could tempt her into the 'dependent circle'.

Of course, the new entrants make this allocation of nations within circles of interest more complicated. It is difficult to visualise Hungary, Israel, Poland, Turkey or Ukraine fitting in easily into a dependent circle. There is no definitive answer to these futuristic questions but the issue emphasises the complexities to be managed in a wider European Union.

The Centre Circle or Hub

Germany

The Germans retain a deep feeling of superiority tinged with an uneasy sense of guilt so that they are unwilling to talk about it but it does affect their own attitude to a united Europe. Of course it would be amazing if all the wartime attitudes had completely disappeared when so much is still in the living memory of so many Germans. Their attitude is probably summed up in the phrase 'Well Hitler wasn't all bad; he did some good things'. To them the 'good things' relate to the elimination of unemployment, the development of the *autobahns* and a general feeling of German success. Would that deep feeling be resuscitated by a prolonged period of high unemployment in Germany? (At the time of writing the unemployment rate in Germany now exceeds the level when Hitler came to power.) So the question still remains; does some or all of Nazi ideology represent something deep in the German psyche?

Defining behavioural characteristics for other nations is difficult and can be dangerous. For example Germany, is a truly federal union (and became a nation through federalisation which partly accounts for their apparent unconcern at the idea of a federal Europe) of very different states or *lander.*

The differences between Berliners, Rhinelanders and Bavarians is as great if not greater than the difference between Parisians and the rest of France, or even between Londoners and Yorkshiremen. Additionally, the political reunification of Germany has complicated the issue with the differing attitudes of '*wessies*' and '*ossies*'. British attitudes to Germany are broadly divided between the views of Eurosceptic and Europhiles. The Eurosceptic favour the traditional view of the aggressive 'master race' German and for many of them the modern evidence is based on the 'poolside towel syndrome'. The Europhile is convinced that the leopard has changed its spots and will instance the undoubted triumph of democracy in Germany since the war. Certainly one can find instances of strong right-wing or even fascist activity in modern Germany but the same is true of France and to a much lesser extent in Britain where it seems to be confined mainly to ersatz football fans. The author tends to the Europhile view though he still feels very uncomfortable in Bavaria, the cradle of Nazism. From a traditional balance of power viewpoint Britain should have some sympathy with the French desire to ensure that Germany does not revert to its past.

There is a tendency to equate the terms 'Prussian militarism' with 'Nazi ideology'. Prussians were certainly militaristic, but rather as a trade or profession, than as an imperialistic dogma. Throughout history Prussian soldiers of fortune or mercenaries were used by several other European nations. It is of interest that Rommel, Guderian and many leading Nazi generals in the Second World War were not Prussians.

Germany is a republic of federated states, which has a central bicameral Parliament and consists of sixteen states (*Länder*) each with its own constitution, parliament and government. The German system of government is often exampled as the model for the European federal state. It isn't and John Redwood's book *The Death of Britain* cogently explains why. However, it is clear that the euro club are driving functionalism in that direction.

The German economy has been the strongest in Europe since the mid 1960s but it is now suffering from the complacency engendered by earlier success. Over-priced labour, over-subsidised social benefits and over-engineered products are beginning to over-price German products and services in the global economy. The high cost of reunion and some acts of protectionism are putting more strains on the much-vaunted economy. We have already noted the high levels of unemployment that, allied to the Turkish immigration issue are causing political unrest. The condition of the German economy is central to the position of the Euro and the future of the EU economy and for that reason is a major element of consideration in Chapter Five – *The Economic Issues of Union* and has some bearing on discussions in Chapter Six - *A Divisive Single Currency.*

In conclusion, Germany is clearly now a peace-loving democracy. Her history, her culture and her economic strength will naturally lead her to want to dominate the European scene. There is nothing wrong with that ambition as long as when it is thwarted, frustration does not lead Germany to reverting to its past. In fairness there is little real evidence of this trend in German policy, particularly under Chancellor Gerhard Schroeder's leadership. Indeed Germany's own sense of guilt is probably the greatest defence against the re-emergence of Naziism. As France's Vincent Auriol said 'We are prepared to forgive, as long as the Germans are never prepared to forget'.

France

The Germans have the largest European population (80 million) but the French have the largest country and a population (58 million) similar in size (if nothing else) to that of the British. The French idea of France begins with the revolution of 1789 and the establishment of the First Republic. The term *republique* in France has great significance because it represents the *constitution* to a French citizen in a similar manner to the American citizen's attitude to their Constitution. '*Vive la Republique*' is as emotive to a Frenchman as 'God Save the Queen' is to a traditional Briton. Each republic is seen not so much a delineating period of history but as a revised constitution or method of government. Currently France is governed by the terms of the Fifth

Republic that was formed in 1958 when General de Gaulle returned to power as Premier.

The impact of the French revolution, the First Republic and Napoleon are much greater on present French culture and national attitudes than all the previous history of France put together. This period is the source of her fundamental method of government, her legal system (the Code Napoleon), her educational system and her logical or scientific approach to most issues. For the majority of the French people this period is also and most importantly the source of their *liberté* or freedom which is jealously guarded. In essence the French are serious people who take themselves seriously and feel affronted when they are not taken seriously in return. But a national culture born of revolution will also have an emotional and volatile element in its nature.

The French love of *liberté* can provoke a volatile reaction if they see a perceived freedom or special interest under threat. The administrators in both Paris and Brussels have quailed in the face of French farmers determined to keep out British lamb or truck drivers protesting against a new regulation. Blocked motorways or blockaded ports have become commonplace and account for a generally-held British viewpoint that the French only implement or obey those Brussels directives that suit them. The number of partially state-owned industries that appear to ignore the laws on competition also contribute to this cynical view of the French commitment to European co-operation.

French national pride and intransigence come to the fore in the language and choice of food. The elite French Academy has fought to preserve the purity of the French language from the incursion of the uncivilised Anglo-Saxon infection. But they are steadily losing the war under continuous attack from the international media and urban argot. When it comes to food the French really display their insularity. A stroll around most French supermarkets will soon convince the observer that there is a dearth of *foreign* produce. It's not just the absence of English lamb, cheese, or biscuits, but port, sherry and many other products from other EU countries. Now that thousands of French men and women are working in London and SE England it will be interesting to see if free market choice invades the French tastebuds.

The serious side of France is seen in politics, academia, business and social life. The French take their language and other aspects of their cultural life very seriously indeed, resisting every possible 'corruption' from the 'uncivilised' Anglo-Saxon influence. The French cannot understand the British self-deprecating sense of humour; to them it seems unpatriotic. The French are also very formal in their communication style. Though the international nature of modern business is certainly influencing French business behaviour, they have not adapted to the easy first name terms of Anglo-Saxon business. The same formality is present in social life and that at times seems archaic to a modern Englishman, but a moment's thought might recall that it used to be called good manners.

The popular Anglo-Saxon perception of the French as an art-loving, romantic nation populated with sexy singers and great lovers is an illusion. 'Ooh-la-la' was a Parisian invention that has been successfully marketed since the era of the Impressionists. In reality the French are logical and scientific rather than artistic. A French school, university or institution is more likely to be headed by a science rather than an arts graduate, the exact opposite to Britain. The French reputation for engineering rivals that of the Scots across the world, and is central to the economic strength of France. Nuclear energy technology, the TGV rail system and their advanced aircraft and automobile industries are all evidence of this facet of French culture.

As one might expect from a logical nation, the French have worked hard at solving the cultural dilemma of the last century in trying to find a balance between the ideology of socialism and the pragmatism of conservatism. Like the Germans they have not wholly embraced the demands of the market and monetarist-led economy as the British did under Thatcher. That is both a weakness and a strength. France has high unemployment, strong public service and industrial unions, state-subsidised industry and a bureaucratic administration. On the other hand the French probably have the finest health service and quality of life in the world.

Two other factors contribute to the overall quality of life in France. The French have a strong sense of family that provides a stability to their culture. Of course all French family life is not a model of love and devotion, but they do seem to have survived the threat to the family as the key nucleus for a successful culture better than most major nations. The cohesive strength of the family is supported by the other key factor of French life, which is the importance they place on the role of food and drink in civilised life.

Again, contrary to popular perception it is not the culinary excellence of French cooking which is crucial (more great chefs come from Belgium than France) but the importance they place on the cultural place of the meal as a concept in its own right. Business breaks for two hours for lunch and the family regularly spends several hours over dinner. Conversation and inter-personal communication play a large part in the French life. This approach is probably helped by the banality of French television that provides little competition to the art and delight of conversation. We must all hope that the French do not improve their television and continue to allow good food, good wine and good talk to predominate.

As one might expect from a country stretching from the warm Mediterranean to the cool English Channel, there are major regional variations in France. For example there are five local languages and distinctive cultures within France. Castilian and Basque in the Pyrenees; the Alsatian language in Alsace; Breton in Brittany; and Corsican in Corsica exemplify this wide diversity of cultural strains. However, like the Welsh language in Britain, they are subservient to the national language. The French constitutional system provides a strong voice for regional differences so that externally the national culture predominates.

However, the French do have two great weaknesses or, perhaps more fairly, facets in their national culture which influence their relationships with their European partners. Both have their origins in relatively recent history and can be summarised as a rather fragile self-confidence and a deep sense of guilt over their part in the Second World War.

The French are said to have an inferiority complex as a nation that probably accounts for the occasional escape into some '*folie de grandeur*'. The general English reaction to the attitude is that they have spent a thousand years of history trying to convince the French that it is not a complex. However, there is an element of truth in this assertion. French self-confidence does seem to fluctuate with events more dramatically than that of other nations. To the extent that this trait is true it stems from the origins of modern France. Following the Revolution, the First Republic and the era of Napoleon started the new nation with incredible success so that France dominated continental Europe and, to some extent, the world. For the French the history of France has been downhill ever since. An example of this sensitivity came in 1989 at the French national celebrations of the 200th anniversary of the storming of the Bastille. The French President's claim that this date had marked the birth of modern democracy and the freedom of the common people was easily accepted by his nation. But Margaret Thatcher debunked this claim and reminded everyone of habeas corpus and parliamentary democracy that started much earlier in England. Perhaps this was an insensitive

80

comment by a guest at the celebrations, but the apoplectic reaction of the French media and her politicians was indicative of an inferiority complex. President Mitterrand tried to get his own back at the Channel Tunnel opening. On the celebratory train journey linking the two capitals he took great pleasure in pointing out the contrast between the tremendous speed of the Eurostar through the plain of Picardy and the much slower pace of the journey through the Kent countryside.

In terms of today's culture and national attitudes the Second World War has left more scars on France than almost any other European country, including Germany. Of course the war made a great impact on Germans, but somehow 1948 and the ensuing years of economic success acted as a new start. Not unlike the effect of the First Republic and Napoleon on the French, most Germans and particularly the younger generations seem to see pre-1948 as almost pre-history. This is why British and other nations' reservations about German objectives or motives often perplex them. But for the French it was a very different experience. In 1945 they were included with the victors and joined in the occupation of Germany, but deep down they recognised that they really had no right to be numbered with the victorious allies. Steadily since the war there have been more and more shameful revelations about the Vichy regime and the level of French collaboration with the Gestapo and other elements of the Nazi occupation. The real level of resistance is now generally accepted to have been way below the legends promoted immediately after the war.

All the attitudes we have discussed help us to understand how such a beautiful country with highly accomplished people should be plagued with so many doubts about themselves and a strong fear of a German revival. However, there are real signs that the French are entering a period of

81

high self-confidence and economic strength. In that mood they make great friends.

Italy

Italy is the joker in the European pack – on balance probably the most civilised nation in Europe. With its incredible artistic heritage Italy is now the clear leader in style and design. Italian names such as Ferrari, Fiat, Alfa-Romeo, Gucci and Versace epitomise everything that is good in industrial design, fashion and business success. However, in the modern world of political machismo the Italians tend to be overlooked, particularly by the British. The fact that Italy has not the slightest desire to dominate her neighbours (even the Italians viewed Mussolini and his Fascist imperial dreams as grand opera) sometimes hides the fact that Italy has a population equivalent to both France and the United Kingdom.

The French phrase *joie de vivre* has more relevance to Italian social life than to France or any other country in Europe. They rarely take themselves or other nations too seriously and have a sense of humour not unlike the English. They have deservedly built a reputation as the greatest restaurateurs in the world. 'Enjoy' is the essence of the Italian restaurant and indeed the Italian family meal. The concept of the family is even stronger in Italy than in France. There are very few old people's homes in Italy as the older members of the family are the natural responsibility of the extended warm Italian family.

Behind the obvious beauty, art and music of Italy there is another side that is far from attractive. Political and business corruption, often linked to organised crime (the Mafia), has been endemic in Italian life for decades. Wealthy individuals and corporations avoid paying taxes and regional investment and public works initiatives are milked of funds. The Venice Lido is a prime example. All of this has helped create an almost lawless attitude across Italy. These factors have exacerbated the wide divide between the wealthy industrial north and the impoverished, arid agricultural regions of the south. Coupled with the bizarre exchange rate for the old lira, this has given Italy the image of the sick man of Europe, which they inherited from the Britain of the seventies. This was a little unfair considering Italy's other economic achievements, including meeting the euro requirements, though with some manipulation of the rules.

But this may well be about to change. A massive transformation has been going on in Italy that has similarities to the impact of Margaret Thatcher on Britain. The nationwide drive against corruption, organised crime and tax evasion is reaching a level of success that could release the economic potential and energy of her people on world markets. Membership of the EU and the decision to accept the euro have been good for Italy. In return Italy may soon provide a new balance at the inner core and be good for the EU and *all* of its members.

Dependent Circle

Austria

The end of the Great War of 1914–1918 brought about the collapse of the Austro-Hungarian Empire of some 50 million people ruled from Vienna, and reduced Austria to a small country of some 8 million. As a result, the international image of Austria as a small Ruritanian state of music lovers and apple strudel nestling in the towering beauty of the Alps, is in reality a delusion.

Ostensibly a freedom-loving democracy, Austria, like her regional neighbour Bavaria, is still at the centre of a living Nazi cancer. As a small nation this aspect of modern Austria should pose little threat to the concept of a united Europe. This fact made the EU Commission's reaction to the electoral success of the Freedom Party led by Jorg Haider seem excessive and an unwarranted interference in the internal politics of a member state. Perhaps so, but this cancer at the heart of a Germanic Austria, naturally dependent on the new Federal Republic of Germany, is a concern for the future of Europe.

Benelux

The independent nations of Belgium, the Netherlands and Luxembourg joined together in the Benelux treaty of 1960 to establish economic but not political union between their countries. It is perhaps appropriate that these three nations play host to the most important of the EU institutions.

The area of these three nations has formed the cockpit of Europe for more than a thousand years. Over that period the armies of other European nations have marched across or fought their battles on their territory. Waterloo, Flanders, Mons, the Battle of the Bulge and Arnhem are just recent examples. Some of the old ethnic regional differences still exist in the Belgian conflict between the Dutch-speaking Flemish and the French-speaking Walloons. The Netherlands, once a great colonial power and scourge of the British, is hardly a dependent nation, but she now appears happy with her new role out of the limelight. However, in the future she could well emerge as a leader of the smaller nations.

Eire

The Irish have always had an influence in Europe and the United States way beyond the size of their nation (population 3.5 million) and its economic power. This is surprising as Eire is a relatively small island on the western extremities of Europe. There are a number of reasons for this high profile. The Irish are a loquacious people with a literary output that is recognised worldwide. But the primary reason for their influence is more than a 'touch of the Blarney' but the fact that for a century Eire has exported more than a third of its citizens to other countries. Indeed, in 2001 immigration to Ireland has exceeded emigration for the first time in history.

In recent years Eire has been a major beneficiary of European funds for regional investment. She has used the funds well and transformed the economy with a series of high tech and service economy initiatives. Eire is a committed and happy member of the EU, but some troubles are gathering on the horizon. Inflationary pressures are building which Eire has little power to curb independently now that she has joined the euro.

On a positive note the traditional enmity between Eire and the United Kingdom on the political front is rapidly disappearing as both governments actively collaborate in the peace process in Northern Ireland.

Greece

Greece is another small and poor country in Europe with an influence beyond its political or economic power. For many, Greece is the fount of European culture, which partly stems from the classical tradition of so many European schools and universities. Ancient Greek mythology and the teaching of her philosophers defined the great issues of life in the minds of many students. Certainly Greek mythology and philosophy is a major element in our heritage but there is one myth about Greece that is often repeated as if it was a truth. The myth that Greece was the founder of modern democracy is palpable nonsense and is only based on the linguistic source of the word and the perorations of romantic politicians. Athens may have contained a forum for slave-owning aristocrats but the concept never developed much beyond the listening circle. History should have taught us all that effective democracy is much more complex and needs constant attention as it evolves.

Greece has found that membership of the EU has meant substantial adjustment and change. The economic disciplines required have caused political disruption and some social unrest. However, it has paid off and Greece has achieved considerable economic growth in recent years and though there was doubt about her meeting the convergence criteria she became a member of Euroland in January 2001. The undoubted success of the Athens Olympics has enhanced her stature in Europe.

Though clearly a dependent nation, Greece is likely to have an influence with new entrants to the EU on the basis of her experience as a poor nation meeting the challenges of the EU. Another issue, which will be touched on later, is her acrimonious relationship with Turkey.

Independent Nations

The importance of the independent nations to this book is the likelihood that they are the countries most likely to resist the euro club's remorseless progress towards the federal state of Europe. They could also have a major influence on the new entrants to the EU over the next decade.

Denmark

Denmark is the one nation that survived occupation by the Germans in the Second World War with their dignity and respect still intact. It is easy to forget that under German occupation when called upon to identify the Jews, the King of Denmark demonstrated his opposition by walking the streets of Copenhagen with the Star of David '*Juden*' sign on his coat. With her referendum result against the euro, the Viking state has once more demonstrated its strong sense of independence. Michael Seidelin, political editor of pro-euro newspaper *Politzken* stated that in 'reality it is a vote on the whole question of Europe'. The Danish position had influence on the other Scandinavian nations. The Swedes have also voted in their referendum against the euro and the Norwegians will be confirmed in their decision to stay outside the EU.

At the time of writing Denmark is the one European country proving that you do not need to kowtow to Brussels and its directives to be successful.

Finland

Finland won her independence from Russia following the 1917 revolution. She again won the world's respect as 'plucky little Finland' resisted the Russian invasion of 1939. Though her size and economic power would tend to place Finland in the dependent circle, her fierce defence of her independence in her short history and her close collaboration with her Scandinavian neighbours places her in the outer circle. Her future position will be influenced by the approach by her neighbours the Baltic states of Estonia, Latvia and Lithuania who joined the EU in May 2004.

Portugal

Portugal is one of the most ancient nations in Europe and Britain's oldest ally. The fact that she has continued as a nation as the smaller occupant of the Iberian Peninsula is proof of her independent spirit. The Portuguese language is indicative of her colonial past and her wider influence in the world. Portugal has recovered from a long period of dictatorship and economic decline and is now winning a sense of self-confidence as her economy grows.

Spain

In area Spain is the second largest nation in Europe and Spanish is the fourth most widely spoken language in the world. Spain has been a great nation for centuries and at one time was the most powerful nation on earth. As Robert Stevens wrote in his book, *About Europe*, 'The character of Spain lies in its people, a proud and assertive race whose culture has swept across foreign lands in the wake of conquest'.

Since joining the EU, Spaniards have become enthusiastic members of the EU. However, having emerged from her long isolation under Franco this proud people are unlikely to allow Spain to be lost again in the State of Europe. Spain demonstrated her independence in joining the USA and Britain (and indeed Poland) in the war on Saddam Hussain. But then the terrorist attack on Madrid in 2004 and the defeat of the government for deceiving the electorate over the source of the attack has brought in a Socialist government highly pro the EU.

Sweden

Sweden's long-standing neutrality and non-alignment with European institutions came to an end when she joined the EU in 1993. It was not an easy decision and was only made after considerable national debate influenced by Sweden's lessening competitiveness and rising inflation.

To a large extent Sweden's international reputation is based on her long time leadership in the cause of peace. The Nobel prizes for peace, literature, medicine, chemistry and physics bring the world's most significant people in an annual pilgrimage to Stockholm.

Her international influence and her reputation for balanced judgement make Sweden a strong ally in the battle to prevent the federalisation of Europe.

United Kingdom

Britain is a set of small offshore islands to continental Europe, but her people have played a leading role in the history of Europe. At one time or another wars, diplomacy or trade have each brought the UK into conflict or alliance with all the other European countries. She used her geographical advantage to great effect, building the British Empire, the greatest empire the world has ever known, in competition with her European neighbours. Britain can claim the lead in developing the global economy with her efforts to develop world trade, ensure protection of sea-lanes, the enforcement of international laws and the establishment of global financial institutions. Overall, Britain's history, her international involvements, particularly with the United States, and her natural sense of superiority have not made her an easy partner for her EU colleagues. But the reader does not need another detailed repetition of Britain's history and her contribution to Europe. More pertinent to the arguments of this book are the evolving attitudes of the British people to the European Union.

The UK joined the Common Market for economic reasons and for a long period her people and perhaps most of her leaders were seduced into the belief that economic collaboration was the main purpose of the EEC. For some twenty-five years the people of Britain were focused on internal social, political and economic change. This era included the disastrous Labour Governments of Harold Wilson and James Callaghan (1964–1979) that led to national bank-ruptcy and was followed by the social and economic upheaval of the Margaret Thatcher years (1979–1990) when the country finally faced up to reality and successfully climbed out of the economic pit. During this long period Europe was hardly mentioned in the media headlines except for Margaret Thatcher's occasional forays with her handbag. Throughout this time the Europhiles were gaining power and influence and those who recognised the political significance of Commission actions were easily branded as outdated extremists and marginalised in all political parties. Towards the end of the Thatcher era the Europhiles became so strong in the Conservative Party that they were able to play a major part in the fall of Margaret Thatcher and imprisoned John Major throughout his premiership. But in the main, the British people were just not interested or involved in the European issue.

It is difficult to pinpoint exactly when this indifference began to change and the people of Britain began to speak. The arguments over Maastricht, Amsterdam and the presence of the Referendum Party at the 1997 election must have contributed, but perhaps it was the protracted disagreement over British beef that really started the process of change. Certainly the European Parliamentary elections in May 1999 came as a big shock as William Hague swept the field with the slogan 'In Europe but not run by Europe'. From then on the Eurosceptic cause has come out into the open and captured the media spotlight. The future of Europe is in focus and the debate has now opened in Britain.

The Europhiles seem flabbergasted and very much on the defensive. Tony Blair's government, ostensibly pro-European, seem a little lost waiting hopefully for the right moment to hold a referendum on joining the euro. The same dithering and lack of direction is evident in the argument over a referendum on the proposed European Constitution. Arrogant opposition to the concept has now given way to what the *Daily Mail* called 'a EU turn' and the British public are now going to get a referendum. Blair himself appears as a scoutmaster taking his charges for a row on the local park pond. There is no need for a sense of direction when the purpose is merely to keep rowing.

Ethnic issues and extremist groups

Several member nations of the EU have internal problems with ethnic groups and separatist nationalistic organisations. They are part of the diversity of interests in Europe, but their particular relevance is that these groups are increasingly seeking to use the EU's supranational institutions to further their cause. The IRA in Britain and ETA in Spain have been out and out terrorists but peace initiatives in both countries have reduced the bombing threat and they have achieved favourable rulings from the Court of Human Rights. On a lower level the Germans have had problems with their Turkish population as has Greece in Cyprus. Algerians and Corsicans cause similar problems in France, and Belgium has long wrestled with the Flemish/Walloon discords. In reverse, we have also seen the intervention of the EU in the internal affairs of Austria with the sanctions imposed over the Haider affair. These clashes provide opportunities for sovereign nations to be put into dispute with the Union and provide another reason for the growing change of mood about integration in many nations.

Regionalisation

Since the Maastricht Treaty in 1992 the steady growth of the EU policy on regionalism has provided clear evidence of the hidden agenda of the Commission. The Committee of the Regions, the European Regional Development Fund and the Assembly of European Regions are the institutions that the Eurocrats are using to transfer power progressively from national governments, through the European regions to the supranational bodies of the EU. New regional committees (often appointed rather than elected) within individual nations are being encouraged to instigate initiatives that appear reasonable but require funding. The European Regional Development Fund will then grant substantial funds on the basis that the national government will make a similar contribution. The British government has already been black-mailed to match European funding by the Welsh National Assembly representing a European region. In that context one wonders how many English citizens realise that England no longer exists on the Brussels European Map. As we noted earlier, Wales and Scotland are full regions but England is divided into autonomous regions or '*Länder*' on the German pattern. With some amusement the English noted that Wales disappeared altogether on one Brussels map.

These divide and rule concepts have a number of long-term perils for the Union. Clearly regions are defined on geographical, economic, ethnic or existing national regions. Currently, these issues are contained within sovereign states and in the main managed without too much rancour. In Britain the Scottish and Welsh issues are amusing but controllable but Northern Ireland is very different. But one can envisage a situation in which Wales and Scotland are gaining so much from regionalism that the United Kingdom becomes insignificant to them. As the union within one nation divides and creates dissension so will the unity of the European Union come under strain.

This same regional concept brings another threat to Europe that could raise some of the issues that led to war in the 20th century. As individual regions build up their independence within states they will tend to look for ways to extend their power within Europe. Some of these regions have an ethnic or local nationalistic basis for their differentiation but are at least contained within national boundaries. But if any of these regions can find ethnic or other identical interests with another European region that lies outside the national boundary, we could witness new divisions. The recent conflicts in the Balkans are one example of the problems raised. Another is the use that the Germans made in the 1930s of German minorities in the Sudetenland and Danzig. The problems of diversity within Europe do not automatically disappear with a European State.

Corporate grouping

Major business corporations are gaining in power as the global market expands. Their revenues often exceed the GNP of nations, and this will increase as they make mergers across international borders. Great national corporate names look far beyond their national origins – for example British Airways with its 'ethnic tail fins' and others who change their names to avoid recognition as regional specialists. Since the late 19th century, great corporations often saw themselves above the law and were influential in the formation of governments. Krupps, IG Farben and others were influential in central Europe, and now another group of corporate giants is flexing its muscles.

Within Europe there are groupings of industrial power that exist outside contemporary regions or national boundaries that are beginning to develop spheres of interest in their own right. The shapes of these areas may indicate a new era of 'banana shaped' republics developing within Europe. A southern banana starts in northern Italy, sweeping through Lyon and Toulouse down to Barcelona. A northern banana starts in the Saar, includes the Ruhr through Liege and Lille and into the silicon valley of south-east England. International capitalists and corporate leaders welcome a federal Europe if only because it reduces the number of governments they need to negotiate with from twenty-five to one. A substantial proportion of the hidden mandarins of the euro club are international financiers and industrialists.

A bureaucratic dream

To conclude this chapter on diversity and hidden agendas, it is worth recalling the old joke about the idealistic view of a united Europe, in which the national skills and characteristics would be combined for the benefit of all.

The utopian dream envisages a Europe in which the Germans run the army, the British are the policemen, the Italians run the restaurants, the Swiss are the bankers and the French are the lovers.

The Eurosceptic reply would be that it is an interesting concept but experience tells us that the Brussels bureaucrats are more likely to produce a Europe in which the Italians run the army, the Germans are the policemen, the British run the restaurants, the French are the bankers and the Swiss are the lovers.

Chapter Four

The Stifling Hand of Bureaucracy

'Don't consult anyone's opinion but your own.'

Persius, AD 34–62

The governance of the European Union is suspect. The suspicion grows that there is a corruption wider and deeper than the cancer brought out into the open by the resignation of the Commissioners in March 1999. That created a furore in the world's media for a few months. It also represented a turning point for the Eurosceptics and put the euro enthusiasts on to the back foot for a time. The majority verdict at the time seemed to be that the shamefaced ending for the Commissioners and the part that the European Parliament played in their downfall would bring about a new beginning. In other words that the Commission would have its power curbed and be more answerable to the European Parliament. There are some new theoretical curbs, but it cannot be said that the Commission has changed much. The other corruption, far more insidious than the venality of some Brussels Eurocrats, remains largely hidden as it has for decades. Yet, this cynical corruption of the institutions of the EU for the purposes of an elite few is yet another reason for Britain and other nations to resist the continuing march towards a federal state.

For Britain and other independently-minded nations the

hidden enemy behind the bureaucracy is the elusive euro club with members in every country. These Eurofanatics, committed to their dream of the European super state rather than to their own nations, use the Commission and the other institutions of the EU to further their aims. The bureaucracy of Brussels, pet hate of the sceptics and the British media, is merely the tool of the euro club. To date the bureaucracy has been the strength of the euro club but paradoxically it could become its nemesis. Any period of retrospective amendment of the treaties or directives could turn Brussels into a bastion of national sovereign rights.

State and Nation

It has become fashionable to treat the words 'state' and 'nation' as synonyms but there is a difference that is pertinent to these discussions. As Bernard Connolly pointed out in his book, *The Rotten Heart of Europe*, it is possible to envisage Europe as a state but it is almost impossible to envisage the totality of Europe as a nation.

The concept of the state is ideological in the sense that it is a political answer to *organising* existing peoples into a viable functional unit. On the other hand a nation *evolves* from the experience of its people. To put it another way, the state has to do with logic and science while the nation has more to do with people, their history and their emotions. In these terms the state represents a *political decision* (not necessarily wrong) at a particular moment while the nation represents a *culture*.

History provides many examples of nations evolving or being organised to establish new nation states. In Europe two examples support the thesis; Britain and Yugoslavia. The nation state of the United Kingdom has evolved and survived but not without difficulties. From time to time the national cultures of Scotland, Wales, and Northern Ireland asserted themselves. Britain needed several hundred years to become a reasonably stable nation state. The state of Yugoslavia was organised by the victorious powers after the First World War to solve some of the problems arising from the collapse of the Austro-Hungarian Empire. It survived a few decades of internal strife until it came under the iron hand of Tito as a Communist state after the Second World War. With the death of Tito and the collapse of Communism the organising or controlling political hand was gone. In no time the stable nation state was blown apart as the strong differences in ethnic cultures sought their nationhood. As a result in the 1990s, for the first time since 1945, there was war on the European mainland. More to the point, major nations within the EU reverted to conflicting traditional stances to the war in the Balkans.

In the wider world context there are many examples of attempts to combine nations or small states into nation states. Three examples, Russia, India and the United States of America serve to develop the point. Russian history is a continuous story of one nation attempting to control or organise disparate cultures into one super state. Most recently we have seen what happens when that kind of state relinquishes or loses its organising control. As with Yugoslavia, the Union of Soviet Socialist Republics was torn asunder and even now, some smaller nations of what remains of that Union, are in armed conflict with the nation state. Students of history will recognise that something similar happened twice before to Russia. In India the issue is more complicated as it can become confused with the battle for independence from Britain, but the lesson is the same. The original politically organised plan for the federation of the diverse national cultures of the sub-continent was overtaken by partition and Pakistan was formed. Even that partition of major religious cultures was not enough. The later formation of Bangladesh

97

after a war and the continuing problems over Kashmir are indicative of this. But the remaining states of India, have not made an easy alliance and to some extent are only held together by the unifying imported culture of the English language. To prove the point try sending a fax from Delhi to Madras in any language other than English and observe the reaction. Madras will ignore a communication in Hindi. It is absolutely clear that super states do not eliminate the strains of diverse cultures. But then there is the United States of America.

The USA is often held up as a model for the United States of Europe by Europhiles and would seem to refute the author's thesis. However, the historical development of the cultural components of the USA and Europe are so diametrically different that the choice of the USA as a model can only be considered as a case of ignorance, naivety or perfidy.

Colonial North America began with two unifying cultural elements, the English language and the shared fellowship of a dream. The original thirteen states were heavily populated by people of English descent, though there was a substantial German speaking minority. Both shared the common experience of escaping religious persecution or other con-straints on their freedom to better themselves. A few also had that restless energy for new frontiers that epitomised the England of that time; in the main this group provided the leaders. In the formative years the colonial states were unified by their allegiance to their original homeland until England tried to levy taxes that the colonies considered unjust. When they resisted, Britain without much thought sent a gunboat (actually a number of gunboats) to sort out these errant children and teach them a lesson. This acted as the catalyst that created the USA. The individual states combined to resist the impositions of the mother country. In a glorious moment of history they came together in

Philadelphia to draw up a 'Constitution' which seemed to express a dream for all those who hungered for freedom from oppression in many parts of the world, but in particular Europe. The fact that they were eventually successful in their 'War of Independence' gave the dream a reality.

Before the new American dream had fully evolved it was tested almost to destruction. Even with the advantages of the common cultures we have noted, new cultural diversities were emerging which resulted in the devastating horror of the Civil War. This conflict, fought less than a century after the War of Independence, was to have an impact on the USA at least equal to the impact of the First World War on Europe. It has not totally disappeared even today.

Popular history has portrayed the Civil War as a conflict about slavery. The Civil War is seen as a clear picture of black and white and right and wrong. Unfortunately history is not quite like that and it doesn't really represent the views of the Americans engaged in the war on both sides. Lincoln the President of the North did not promulgate the emancipation of the slaves until halfway through the war. Slavery was the issue that sparked the confrontation between the states but the issue of principle that provoked the war was the right of an individual state to govern itself, despite the view of a majority of the Union. Slave and non-slave states had co-existed since Independence without too much difficulty. The growth of new states and their right to make a decision on slavery provoked the Civil War. Essentially the South believed it was fighting for 'States Rights' and the North believed that it was fighting for the preservation of the Union as defined in the Constitution. In the hindsight of history we can all recognise that the issue of slavery was a matter of human rights that transcended any political polemic. However, the point remains as we consider European issues; the Civil War started over the rights of the equivalent of a nation state in conflict with the objectives of the super state.

Following the Civil War, the USA became the mecca for the oppressed and downtrodden people of the world, and expanded rapidly to become, in the 20th century, the greatest single power the world has ever seen. Millions of people emigrated from Europe and other parts of the world. All the immigrants were happy to accept that they must conform to the unifying culture of the English language and to the rules of the Constitution. They all took part in an examination on both these elements before they could receive their citizenship. (The USA may eventually rue its recent relaxation of those unifying rules.) However, that same Constitution allowed them to retain the social elements of the culture they had abandoned. A strong thread of Italian, Irish, Polish, German, Swedish and Jewish social cultures survived in the USA but were always secondary to the unity of America. The immigrants understood the importance of being American first and Italian or Irish second and so the Union has not only survived, but has grown in strength.

Some Europeans, including the British, have found it easy to sneer at this polyglot nation and dismiss America as 'Johnny come lately' with no real experience or understanding of international diplomacy. At one time the phrase the 'Ugly American' became very fashionable in Europe. However, a glance at history shows that the highly experienced and diplomatic masters of Europe had somehow allowed themselves to be plunged into two devastating world wars and in the end only survived with American help. Of course the USA has made some naive mistakes, but the real lesson of history is that this is the first time that a super power has emerged with the self-confidence not to need to conquer or colonise the rest of the world. To quote Alistair Cook, 'The only time Europe wants American values is when it needs them'.

The possible development of a United States of Europe would have no relationship to the development of the USA.

Europe is not an empty continent ready to welcome a massive influx of volunteers eager to embrace a new culture, a new language and a new form of governance. On the contrary it is a heavily-populated area with a wide diversity of ancient and ingrained cultures, languages and political institutions. Economic circumstances have created a need to collaborate, but there is little evidence that the settled peoples of individual nations are ready voluntarily to merge their cultures, languages and political traditions to build a new European dream. Why should the wonderfully diverse peoples of Europe be subjugated to the will of a few powerful people who believe that they know best?

Nevertheless, the euro club is still convinced that it can establish a cultural identity across Europe. They have now launched a new Constitution for Europe to help bring this identity about. Again they forget their history. Unifying constitutions come from extreme pressures that involve the total population. This is what really creates the identity of interest. This is what happened in the USA, India and the new Germany and other instances. Where is this feeling of common identity in Europe that will fully engage their peoples? The functionalists early on decided that one way to encourage this identity or common culture was to drive for a single currency. We will examine the efficacy of this argument in more detail in Chapter Six – *A Divisive Single Currency*.

One essential facet of a common culture is slowly evolving in Europe and relates to the development of federal states in the USA and India. A common language for Europe would do much to provide a shared identity that could break down other traditional cultural barriers. That common language would have to be English if only because it has become the *lingua franca* of international business. For many years the citizens of those EU countries with non-international languages such as Swedish, Dutch and Danish have regularly used a second language: English. The Germans, Italians and to a lesser extent the French are putting more emphasis on learning and using English for both business and international communication. English is the official language of the European Central Bank, even though the Bank is in Frankfurt and Britain is not a member of the European Monetary Union.

There is a strong logical argument for a European common language as a unifier and for English to be that common language. The principle objective of the EU, as we have been told, is to enhance the economic position of its members in the competitive global economy. How better to achieve this economic objective than by making the language of the global business community the common language of the European community. This could provide the euro club an opportunity to progress its dream of a European super state.

In all logic the Commission should be proposing a new directive to make English the *only* language of the EU. In other words a similar directive to the one that enforced the continental method of weights and measures on *all* EU nations. Despite the French love of logic they could be expected to brandish their veto. One can imagine the debate on the decision. The British representatives would tentatively accept the directive but express a deep sympathy for the viewpoint of their European partners. The Germans would explain with ponderous calm that though they accepted the long-term inevitability of the directive, they could not accept that it applied to the *Reichstag* or the individual *Länder.* The Italians would exclaim *Si!* and explain that it was an essential element of their culture to write all menus in both English and Italian. The Irish would claim that they didn't really understand the need for the directive as they already spoke English and the Danes would die laughing. There is no polite way to describe the French reaction.

Perhaps a perverse English sense of irony has been allowed

to intervene but the purpose of irony is to highlight the essential ridiculousness of the proposition. In the long term international pressures may ensure that English will evolve as the dominant language of Europe. However, that is a long way off and will only play a limited part in creating a unifying culture for the EU. If that is so, then the only unifying culture available to Europhiles to exploit is the economic issue. The question then arises, is it possible for Europe to survive in this fiercely competitive world without political union? That issue will be examined in Chapter Five – *The Economic Issues of Union*.

The euro club elite

Every nation in Europe has long had an elite group of people who believe that their position, power or sheer intelligence makes them ideally qualified to make decisions for other lesser beings. At their centre are the mandarins of the national civil service who continuously keep their hands on the levers of power and control the implementing bureaucracy. They are by nature and inclination skilled networkers who have quietly used their educational institutions and positions to move easily among others who wield power, through the ownership of land, title or great corporations. They tend to arrogance and to be impatient with all the 'nonsense' of democracy such as elections and other means of seeking the opinions of the *lumpen proletariat* or even with parliaments who have the impudence to want to call them to account. They also tend to shun the limelight and so remain hidden and elusive. Yet they have large armies of bureaucrats at their command. The average citizen only makes contact with the lower foot soldiers of those armies; the much-despised bureaucrats. There are exceptions: the bureaucrat in India is recognised as a leader and is shown great respect. The author remembers watching the parades for the Indian Republic Day in New Delhi on television. The commentator explained that the stands surrounding the saluting base were reserved for 'bureaucrats and other VIPs'.

National elites have networked across country borders for centuries, though the general slowness of communication and constraints on travel sometimes made this an ineffective process. At some stages in history the church represented an alternative power clique and operated its own networks. Then the catastrophic impact of the First World War changed everything. The collapse of the old order and the sense of staring into the abyss brought the elite of Europe together into almost endless international committees and conferences. With hindsight it is now clear that the foundations of the euro club were laid in the 1920s and 1930s. Their growing collaboration was based on two shared fears. First was the fear that Germany might start war all over again. Second was the fear that unless they organised a rapprochement in the centre of Europe the future was anarchy and for most of the elite that meant Bolshevism. The arrogance of the elite is founded on a basic insecurity; a fear that the whole pack of cards could collapse if a wider audience found out what was really happening. It was in this atmosphere that the euro club was born.

From the outset the euro club was dominated by the French. Initially this was partly by accident, but after 1945 it was mainly by design. The first leader of the group was Briand, followed by his protégé Monnet. They were both fiercely intelligent, natural networkers and masters of the technocracy of planning and managing bureaucracies. They were both noted alumni of the elite French educational system with its heavy bias towards logic and science. Armed with these talents, they developed logical answers to the fears of Germany and anarchy. Their solution was based on a federal Europe that would both curb Germany and expand

104

the opportunities for the elite to guide the future. Their plans were not overtly fascist or communist but they were functional and anti-nationalistic. Though mainly driven by French functionaries, their dreams of a federal Europe appealed to many others in other national elites. In time the concept had a greater call on their allegiance than that to their own country. In their arrogance they had decided that their solution was in the best interests of their own countrymen. We will consider the activities of the Bilderberg Group as an outward sign of the elite euro club in an appendix.

The worldwide depression of the 1930s brought about a change of focus and resulted in the rise of Hitler and the Nazi Party. The German elite at first despised Hitler but soon compromised as he manipulated them with a series of direct actions that put an end to the recession and the chaos in Germany. First in 1934 he eliminated Rohm and the S.A. hooligans who were challenging the army. Then he launched major capital programmes to rejuvenate German industry and expand the armed forces. In addition, he liquidated the unions and imprisoned other dissidents in the new concentration camps. In no time at all the bureaucrats, the industrialists, the financiers and the armed forces were taking the oath of loyalty to Adolf Hitler rather than to the nation. The German elite explained to their European colleagues that Hitler was their chance to rid Europe of anarchy and to build a greater European state. They advised sceptics to forget the fear of German domination, because we will soon curb the excesses of Nazism, and in any case Hitler is not an intellectual and therefore cannot last.

Already in the 1930s the insidious strength of the euro club was permeating the national policies of once great nations. France, who had suffered greatly in terms of casualties and the loss of national morale in the Great War were so susceptible to the compromise approach which they were eventually to take to the extreme in the Vichy culture.

The Italian people didn't seem very interested in what was happening north of the Alps, but in any case already had their own Fascist regime. Its bombastic leader, Mussolini, saw opportunities to gain the laurels of a Roman Emperor and so provided support to the new order. But his foreign minister and son-in-law, Count Ciano, kept his own channels open to the euro club.

The euro club network included many in Britain of whom the most notable were the Cliveden Set. This elite group were based on the hospitality of the Astors at their great house, Cliveden, on the River Thames a few miles from London. The British Foreign Secretary, Lord Halifax, his assistant R.A. Butler and Geoffrey Dawson, editor of *The Times* were among those prepared to accept compromise and appease Hitler. Neville Chamberlain, the British Prime Minister, was bemused by events 'in far-away countries between people of whom we know nothing' and was easy meat for Halifax and the appeasers. The Cliveden Set and others contrived to foster appeasement and prevent war with Hitler's Germany but it has to be said, in fairness, that they were supported in this by the majority of the British population. Even in late 1940, after the Battle of Britain, Halifax and his supporters wanted a negotiated peace with Hitler. In later years the British were vociferous in their condemnation of the Vichy regime and the collaboration it represented but in 1940, in Britain, there were plenty of elite leaders who would have been ready to settle for a Vichy-style government. Luckily for history and the British there was another leader to hand in Winston Churchill. He detested appeasers, was a difficult iconoclast who distrusted 'functionaries', had a clear set of principles and had the towering ability to convey them to the British people and the world.

By 1948 the French had again taken control of the European movement. They still feared the Germans but they were now taking part in the occupation of Germany and the management

106

of them with the USA, UK and USSR. They considered that the federal solution would integrate and emasculate the Germans and that the brilliance of their own functionaries would mean, in effect, that the French ran Europe. But other French insecurities now came to the fore, some of which had been exacerbated by their experiences in the war. For historical and emotional reasons the French hate the Anglo-Saxon way of doing things. For them the Anglo-Saxon has replaced the Hun and the Visigoth as the barbarians at the gates ready to tear down French civilisation. In more recent years, as they have become involved in the global market, the Japanese have been added to this pantheon of terrors and they will stop at nothing to keep all of them from the centre of Europe.

The euro club elite is a conspiracy of federalists and they operate in every country of the EU. They include corporate leaders who have an interest in reducing the number of governments with whom they have to deal, politicians with a love of utopian answers or a desperate need to *modernise*, and of course the leading academics and technocrats who believe that they should be in charge.

In recent years a number of books have attempted to raise the veils of secrecy that surround this conspiracy. One book towers above them all. With its meticulous research and an insider's account of what is happening, Bernard Connolly, himself a disaffected senior Eurocrat, describes in great detail the progress of the exchange rate mechanism (ERM) and the euro currency. His book *The Rotten Heart of Europe* exposes the insidious tactics of the euro enthusiasts.

Bureaucratic directives

Jean Monnet decreed that the objectives of federalism would only be achieved by the steady application of *functionalism*.

It was all in the open and everyone seemed to agree without the slightest idea of what it meant. It actually meant that the functionaries in Brussels would search for 'little local difficulties' or obstacles to free trade and produce a directive to overcome them to *harmonise* an international approach for Europe. They were well-trained and assiduous Eurocrats and soon the directives flowing from Brussels were being numbered in hundreds. Each new treaty was designed by the Commission to open new areas for directives. They seemed reasonable to heads of state who didn't have the time or inclination to delve too deeply. Following Maastricht, the flood-gates were opened and the red tape began to unroll in kilometre after kilometre. Each piece of red tape slightly restricted a nation's right to make its own regulations in an increasing number of areas. They include food safety, product definitions, workers rights, advertising, transportation and many others. As Monnet intended step by step the diverse countries of Europe are being standardised. The Commission is now driving at even more fundamental directives designed to standardise taxation, state banking, currency and create a European army.

There are a number of problems in resisting this remorseless march of directives which can be summarised as:

- They are not all bad.
- The British media often misrepresents them.
- The supine behaviour of the British bureaucrats.
- The failure of British politicians to reduce the number of broad directives that can produce thousands of small directives which need no return to the table before application.
- The failure of British politicians to fight for a reduction in bureaucracy in line with its national economic policies.

Not all directives that emanate from Brussels are automatically bad. They often start with a fundamental point of safety or perceived difficulty in common product descriptions. Until relatively recently the British paid little attention to the process of developing a directive and thus were suddenly hit by new regulations with little or no notice. Commission directives go through a green paper/white paper series of drafts not unlike the British system for introducing new legislation. The British media will then leap upon an initial draft and scream that the Brussels' bureaucrats are about to ban the British sausage. They have no intention of doing anything of the sort. They do have a problem with the fraudulent description of continental sausages that are a totally different product. The differences between the British and continental versions can be argued at the draft stage and were; as a result we still eat British sausages. This leads to a lot of media hype that creates a situation of crying wolf, to the degree that a really dangerous directive can escape any critical comment, particularly if it is complicated.

Christopher Booker, the journalist and writer, has produced substantial evidence that one of the worst sinners is the British Civil Service. It appears to stem from their own arrogance that they are better at producing regulations than their Brussels counterparts. While the original directive may have loopholes which allow for some local discretion, the UK Civil Service hunts them down and closes every loophole. In the process they create ludicrous regulations with horrendous consequences for small but legitimate entre-preneurs. They add all sorts of requirements never envisaged by the Commission. One such example quoted by Booker is the Workplace Directive 891/654, which contained just 34 lines relating to fire safety. Whitehall officials managed to turn those 34 lines into 20 pages of a regulation, plus more than 100 pages of explanatory guidance. The original 34 lines were ... successfully expanded into 3,500 lines and Sir Humphrey beamed his approval. It is high time that

British politicians took a very sharp axe to these red tape factories. That would be real modernisation!

However, even taking all that into account, there are still far too many directives which are restricting British opportunities to build an entrepreneurial economy fit for the global market. In other words we are allowing the Commission to achieve Monnet's objective of restraining the Anglo-Saxons. We are running out of time but there is still a chance to reduce the current pace of directives and even a possibility of reversing the whole process. Our politicians must find the courage to fight the process and beat the euro club at its own game; *functionalism*. A step-by-step approach to reduce regulation and free the entrepreneurial potential of all the peoples of the Union. Politically we must use every opportunity for referenda on key directives or major new moves. The argument has to be taken over the heads of the apparatchiks to the people of Europe.

Our own functionaries must be directed to pay attention to the detail so as to build up the evidence for reforming battles against the functionaries of Brussels. Gathering this evidence should not be too difficult. Christopher Booker has developed hundreds of examples of red tape bureaucracy in his *Sunday Telegraph* column and his book, *The Castle of Lies*, written in collaboration with Richard North. The book develops the argument that how, compared with other European nations, Britain is making a unique mess of this new form of government, whose centre is no longer London but Brussels. The book is much more than a set of examples but provides a powerful focus on the 'New Totalitarianism' with all its deceptions.

Christopher Booker's case that Britain is being strangled by red tape is supported by dozens of well-documented examples. Rather than develop another list of examples (my references, press clippings and research under this area contain two packed filing boxes of papers detailing ludicrous

110

examples of the imposition of EU directives on our daily life) to fill this book one example from the prologue to Booker's book, *The Castle of Lies*, which is entitled 'The Binding of Gulliver', provides a good flavour of all this nonsense.

'One of the more haunting images in English literature is that of Gulliver waking up on the beach on which he has been shipwrecked. He finds to his alarm he cannot move. Gradually he realises that, while he has been asleep, an army of Lilliputians has tied him down in a mass of silken threads. He is a prisoner.'

All over Britain in 1995 and 1996 people began to feel they had been through a not dissimilar experience to Gulliver's. They were gradually waking up to the fact that something very strange had happened to their system of government.

One morning in April 1995 farmers gathered in the north Yorkshire market town of Malton, as they had done for centuries, to sell their animals. Suddenly from all sides of the market place came a crowd of policemen and officials. Business came to a halt as dozens of farmers were interrogated about the weight of the Land-Rovers and trailers in which they had brought their cows and sheep to market. Most were then told, to their astonishment, that they were committing a criminal offence. The combined weight of their vehicles, trailers and the animals in them came to more than 3.5 metric tonnes. This meant, under new regulations, that their farm vehicles should have tachographs, the 'spy in the cab' devices fitted to heavy goods vehicles to record the exact times and distances drivers spend on the road on long journeys. When a farmer who had heard of the new law protested that surely it didn't apply to farmers driving to their nearest market, a policeman asked where he came from. Egton, on the Yorkshire Moors, was the reply. 'Then Malton is not your nearest market' the policeman told him. There was a tiny mart on the moors, at the little village of Ruswarp.

The farmer indignantly explained that he didn't use Ruswarp because he could get £60 more for his animals at Malton. This was irrelevant, said the policeman. Under the law Malton was not his nearest market; he would therefore have to spend £700 fitting his Land-Rover with a tachograph.

What none of the policemen or officials bothered to explain was that these new rules came from EC Council Regulation 3820/85 on 'the harmonising of certain social legislation relating to road transport'.

In August 2000 the Confederation of British Industry (CBI), which has traditionally supported the euro cause, produced a report that their research indicated that the directives implemented in Britain over the previous two years had cost industry about £13 billion. Other bodies over the years have estimated that the overall cost of implementing EU directives since the UK joined the EEC amounted to hundreds of billions. All of these estimates are the subject of criticism if only because of the limited provision of evidence and all the issues of double counting. Nevertheless, the balance of evidence does indicate that Britain is paying a massive price to remain in the European Union. It is possible that it may all be worth it and represent a good investment for the future. But surely the onus of proof must be on the euro enthusiasts who are urging the nation to follow that route. To date that has not happened.

UK leaders over the years have appeared to be in thrall to the Europhiles. With the honourable exception of Margaret Thatcher, all UK prime ministers have either been Euro fanatics like Edward Heath or have been at pains to prove themselves as 'good Europeans' and aiming to position the UK at the 'heart of Europe'. All (including Heath) have denied that they intended to surrender British sovereignty to the concept of a federal super-state. The question then arises, how have they allowed both the UK and Europe to get into the current position?

Before answering that question the authors must make it clear that it is not their objective or the objective of many other sceptics to destroy the EU or even for the UK to leave the EU. They still support the development of a strong collaboration between European nations to the economic benefit of all. They even accept that this objective will entail some constraints on their freedom to act independently, as would any alliance. However, they do believe that the power of the Commission (supported by France and Germany in their national interests) has gone too far and must be restricted or reversed for the benefit of all the present and future members of the European Union. Further, they believe that this has always been the role of Britain and that in general it has proved in retrospect to be to the interest of the whole of Europe.

In that context where have British leaders failed and what should be their attitude to the current position of the EU? Most certainly it is to recognise the mistakes of the past but not just to accept them: they must ensure that the mistakes are not repeated. For the sake of the UK and the EU, what is needed now is a vigorous policy to support the original concept of the EU that the UK and others joined. This will entail a difficult period of direct confrontation with the multi-headed elements of the euro club and their chosen front men, the Commission. Part Three of this book will concentrate on the winning vision of this policy. Now we have to return to other elements of the stifling hand of the euro bureaucracy.

Corruption exposed

From time to time minor corruption has been exposed in British politics. The 'Poulson Affair' in the 1960s was one such incident, but in the late nineties the British electorate became obsessed with 'sleaze' and the easy corruptibility of their politicians. But these were all minor peccadilloes in comparison with the widespread corruption common on the continent. The long-drawn-out investigation into the financial probity of former Chancellor Helmut Kohl has highlighted the penetration of corrupt practices at the highest level of German politics. Long before the excesses of Mme Edith Cresson were exposed French politics were also riddled with corruption at every level. All this probably accounts for the limited impact on European politics of the resignation of all the Commissioners of the EU in 1999, accused of widespread corruption. The President of the Commission, Jacques Santer, paid the price, but most of the other Commissioners survived to fight another day. Even though not guilty of personal culpability there surely had to be an element of 'looking the other way'. But no! One of the Commissioners who resigned on the basis of collective guilt, Neil Kinnock, was reappointed and even given the role of ridding the EU of corruption.

At first the Eurosceptics welcomed 'the growing strength' of the European Parliament, which had been castigating the Commission for a long time over fraud and mismanagement. Lord Tebbit said that the row had demonstrated the 'institutionalised corruption' in the Commission and called for the removal of power from both Brussels and the whole of the EU. Eurosceptics and Europhiles alike took solace from the possibility that a 'proper public service in Brussels would arise and that Europe would be better run'. The general British reaction was that it was good to see that the Commission had been held 'accountable' by a 'democratic institution'. In other words that the European Parliament was now acting like the British Parliament. But some had doubts.

The doubts began with the general reaction of the errant Commissioners. Jacques Santer and later Edith Cresson displayed no sense of guilt. Later many Commissioners returned to office mouthing words of reform but appeared to accept no personal blame for the fiasco. Neil Kinnock now heads the reformers, while Leon Brittan has retired and has since published a book, *A Diet of Brussels*. He describes his work in Brussels and seems to believe that the whole question of corruption is not worth discussing. Yet, these people were the senior executives of the whole sordid enterprise.

The root of the problem lies with the structure and working practices of the Commission. As the EU correspondent of *The Times* Toby Helm noted at the time 'they will have to overhaul the staff de-motivating rules that govern the Commission. These prevent able young officials being promoted on merit and, instead, ensure progress is based almost entirely on time served. It has long been the combination of job security, boredom and cerebral atrophy in the Commission that has helped foster corruption and inefficiency'. He concluded 'The promises to reform the commission and turn it into a squeaky clean, dynamic and motivated executive engine look over optimistic'.

In fairness to the Commission and its staff, the EU civil service is severely stretched. As part of the Monnet strategy, Brussels has not created the *size* of bureaucracy that might have been expected. Quite apart from the continuing battle of the budget, the Commission has carefully maintained its approach to promulgating the general principles of directives and insisting that the subsidiary national bureaucracies worked up the detail. However, the work involved in supporting the numerous Councils of Ministers and the regular meetings of the 'heads of state' have stretched the Commission's resources.

The natural answer is to battle the budget pressures and provide increased resources to the Commission so that it can efficiently carry out its workload. That is what is likely to happen. An alternative that Britain and the independent circle should fight for is the simpler answer: reduce the workload. A steady evolving reduction in the powers and duties of the Commission would solve the problem without the crisis of over-dramatic change. It would also carry a strong Thatcherite message to the powerful staff unions who call Eurocrats out on strike at every stage of change. This change of attitude would require a massive reversal of the semi-socialist beliefs of the French and German politicians. On the positive side there are some indications that Gerhard Schroeder, the German Chancellor was making tentative moves in that direction, but recently electoral problems seem to have put these moves on hold.

The gravy train

There has been considerable criticism in Britain over the array of perks available to members of the Commission and the European Members of Parliament. Clearly the duty-free supermarket available exclusively to Commission and Brussels diplomatic staff was a gross act of greed. This was a particular red rag to a bull when it continued after the corruption scandal and after the end of duty-free concessions for European travellers. Public reaction has brought about the end of this perk but it is yet another example of the 'elite' not being subject to the rules governing the *hoi polloi*. Some of the disquiet has been caused by the comparison of salaries with counterparts in the UK. However, UK parliamentarians have long suffered from such comparisons with their equivalent worldwide. Nevertheless, citizens have a right to be angry at the obvious systematic abuse of expense allowances. Stricter regulations, clearly spelt out and properly audited by an independent body are long overdue in all the institutions of the EU.

The judiciary

The whole issue of the supremacy of the EU law and the laws of bodies such as the Court of Human Rights over national laws is a major area of principle for the future of the EU. This will be discussed in Chapter Seven – *Widening and Deepening*.

Chapter Five

The Economic Issues of Union

'Practical men, who believe themselves to be quite exempt from any intellectual influences, are usually the slaves of some defunct economist.'

J.M. Keynes

A fascination of the European debate is that it abounds with paradoxes that tend to confuse the logical arguments of both the Europhiles and the Eurosceptics. The paradox of diversity clouds many of the economic issues of the union. There are elements in the diversity of economic practices in the member states of the EU that call out for amendment and integration. At the same time there are areas of diversity in economic culture that would inhibit successful integration. For example, a wide diversity of customs duties, weights and measures, product recognition and other standards would clearly make it very difficult to maintain an economic community. Yet, at the same time the diversity of economic and political strategies between member states could make deeper integration a dangerous option for some nations and indeed the overall economy of Europe. The biggest single issue to exemplify this paradox is the decision about the euro or single currency (and both sides of that argument will be discussed in the next chapter) but there are underlying economic divisions that influence every facet of the future of Europe.

Euro-enthusiasts have little time for all the niceties of the diversity argument. To their mind the whole purpose of integration is to eliminate diversity. In the United States of America the economic strategy is a federal issue to be decided at the centre. Therefore the economic direction must be imposed to ensure that it is the same for all or 'one size fits all shapes'. There is some logic in that argument but as with all logic it depends on the premise. Yet there are few 'heads of agreement' on the direction of the European economy to provide a firm premise. Integration on its own does not select the right economic direction for Europe and in today's global economy to select the wrong strategy could be suicidal. If there is ever to be a single European economic strategy it must be allowed time to evolve; the inner circle cannot just decree it.

The independent circle of nations, which includes the UK, is extremely hesitant about this argument. These countries see a strong contrast and contest in the global market between the highly over taxed and over regulated economies of Europe and the much freer economic strategy of the USA with higher rewards for hard work, risk-taking and enterprise. As a broad generalisation Germany, France and to a lesser extent Italy favour the controlled and regulated economy in thrall to trade union power while Britain and others tend towards the American answer. For the 'reasonable man' it would be disastrous for the UK to sacrifice more sovereignty in the cause of a false unity, which it would be if the EU were to follow the disproved German and French model. In reality diversity is still the strength of Europe and rather than inhibiting decisions it maintains the power of choice. A decision to halt or even slow the pace of European integration to provide a period for deeper thought and general economic evolution would be a positive rather than a negative step.

Since Maastricht in 1992, tactical integration has moved ahead at a fast pace as thousands of directives have emanated from Brussels. A whole series of barriers to trading across national boundaries has been dismantled (including for many the actual boundaries) and in the main have proved to be successful. This has naturally encouraged the Europhiles to demand that the pace be maintained to remove remaining barriers including disparate tax systems and individual currencies. However, the mood has changed in countries like Britain and Denmark. The mass of directives may have achieved the Commission's objective but their implementation has caused problems in the UK. The principle of subsidiarity, which means that each country implements a directive through its own parliamentary/legal system, has actually put a 'spanner in the works' of Monnet's theory of *functionalism*. The UK civil service has managed in nearly every case to take a broad directive and turn it into a pedantic set of regulations that strangle business with red tape, cripple initiative and in many cases add horrendous costs which can destroy small businesses. The common law precept of 'what a reasonable man might expect' has been drowned in bureaucratic statutes.

Steadily as this approach has become apparent, there has been a growing anger in the country at what is seen as the imposition of foreign laws from the EU. This change of mood has caught the Europhiles by surprise, and allowed the sceptics their time on the stage. But at least the delays provides some time for thought and perhaps more serious debate about the more important economic barriers to integration.

The attitude of Britain towards integration and a European economic strategy has been complicated by internal political change. The period of purposeful confrontation and certainty under Margaret Thatcher was replaced by the 'nice man' compromises of John Major. The 1997 election brought about another political change with the election of the New Labour government. The new Prime Minister, Tony Blair, seemed to bring a new certainty as a declared Europhile pledged to

121

'put Britain at the centre of Europe'. But Blair has found this stance increasingly difficult and frustrating. For one, the French and Germans were not about to share the leadership with Britain and, for another, he was facing unexpected opposition back home from elements in his own party, including Gordon Brown his Chancellor of the Exchequer, and a growing awareness by the public at large.

In terms of Europe and many other issues the New Labour Party was not quite certain what it stood for and what exactly were its new principles. The success of the Thatcherite principles had forced the old Labour Party to shed its socialist principles if it was ever to be electable. Since then it has been desperately trying to find or to invent some new principles. It finally and successfully fought the 1997 election on the principles of ethical politics and modernisation. In no time at all ethical politics had to be abandoned as they didn't accurately describe New Labour politicians in action, but modernisation continued to hold sway. The difficulty with modernisation is that it is impossible to define as a guiding strategy and so quickly becomes mindless change or a pious hope rather than a principle. So on one hand Britain has experienced a government dedicated to modernising everything to little purpose and on the other hand being tempted back to its old principles of tax and spend. The General Election of 2001 brought more focus in the sense of improving or modernising public services and that became the new strategy. But a party with no principles, just as a party that has temporarily forgotten its own principles, is forever looking over its shoulder trying to gauge public opinion to seize political advantage. This is a little like trying to find directions in a desert storm without a compass. Typical examples have been the reform of the House of Lords together with the intended elimination of the post of Lord Chancellor. A growing scepticism about the modernisation of public services and further loss of 'Britishness' in the public perception is the 'sandstorm' for the present government.

Tony Blair, the UK Prime Minister, has a natural affinity with the Christian Democratic Socialism of continental Europe and so came to power with a natural sympathy for the Europhile arguments. He also seemed to believe that his personality and keenness on the EU would achieve much greater influence for Britain in the corridors of power. It is true that Blair's immediate acceptance of the Social Chapter which brought constraints on the flexibility of labour and his introduction of the Minimum Wage to Britain gave him some credibility in the EU, but in reality his positive stance achieved little as a series of policy differences were soon to make clear. France and Germany smiled at British naivety and continued on their merry way. Blair lost his virginity in the long-drawn-out-saga of British beef and French perfidy. The same saga brought about a stirring of English public opinion and a growing suspicion of where the EU concept was taking the UK. At the same time internal divisions in the government were beginning to contribute to a more tentative attitude towards the EU. The Chancellor of the Exchequer, Gordon Brown, committed to his objective of a stable growing economy, almost became a Eurosceptic. He was not prepared to duplicate the mistakes of John Major and his Chancellor Norman Lamont, over the ERM, and allow a too quick and eager entry into the euro. Brown, more than any other Labour politician, recognised the perils to the British economy of irretrievably locking itself into the economies of Germany and France. Though New Labour is ostensibly a strong supporter of a growing British involvement with the EU, the doubts are growing. Labour continues to use the term 'extremist' to describe the Conservative opposition but in reality are becoming more wary of the growing scepticism of the electorate. Interestingly, as the European elections in June 2004 showed it is becoming increasingly clear that a more sceptical approach to the EU is now coming to the fore in the British government.

In September 2000, in the midst of all the indecision over Europe, the British people provided a singular shock to its New Labour government. During the summer the fuel price crisis spread across Europe. Crude oil prices had risen from $10 to $30 a barrel, which together with government imposed duties, created a crippling price per litre at the retail pump. The protests began in France with fishermen blockading the Channel ports, soon followed by the farmers with their tractors, and then the hauliers with their trucks, closing the Channel Tunnel and bringing chaos to all traffic movement in France for both business and holiday-makers marooned at the ports. In traditional fashion, the union-dominated French government caved in to the protesters and effectively subsidised the fuel price. Quickly Belgian, Dutch and German road users initiated similar blockades and go-slows to create chaos and calling for the same treatment as the French. For a time the reaction of the British drivers was also traditional. Though they had a greater cause for grievance because the Labour government had increased the duty on fuel so that the pump price was much the highest in Europe at about $6 per gallon, they seemed at first to take the attitude of 'grin and bear it'. During this initial period the British media castigated the lawless French and their supine police and government for daring to inconvenience UK travellers and truck drivers going about their lawful business. But this was all about to change dramatically.

For a moment revolution was in the air, but it soon became clear that it was a peculiarly British revolution. It began with protesting farmers and hauliers 'blockading' an oil refinery to prevent petrol tankers supplying the retail outlets or petrol stations where the majority of drivers purchase their fuel. Within hours the protest was being taken up across the country and within two days every refinery in the UK was 'blockaded'. This was not a blockade in the French sense. Vehicles did not 'obstruct the Queen's Highway' for that would have been a criminal offence. Fuel tanker drivers were approached but with close police surveillance there was little or no intimidation. Indeed, the protesters generally took great care not to look like the industrial pickets of the eighties and were moderate in their language and attitudes. Within four days the country virtually ground to a halt. The government was caught totally by surprise and so reacted in panic. First, they were determined to demonstrate that the Blair government was not a lily-livered soft touch like the French government, so they adamantly refused to adjust the excessive tax duties levied on fuel. Next, they tried to win over public opinion by castigating the protesters as a conspiracy of vicious intimidators who were putting lives at peril by bringing the National Health Service to a halt. But, to their amazement, they had misunderstood both the nature of the protest and the mood of the public. To begin with this was not a union-dominated blockade of the Thatcher era and there was virtually no evidence of any intimidation. Indeed, there was no need for intimidation, as almost everyone, including the frustrated motorists agreed with the protest. Further the protesters had taken account of emergency services and supported the supply of fuel to these segments. Far from creating another 'lawless' society the British were demonstrating to the politicians that they no longer enjoyed the trust of the electorate and that they had better start listening to the majority opinion. Rather than a violent riot or revolution, they were giving notice to the politicians that their opinions counted between elections as much as on polling day. As the argument continued in the UK, it became clear that this attitude embraced a much wider spectrum than fuel prices. To the horror of the Europhiles the whole concept of Europe was included in the wide distrust of political leadership.

125

The Eurosceptics have argued that there are fundamental differences between the UK and its continental partners that prevent economic integration. An element in that argument has been the British attitude to politics and the rule of law. The Liberal Democrats (Britain's third largest political party) and other commentators in the USA and the continent argued that the fuel crisis demonstrated that the British people had become more like their European neighbours in this crucial area. In other words they argued that the evolution towards the United States of Europe is happening much faster than the Eurosceptics like to believe and that the sceptic will soon be consigned to the garbage can of history. At first glance this is a tenable argument but it doesn't really hold up under close scrutiny.

The British are not deeply interested in politics and retain a healthy scepticism about government and authority in general. Much of their humour is based on the pomposity of authority. They have endured the traumas of two world wars, loss of empire and the resultant loss of world influence with occasional quivers, but have emerged intact with an inherent self-confidence. As a result they are law-abiding and pay their taxes. They elect a political party to power and tend to give it time to implement its manifesto until events or the political pendulum indicate that it is time for a change. This attitude is possible, because, unlike their European neighbours, they have adopted the political system of 'first past the post'. To date, the British people and their political parties (with the obvious exception of the Liberal Democratic Party) have not fully embraced the continental system of proportional representation. Though theoretically more democratic, to the British way of thinking proportional representation produces fudge and continuous compromise. Despite this, the British are not extremists, and it is worth noting that throughout the political extremes of this century only one communist and no fascists, standing under that label were ever elected to the British parliament. This in itself is an incredible contrast to their continental neighbours. Given that background it is possible to argue that Europe needs Britain more than Britain needs Europe.

This is not to claim that the British are strangers to organised social dissent or violence. In 1979 Britain ended a long period of inertia and an extended attempt to create a false consensus around the 'one nation' concept of social democracy. The ensuing period brought about violent confrontation between the government and the mineworkers and other bastions of union power, which ended in defeat for the unions. Within a few short years Margaret Thatcher had destroyed, possibly forever, the possibility of socialism in Britain, and the concept of the national ownership of the 'commanding heights of the economy'. Britain came out of all this turmoil with a market-led economy in contrast to the semi-socialistic economies of her European allies. For the UK greater economic integration would be a retrograde step.

Whatever the current New Labour myths about the 1980s and the horrors of Thatcherism, the fact remains that while this revolution was being accomplished the British Conservative Party won four consecutive general elections. In short the change in political, social and economic direction had the support of the majority of the British people. New Labour will forget that fact at its peril. Yet this is exactly what Blair's government did in its opening years. Secure behind a massive majority and with modernising zeal, the new government began to dismantle many of the parliamentary checks and balances that had been evolved over time to make governments accountable and to keep them in touch with the mood of the people. Despite all the propaganda about the people's government, devolution and focus groups, the Labour Party was steadily introducing a presidential form of government. As a result, the people brought about a calmer British version of the typical French protest to out-of-touch governments. But as the debate raged and the breadth of the fuel protest was apparent it became clear that the people were saying that they did not like the methods of this government rather than just about oil prices. The message for the government was that stealth taxes, grandiose follies like the 'Dome', the euro and crony jobs for the boys were not what the electorate voted for in 1997. In 2001 the British electorate again returned New Labour with a still massive majority, but it was clear from the turnout that it was not an enthusiastic choice, and to a large extent was based on a continuing distrust of the Conservatives.

Economic survival

A central core of the Europhile argument is that Britain will not long survive in the fiercely competitive global market without economic and political union with Europe. To remain independent would entail a grudging acceptance of survival as a small insignificant nation with a steadily falling standard of living. Many doubters with strong reservations about the political implications of integration have found this view of the economic need conclusive. Indeed the euro club rely on this implicit fear to continue the progress towards the European super state.

In reality this is a tenuous argument that cannot survive rigorous examination. The obvious truth is that economic collaboration is advantageous to Europe as a whole and to the individual member nations. However, there is no guarantee that close integration would be equally advantageous. Indeed, to the contrary, there are several factors in the world today that argue that such a strategy would inhibit Britain's economic success.

To a great extent the Europhile case depends on the big

versus small syndrome. This is a far too simplistic argument. For example how big is big? In other words how big has a nation to be before it has the leverage to act independently in the world market. Population is not really the measure of economic power. The world's greatest economy, the United States, is approximately one quarter the population size of China or India. Japan is under half the size of the USA. Britain and France are each a little less than half the size of Japan, with Germany between them and Japan. South Korea and Taiwan are both well below the size of the UK. In economic terms the USA are followed by Japan with France, Germany and the UK vying for third place. In simple population terms there are many nations much larger than the UK but in economic terms the UK is clearly one of the leaders. If Britain is already the world's third, fourth or fifth most powerful economy where is the evidence that she needs to merge her sovereignty just to survive? It is not as if the UK was in steady decline and could expect to tumble from its present position. In fact, the trend is positive and Britain has been rising in the economic measures.

The global political and cultural trend is very much against bigness. Nationalism, ethnicity, and small, in the sense that people feel an identity with the group, have been the political direction since the end of the Cold War. The giant Union of Soviet Socialist Republics has been dismantled and returned to cultural and national groups last seen more than a century ago. As we noted before, Yugoslavia has gone through the same process. All around the world historic ethnic or national groups are fighting for their independence. Many member states within the EU have some ethnic or nationalist issue, which though not involving armed conflict, are certainly divisive. In the United Kingdom it is called devolution but it is the same dragon under a different name. If the underlying world trend of its people is a desperate attempt to retain individuality in smaller groupings, what on earth is the point of the European Union going in the opposite direction? History shows that sooner or later national pressures will erupt again and bring chaos to Europe. Surely the sensible way forward is to continue to find ways to collaborate economically while resisting any tendency to further centralisation and reduction of national sovereignty.

Competition

The global economy is not for the faint-hearted or the incompetent. There are hungry sharks out there and the competition is fierce. The ability to compete effectively in such a widespread market depends on knowledge of the diverse cultures, the exportability of core competencies, flexibility and speed of response. Dependent upon the industry in which they operate, this can be a difficult test for even the biggest corporations. As a result, a series of mergers or strategic alliances, often between erstwhile competitors, are taking place, enabling the new group to compete across the board. Corporations need to be certain that not only are they fit to compete but that their national base is in support and can respond as flexibly as situations demand. But this does not mean that only giant corporations are suited to the global economy.

Small is Big

There are a number of reasons why the global economy provides opportunities for small or medium-sized companies:

- As in nature, great corporate sharks need parasites to provide a host of specialised services. Of course the majority are found in specific operational areas but high technical knowledge or competency follows the big corporations.

- Giant organisations are themselves breaking down their bureaucratic organisations into confederations of small entrepreneurial companies. They tend to form partnerships with other small entrepreneurial groups with specialised knowledge.
- The latest technology is now cheap enough to be available to the small company, which gives it great mobility.
- De-regulation and globalisation of financial markets have given relatively small companies access to the investment capital once denied to them.
- Since liberalisation, it is much easier for the small company to gain access to new markets.
- Bright young entrepreneurial people in Britain and other EU countries no longer automatically seek the large corporation. They want more responsibility and challenge at a much earlier age. They are attracted to join the small company, or group together to set up their own.

Jack Welch, the legendary CEO of General Electric, in a company report, says, 'Think small'. He adds, 'What we are trying relentlessly to do is to get that small company soul, and small company speed, inside our big company body.' He explains further, 'We are trying to get the small company benefits of quickness in time to market, decision making, and the elimination of bureaucratic activities.'

Economic survival for Britain and Europe depends on creating an environment in which all these factors are encouraged and nurtured. To date the central European social democratic model has produced big government, high taxes, rigid labour markets and lavish social welfare. The American free-market model works with moderate government, low taxes, reasonable welfare and flexible labour markets. The British economy is still in transition, but even under the New Labour government it still leans strongly towards the American model. The free-market American model is a huge job-creating machine. In the last twenty-five years, despite the massive impact of global competition, the American economy has generated nearly fifty million new jobs (that is nearly the population of the UK), while central Europe has struggled to about four million. It would also be wrong to assume that these jobs were all in low-paid service areas or part-time. The US Council of Advisors has reported that 70 per cent of the new jobs are in high wage occupation, including 60 per cent in the professional or managerial capacity.

As journalist Andrew Neil has pointed out in many articles, the central European model has little to teach the world; it is moribund. He notes that it has 'ceased to work; it no longer provides jobs for its people'. The jobless rate in France and Germany is three times more than that in the USA and more than twice the rate in the UK. In addition France and Germany spend billions in expensive employment and 'make work' subsidies. These disparate performances within Europe and the international comparisons are important outside the economic sphere. They are creating strains within Europe as the European Union adopts the single currency. A great international experiment is encountering storms in which the whole concept may founder unless Europe wakes up to a real understanding of a market-led economy. The European Union can change, but it requires leaders of courage prepared to take on the vested interests in their own countries and the Commission, and time is running out. Clearly Chirac and Schroeder are not such leaders.

Initial economic verdict

The economic argument for further integration is not sustainable. Indeed, the Eurosceptics should reverse the economic argument as the principal reason not only to halt further moves along the Commission route but also to start the task of reversing the process. If the European Union is to be a viable entity in the future global market place it needs substantial reform to free its individual economies and to reduce the bureaucratic directives from Brussels. The only alternative is a slow strangulation of the entrepreneurial spirit that is so essential in the global market place.

British Europhiles are unlikely to accept this logic, and would claim that it is far too late to leave the Union, and in any case we are already so involved that the loss of trade would be too great to bear. They would rightly claim that more than 50 per cent of our trade is now with Europe. Therefore, in their opinion, we must become even more committed to Europe and walk in step with our EU associates.

The exact opposite is in fact the case. The size of the UK market in a successful European economy is now so great that our EU partners cannot afford to lose the UK trade. Additionally, Britain is a nation of shopkeepers or to be more precise, a nation of small businesses. In other words Britain is more fitted to be successful in the global market, and with its links to the USA and the Commonwealth is also in a position to overcome some loss in the European market.

However, that is not the Eurosceptic logic. The authors are *not* arguing that the UK should *leave* the European Union. Rather they want to enhance the collaboration with Europe to reform its original treaties and some of its entrenched policies to benefit the Union so it can take its place in the competitive global market.

133

Priorities for Reform

Château Management

If the competitive global market is relatively easy to predict and define, why do so many EU members and the Commission fail to adapt their economies to meet its challenges? Why do so many seem unable to escape their past, with all its fears, and envisage a new future?

In essence, they have lost touch with the world outside. Many of the political leaders and the mandarins of the Commission act like the Generals of the First World War. They and their staff sit in the chancelleries and the Brussels headquarters or *châteaux* way behind the economic front line. In 1916 Generals Haig and Gough of the British Army in France, in a château some 40 miles behind the front, after losing 60,000 men on the first day of the Battle of the Somme, constantly pressed for more futile and costly attacks. Soldiers could barely move without attracting a swarm of machine gun bullets and land was churned up by the constant artillery exchanges. In 1917 Haig's Chief of Staff, General Sir Lancelot Kiggell, who should have warned him of the conditions at the front, was himself based in the same château. Nearly two months after the battle of Passchendaele had started Kiggell decided to visit the battlefield. While still a mile away from the mudbath he commented to the local commander that he hadn't realised how bad the conditions were. The officer laconically replied, 'It's worse up front, sir'.

Too many politicians, civil servants, commissioners and other VIPs act like château generals. The leaders lose contact with the reality of public opinion and the world market place. As a result, they are blinded by the brilliance of their inter-treaty strategies and do not feel the need to be challenged by the truth. When change eventually catches up

134

with them, they react in panic. It is time to expand the vision of the EU leadership and make contact with the ordinary people of the member nations. A good start would be to evacuate the bureaucratic *château* in Brussels and devolve power to the member nations. Centralisation must be rolled back.

Harmonisation of taxes

Following the establishment of the euro, the next step forward for the Commission is to gain control of taxation and budgetary policy. Should the Commission objective be achieved, the EU for all practical purposes will then be governed centrally from Brussels. Twenty-five sovereign nations will have abdicated their power and their hard-won rights to control their own economic destiny. Further, on the evidence of recent years, the EU is likely to be condemned to high taxation, subsidised industry, commerce and agriculture, inflexible union-dominated labour, welfare dependency and restrictive red tape. In other words a semi-socialist regime ill-equipped to meet the competitive challenges of the global market.

The Commission and the euro club know full well that it would be impossible to move directly to the control of taxation. It will never be a declared objective, but Monnet's influence still reigns, and so once again *functionalism* is the chosen strategy. The Commission's policy groups will be searching for opportunities to propose minor directives in the area of taxation, nibbling away at independent control of taxation. This latest assault on British sovereignty is launched under the non-aggressive title of harmonisation of taxes.

The Germans provided the first opportunity for the Commission to move on the harmonisation of taxes. They proposed to implement a withholding tax to act as a powerful disincentive to take savings out of one EU country to another. The penalty or tax proposed was a flat rate 20 per cent on the interest payable on all investments made within the EU, but outside the investor's home country. The EU commissioner Mario Monti seized the opportunity saying 'Brussels could not allow the creation of a tax haven in Luxembourg or Britain while consigning the rest of the EU to a tax hell'. The potential impact of this proposed new tax on Britain would be devastating. At one level the UK's own offshore tax havens of the Channel Islands and the Isle of Man would be badly hit by such an imposition. But the real impact would be on the City of London as a financial centre. The tax would decimate the Eurobond market that is totally dependent on out-of-country investments. London is the European centre for Eurobond trading worth a massive £3 billion a year. Financial institutions say that the new tax will simply drive the market out of the EU altogether either to Zurich or New York. For London it could lead to the loss of 10,000 well-paid jobs.

Britain held the pass for a while at the Helsinki EU summit, threatening to use their veto if the proposal was tabled. A fudge was agreed in setting up a high-level working party to find an answer to the issue of tax avoidance versus just moving the market outside the EU. The battle was postponed, hopefully providing a pause for more careful thought.

The dispute over the withholding tax has brought into focus the crucial difference between the UK and her part-ners over taxation and economic strategy. Mario Monti deployed the seemingly reasonable Commission viewpoint, 'Member states cannot preach the virtues of an open, integrated and competitive financial market on the one hand, while turning a blind eye to the remaining tax obstacles. On the contrary, it is precisely by reducing tax avoidance and the beggar-thy-neighbour measures which give rise to an erosion of the tax base that member states can reduce overall tax rates'.

But these saccharine phrases hid the real issue and were the reason why the Germans took the lead in sponsoring the withholding tax. The German government was fed up with the way that German people and businesses were exporting savings because of high German taxes. Indeed hundreds of German firms were going further and were also considering moving production out of the country because of crippling labour costs and taxes. Hans-Olaf Henkel, president of the Federation of German Industry, was against harmonisation of taxes because, he said 'We should not try to eliminate competition between EU countries'. He continued 'Europe has to compete against the rest of the world, and that would be difficult if all member countries followed Germany's example on tax rates and labour cost', adding 'Britain was setting the right example. Corporate tax in Britain is 31 per cent, in Sweden it's 28 per cent and in Germany it's 56 per cent'. With Germany still pursuing old-style socialist 'tax and spend' policies many German companies are actively looking to Britain for future investment plans, said Mr Henkel. Britain's liberal labour market and favourable tax regime are proving an irresistible attraction.

The concern of German business and from the opposite standpoint, the German government, are understandable. The German tax burden is very high, with a top income tax rate of 53 per cent compared with Britain's 40 per cent and the average German worker surrendering more than half of their wage packet. It is little wonder that Germany, like the Britain of the seventies, has become a land of creative tax evaders. Instead of vigorously reducing taxes (though Chancellor Gerhard Schroeder has made some tentative steps in that direction) the German government has responded to their internal threat of tax evasion by trying to use Brussels to push up the overall European tax base to its own level and thus ensure that Germany remains competitive. At best, though, this is a flawed concept. While it may ease Germany's competitive position within Europe, it would do little for Europe's (and Germany's) competitive position with the rest of the world.

But the concept of tax harmonisation spreads far beyond such somewhat specialised taxes as the withholding tax. Yves-Thibault de Silguy, the EU Finance Commissioner has taken several opportunities to make clear that the Commission intend to include VAT and even Income Tax in its harmonisation plans. M. de Silguy has also warned that Britain's influence would be diminished as long as she remained outside the single currency. As part of the battle to remove the member countries' veto on such moves, the UK could lose its right to vote on these issues because it is outside the European Monetary Union. Any move in these directions would be disastrous for Britain because the UK is currently one of the lowest-taxed economies in the EU. Harmonisation of VAT would end zero rating on food, children's clothes, books and newspapers. *In other words taxation without representation; which raises the question of when the UK should hold its own tea party.*

At the centre of all the arguments over tax are the costs of high taxes on our competitiveness. A crucial area is the burden of social costs on Britain's manufacturing and commercial businesses. This has played a large part in Britain's economic resurgence in the last decade. Far from accepting the Commission's attitude to taxation and their 'level playing field' demands, Britain should be fighting for its own enterprise culture and adherence to free market principles. As the Unipart chief John Neill said 'We should be demanding that the Commission should level up their game to our standards, not levelling down our game to theirs. If we load 30 per cent on to our employment costs, employees will not get any extra in their pay packets. But they will cost 30 per cent more to employ. And, logically, that means 30 per cent fewer people being employed'. Statistically suspect but it makes the point.

Fraud and mismanagement

There is no political system and hardly a government in the world that has not been accused of fraud and mis-management. Despite the fact that most accusations are proved right, and with no desire to condone such corruption, it is important to retain a sense of perspective in criticising the EU. Clearly the level of fraud and corruption found in many areas of the world, overt in the example of Nigeria, and perhaps more subtle in say India or Pakistan, does not exist in the EU. Nevertheless, from a British standpoint, the level of fraud and mismanagement in the European Union is far too great and makes an economic impact through the EU budget. The UK is not blameless, but on the whole the standards of probity in public life and the conduct of government in Britain are among the highest in the world. From time to time there is a minor scandal in the UK, often related to local planning permission or political party funding, but never scandals on the scale of those involving President Mitterrand, President Chirac, Madame Cresson and Chancellor Kohl. Perhaps our continental associates have become so used to corruption that it has lost its ability to shock. But shocked all the members of the EU should be.

Fraud, mismanagement and general corruption of the EU government takes several forms. At one level, national governments totally ignore the rule of law and happily ignore laws and directives that they endorsed when they were formulated. On another level, Commission agencies and commissioners use their powers to suit their own objectives

139

rather than the purport of particular directives. Across the board EU projects and subsidies are milked of funds by a wide network of officials and crooked applicants. Under the leadership of the New Labour government there is disturbing evidence that a corrosive attitude is developing in the UK. The number of Ministers forced to resign over corruption or failure to accept responsibility for their acts is becoming a farce.

The rule of law

Fraud, mismanagement and seeming contempt for the rule of law are endemic in the Commission, and in many of the continental member nations of the EU. This incipient cancer is now rearing its head in the UK. In the view of most British people, France is the major culprit in ignoring EU laws if it suits her national interest. That view has been coloured by the long-running dispute over British beef and repeated instances of holiday chaos at French Channel ferry ports. Though the French do provide some of the most obvious examples, the same attitudes are rife in Germany, Italy and to a lesser extent in the Netherlands, Belgium and Spain.

This lawlessness is the cancer that could undermine the whole concept of economic union. The lack of trust that it engenders among nations inhibits open collaboration. The focus of the Union is turned inwards, attempting to resolve disputes rather than developing an economic environment for successful competition. We can already see the effect on the citizens of Europe. They are losing any respect for the Commission and the direction in which their own governments are taking them. Their lament that the rulers have lost contact with the aspirations of the people is now evident in Britain. Similar reactions have also been recognised in many member nations. The Danish and Swedish people trumpeted the message loud and clear in their referendum vote rejecting the euro. In Denmark the pro euro campaigners included the government, the main political parties, most of the establishment, all the national newspapers and nearly all the other media, yet the electorate voted 53 per cent in favour of rejection. In fact the issue of the euro had very little to do with the vote, as in economic terms it made little difference to Denmark where the kroner already shadowed the Deutschmark. No, it was a political statement that 'we do not like what we see and we want to retain our independence'. It was a similar story in the 2003 Swedish referendum.

Time after time, it is the French who break ranks, who ignore treaties and put their own national interest, first. The historian Andrew Roberts argued in the *Sunday Telegraph* that it reveals a nation that is stuck in the past, and declared that 'perfidious France needs a dose of Thatcherism'. He noted that every year tens of thousands of Britons are caught up in some domestic French industrial dispute that has absolutely nothing to do with them. Every year a different sector of French commerce is involved. One year it was fishermen, in others it was their dockers, farmers, lorry drivers, Sea France crewmen or shore staff, Calais port workers or Eurotunnel's Le Shuttle workers. Similarly the grievances alter from year to year. In 2000 it was the price of diesel fuel, but in 1995 they chose welfare reform, in 1996 shorter working hours, in 1997 pensions, in 1998 the scrapping of duty free allowances, and in 1999 British beef imports. As long as the British holidaymaker is the principal victim the French government doesn't have to do a thing.

But the British have seen it all before. France is going through the same industrial relations problems that Britain experienced in the 1960s and 1970s culminating in the 'Winter of Discontent' in 1978–1979. As Roberts pointed out, the crucial difference is that there is not a French

Margaret Thatcher even on the horizon, let alone waiting in the wings. The Socialist Jospin government was trapped precisely in the same anything-for-a-quiet-life frame of mind that paralysed so many British governments. 'How one would have loved to have seen a Gallic Iron Lady deal with the situation: blockading fishing boats boarded and towed away, mounted police charges at the tunnel, union funds sequestered, and the rest'.

The French economy does seem to be improving, but in the field of industrial relations it is still stuck inside a weird time warp. In France it is even considered politically incorrect to complain too much about strikes, as though one were questioning the basic human right of the worker to go on strike. As Andrew Roberts noted 'while the era of over-mighty trade union barons is now part of the British history syllabus, in France they are still part of everyday life'. As *Le Monde*'s correspondent pithily put it 'Strikes work in France'.

This is not just an internal matter for France. A key element of the EU is its commitment to the 'free movement of people, goods and services' which France signed up to. But will Brussels ever force the French to pay compensation to the businesses and individuals of other countries for the scandals of traffic harassment in France? In the EU, and in international affairs generally, time after time it is the French who cause the most trouble. From Rwanda to Kosovo, from the beef ban to the 1996 road haulage fiasco, from the American bombing of Tripoli to the sanctions and finally war against Saddam Hussein it is the French who break ranks first to safeguard their narrow self interests. Chirac may preach the spirit of *'Communautaire'*, usually when lambasting the British for expressing doubts about some Brussels initiative, but it is the French who never truly believe that the European rules apply to them. If France is an example of the future of the EU, Britain should have nothing to do with it - they have been there before and know the cost. Britain should take the lead in protecting the EU from the excesses of France.

Italy, as we noted earlier, is making progress in freeing its economy from the stultifying effect of the Mafia or other special interests on both organised capital and organised labour, but has a long way to go. However, Germany in a quieter way, exhibits many of the tendencies so obvious in France. A study on the reliability of international car models published by the Consumer Association in August 2004 stated that the three most unreliable cars on the market were all German. Car manufacturers in Germany have always achieved quality by inspection unlike, for example the Japanese, but the growing cost of labour in Germany, has led their car makers to save money on inspection. Union strength has been the prime mover in the high tax, high welfare system in Germany that is steadily eroding her competitive strength. As a result she is flagrantly breaking EU directives on tax incentives to lure investment away from other EU countries, and in another direction she ignores EU rules to protect her own industries and cartels. The actions of German regulators in the Cadbury/Coke deal and their thwarted action over the Vodafone acquisition are similar to the long running saga of French illegal protection of Air France. Perhaps the most worrying factor for the British in deciding their European future is the apparent dominance of the French and German point of view in Brussels. Even the British Commissioner for Transport, Neil Kinnock, was totally incapable of preventing the French from halting 'free movement' and illegally subsidising Air France. Now he has been appointed to root out fraud and corruption in the Commission and EU projects. Kinnock's approach to 'whistle blowing' civil servants shows that nothing has changed. Everything is still brushed under the carpet. The organised and highly-experienced criminals who

143

are responsible for much of the fraud in the EU must be toasting their luck.

Syndicalist Europe

There is another real barrier to Britain's wholehearted commitment to greater integration in the EU and that is the socialist-dominated policies of the Commission and the inner core nations. As *functionalism* has moved forward and veils have been lifting, the crippling cost of the centralist bent of the Commission is becoming clear for all to see. We have already noted the impact of trade union power in France. We will now touch on the constraints of state-owned or-dominated industries. However, there is an aspect of the welfare state which provides a perfect example of the dangers ahead – the Commission's aim for a pensions policy.

There is a growing gap between public and private pension provision among member countries of the EU. There are dramatic differences between the pensions industry in Britain and the rest of Europe. In many countries, the general message is that state pension schemes are much more generous, so that there is no need for private provision. Around £526 billion is held in British pension funds that equals the combined total in Germany, France, Italy, Belgium and the Netherlands. Thus, over the last decade the UK has made a head start over our continental partners. The funds are held in different schemes and the Commission has plans to harmonise these systems across Europe. Following the single currency will come the single pension policy. The very real danger is that the Commission will raid the private pension funds to organise their scheme, and, of course, the United Kingdom has the largest funds. Britain has already experienced the disastrous effect of such policies when the socialist Chancellor George Brown raided British pension funds.

The political battleground over pensions was illustrated

144

by the reaction in France to Socialist Premier Lionel Jospin's attempt to raise the French retirement age by two-and-a-half years. The change is needed because as pensioners live longer, the state needs to collect more money from those who have to pay for them. Already future liabilities well exceed the future tax revenues that are supposed to pay for the pensions. In the case of five countries, Belgium, Denmark, Portugal, Spain and Sweden, the deficit is more than twice the annual gross domestic product. The prospect of raising taxation to the levels needed to maintain state pensions is daunting to an already over-taxed Europe.

A salutary example of the reckless standards and conspicuous extravagance of government-managed projects comes again from France (the British had their own example in the Dome). The project to improve passenger traffic at Charles de Gaulle airport outside Paris can rarely have been equalled for incompetence and waste. At attempt to link the airport's terminals with a new railway shuttle system has been abandoned at a cost to the European taxpayers of more than £100 million. Launched with a great fanfare in 1991, the system of driverless people moving trains had to be abandoned as a complete failure in 2000. The cost of installing a replacement system would exceed £200 million. In the French manner, not a single resignation has followed this stunning indictment. A cynical Englishman might note that the current British government, emulating their continental colleagues, have followed the French pattern over accepting responsibility for the Dome and other white elephant projects.

Subsidy

From the beginning as the EEC and now as the EU, the Commission and the Treaties have been dominated by the socialist principal of public funding and subsidy as the system for major projects. Experience has taught us in Britain that this route is inflexible and tends to create new problems that haunt the project to the bitter end. We will touch on several aspects of this philosophy in the EU but the prime example is the Common Agricultural Policy.

The Common Agricultural Policy (CAP) is a protectionist system for supporting agriculture in the EU. Established by the Treaty of Rome in 1958, it was for many years the only significant Community policy, accounting for over two thirds of the budget, providing vast subsidies, and substantially raising the cost of food to customers. The CAP also serves as an unwilling accomplice to fraud, imposes prohibitive levies on imports, and disrupts international markets through subsidised exports and the creation of unwanted surpluses disposed of by intermittent bouts of dumping.

Its original purpose was to provide a stable income for European farmers, incentives to modernise agricultural production, and to ensure a secure supply of food for European consumers. In fairness to the CAP, most of those original Treaty objectives have been fulfilled. Productivity has been increased, farmers' incomes have risen, Europe is self-sufficient in temperate foodstuffs and prices have been reasonably stable, though much higher than, for example, in the USA. But it has been achieved at a huge cost to both taxpayers and consumers and the pressures on the EU budget are growing. If the CAP continues on its present course and levels of subsidy, especially now that the countries of Central and Eastern Europe have joined the EU the Union would be insolvent. Poland, Hungary, the Czech Republic and Estonia are poor countries with large rural areas and inefficient farming that would so increase the EU budget that it will exceed the EU's financing capacity. Britain and Germany are not prepared to foot the bill, and yet Brussels and the Council of Ministers have been unwilling to face up to the political storm that would arise if the CAP were radically reformed.

Britain has Edward Heath to blame for the parlous state

of the CAP. At the time of the UK's entry the other members of the EEC viewed the UK as a massive new market for their agricultural products and a new source of funds for the CAP subsidies. Their only concern was the traditional UK commitment to free trade and the Commonwealth preference that provided cheap food. Heath, instead of negotiating for modification of the CAP (and incidentally the Common Fisheries Policy), almost immediately conceded all of Britain's negotiating points. An early opportunity to reform the CAP was lost to one man's vanity and intense desire to join the EEC.

There have been attempts to reform the CAP over the years but without great success. Attempting to reverse market trends by decree from Brussels is a recipe for disaster. As a result market discipline was abandoned. Unlimited intervention to purchase produce which could not be sold at a higher price on the open market, brought about the wine lakes, butter mountains and large surpluses of dairy produce, cereals and sugar. The consumer faced overpriced food and the taxpayer bore the cost of storing and disposing of these vast stockpiles. In an attempt to change that situation the CAP was reformed to compensate farmers for not producing food. This led to the 'set-aside' scandals. A series of other directives have tinkered with the problem in the Agenda 2000 reforms. In broad principle Agenda 2000 capped or pegged CAP spending at £27 billion and cut the price producers are paid for milk, beef and corn by up to 30 per cent. This had the effect of bringing 40,000 farmers to Brussels to protest and ended in a massive clash with 5,000 riot police and as a result little changed.

The primary barrier to radical reform of the CAP is that the member states have never been able to agree. This is not at all surprising as each country has different farming interests and thus a separate agenda. The CAP, like the EU, does not recognise diversity, a continuing theme of this book. Britain

147

has some of Europe's most efficient farms. Italy and Spain have many tiny and inefficient farms. Germany has a large number of part-time farmers. France has the most politically active farming community, adept at holding their government to ransom. Ireland relies on the land for 4.8 per cent of its national product while for Sweden it is only 0.4 per cent.

The CAP is an incredible burden on the economy of the EU that has to end. One way to change this situation is to scrap the CAP and allow every nation to make its own decision as to the degree they wish to subsidise their farming. In conclusion, the EU has to recognise that the CAP has failed and brought the whole central direction of EU policy through the Commission in Brussels into disrepute. The EU should put the responsibility for farming back into the control of independent national parliaments.

The lessons for the EU from the failure of the CAP can be summarised as follows:

- The socialist tenet of subsidy rarely works.
- The authoritarian imposition of 'catch all' policies to meet highly diverse situations almost always fails.
- The development of directives to solve the issues of two nations at the expense of others is divisive and eventually destructive for all.
- The diversion of funds imperils other areas for development assistance.
- *Quite simply such systems just do not work.*

Common Fisheries Policy

As Oliver Hardy might have said, 'This is another fine mess that you have landed us in, Mr Heath'. To quote Rodney Leach in his book *Europe*, 'the saga of the Common Fisheries Policy (CFP) is an unhappy episode in the UK's relations with Europe'. In 1970 the UK, Norway, Ireland and Denmark

148

were negotiating entry into the Common Market. These four countries were rich in fish, which the existing members of the community coveted. Having no legal justification for their ambitions (the Treaty of Rome covered only fish products) the Six hastily created the CFP, under which all member states would have access to Community fishing grounds, which would become a common resource. Once again, anxious to secure the prize of membership of the community, Edward Heath gave way. Despite public assurances that the CFP was unacceptable, he contented himself with a ten-year derogation, which temporarily protected only coastal fishing. The UK signed the Treaty of Accession. Later that year, a braver Norway rejected the CFP and voted against joining.

A series of shenanigans over derogation ensued. The entry of Spain and Portugal and the consistent use of the European Court to overrule the British courts, allowed Danish fishermen to ignore derogation rules and Spanish fishermen to sail under the British flag to catch against the British quota. 'Quota hopping' was born. Added to this, reduced quota, problems over mesh sizes and species-by-species targets have decimated the British fishing industry. Thousands of jobs and 6,000 fishing boats have gone since the UK entered the EU and there seems little that can be done about it. Given the multitude of conflicting national interests, no equitable solution is likely to be found. The bureaucrats, in defining species-by-species quotas, have created a major environ-mental catastrophe. Fishing nets cannot differentiate between species, so each fishing trip results in thousands of legally unsellable fish in each trawl. Naturally the unwanted species are thrown overboard. Steadily, masses of dead fish on the seabed are contaminating the marine environment and killing other fish. It is high time that British governments fought to hold back Brussels and to start the reversal of elements of the CFP.

Community interference and waste

Three examples from different areas must suffice to illustrate the restraining hand of the Commission on economic success with its interference, waste and corruption.

Textiles

In April 1998 Jacques Santer, President of the European Commission overruled the wishes of a majority of EU governments at the behest of President Chirac of France in the interests of a small group of French weavers.

The European textile industry, which directly employs 2.5 million people, relies on importing huge quantities of unbleached cotton cloth, mainly from Asia, which is then dyed and made up into clothing and finished items of all kinds from curtains to furniture coverings. The Commission, on the excuse of dumping but in reality reacting to lobbying by President Chirac on behalf of the French weaving industry (which employed 5,000), imposed hefty new duties on all unfinished cotton shipped into the EU. These duties made it very difficult for the EU textile firms to compete with imports of finished cotton products. A similar imposition had endangered the textile industry in 1995 but had been reversed in 1996 when it was proven that the Asian exporters were selling at fair market prices. That experience reduced the import of unfinished cotton by 55 per cent, while imports of finished goods rose by 57.3 per cent.

President Chirac continued his lobbying but the Council of Ministers refused to confirm new levies and that should have been the end of the story. But five days later a new request was made for the duties to be re-imposed. As a result the advisory committee representing EU governments met and voted 9–5 against renewing the levies. France was supported by what has been called the 'Club Med' countries of Spain, Portugal, Italy and Greece. But amazingly Santer,

150

under pressure from Chirac, insisted that the decision by elected governments should be ignored and the Commission was to be obeyed and the duties came back into force. Such arrogant erosion of democracy has been typical of the Commission's edicts.

Chocolate
A twenty year battle over British chocolate was finally ended in 2000, when MEPs voted to allow chocolate made with up to 5 per cent vegetable fat to be marketed in all 15 member states. This ended discrimination against British chocolate in particular from France and Belgium who blocked imports from Britain.

When Britain, Eire and Denmark joined the EU in 1973 they were granted an exemption from a EU ban on making chocolate from anything other than cocoa butter. Sweet UK-style milk chocolate has always been considered inferior on the Continent. France and Belgium led the drive for British chocolate to be renamed 'vegelate' before it could be sold abroad, but they lost that battle.

Now an updated EU chocolate directive obliges all EU countries to accept all chocolate, as long as the vegetable fat content does not exceed 5 per cent of the product and there is clear labelling. In the EU English 'milk chocolate' will now need to be a 'family milk chocolate'. It took more than 20 years to be able to a buy a Cadbury's Flake as easily in Paris as in Manchester.

Another example of bureaucratic nonsense and French intransigence in defending it's own markets.

Waste in Paraguay
The Commission provides many examples of waste and corruption so typical of socialist governments the world over. This example is from the EU support for the Third World in a project called the 'Prodechaco scheme for the sustainable

151

development of the Paraguayan Chaco'. Launched in 1992, the project was to provide a new life for Indians who live in overcrowded poverty on just 2 per cent of the vast Chaco region. In 1994 the EU ruled that the final stage to resettle the 20,000 Indians on their ancestral land, bought with £10 million from the EU taxpayers, should not begin until their land claims had been settled. Then an independent report compiled for Survival International showed that 82 per cent of the claims remained unsettled but that most of the EU money had been spent.

Surprise, surprise! The money had been spent buying either waterless desert up to 100 miles away, or land regularly flooded by the Paraguay River. Much of the money handed over by Brussels to the Paraguayan government had been used to pay landowners anything up to 10 times their land's market value. There was also evidence that money had been recycled into the funds of the Colorado party, which has ruled Paraguay for decades. Despite this report, Brussels, not wanting to admit corruption, continued to send cash to Paraguay without any proper checks as to where it went.

Privatisation

There is one hopeful sign for the economic future of Europe. The pressures of the global free market are finally forcing countries such as France, dominated by state ownership, to move reluctantly towards a greater degree of privatisation. In the highly competitive world market some major industries and commercial corporations need to operate on a scale that cannot be resourced by one nation alone (with the possible exception of the USA) and call for alliances with other corporations that may be in another country. For example industries like defence, information technology and aerospace demand resources, skills and knowledge not often contained in one national corporation. Additionally, service corporations are looking to the size of market and economy of scale that transcends national boundaries. As a result the world market place is dominated by a growing number of mergers, alliances and take-overs to fit those corporations for global opportunities.

But these international corporations want to control their own destinies. They are not prepared to work in alliance with companies that are wholly or partly owned by the government. For example, consider the protracted negotiations to put together the Airbus consortium and the Eurofighter programme. Germany's Daimler Benz Aerospace (Dasa) and Britain's BAe were not prepared to join either consortium unless the French government privatised Aerospatiale. The then French Prime Minister Lionel Jospin resisted privatisation and attempted to put together a 'French-French' solution of mergers between French defence companies. Finally Paris was forced to bite the privatisation bullet, albeit only partially, when Dasa and BAe ran out of patience and started its own merger without Aerospatiale. Similar battles were fought over Thompson CSE, the defence electronics company, and Bull, the computer systems corporation. The French must accept that major corporations are not going to accept as a major shareholder the French government using its veto to block commercial decisions such as cost cutting and lay-offs that are politically unpopular. In different circumstances the German government has met the same hostility when it tried to interfere in the Vodafone-Mannesmann deal.

Though the move towards privatisation is an encouraging sign, it is all happening far too slowly to envisage a convergence of the UK and continental economic strategies for a long time to come. Once again it highlights the folly of forcing a single economic approach on such diverse national economies. It is not extremism to resist that approach: it is simple common sense.

The EU Budget

The Treaty of Rome decrees that the EU must run a balanced budget. On the revenue side, to give the Community financial independence, contributions from member states were replaced in 1970 by a system of *own resources*. This had to be revised again in 1988 after the Single European Act had reduced the income from duties and levies. Own resources is dependent on four classes of revenue, namely:

- Tariffs on imports
- Agricultural levies and sugar duties
- Percentages of each member state's VAT revenue
- Member states' contributions related to their own GNP

Of these revenue streams, the tariffs and levies account for a declining share of the budget, now well under 20 per cent. The VAT revenue (an area of dispute) is being reduced annually: at its height it accounted for over 60 per cent of the budget, but by 1999 this had fallen to around 30 per cent. The GNP related revenue originally a mere balancing item, is rising rapidly and by 1999 it financed more than half the budget. Forgetting for a moment the battle over the British rebate, the overall present system is a fairer way of establishing member state's contributions.

Margaret Thatcher achieved an annual rebate for the UK ('give us our money back') based on Britain's disproportionate contribution to the EU Budget as a result of the workings of the CAP. The rebate was agreed in 1984 and was due to finish in 1999. It cannot be formally changed without the UK's consent, but the other nations, and in particular Germany (who now considers it is paying too much), are adamant that the rebate must be ended or renegotiated before enlargement of the EU. In 2000 Prime Minister Blair was able to put off revision of the UK rebate. As the CAP is reduced, this issue becomes more emotive than economically crucial from either standpoint. In any case the whole budgetary system and accountability needs a substantial re-organisation to fit the EU for enlargement.

Though there are still disputes over the source of revenue, the argument now centres on expenditure. Until recently the battle has concentrated on how the budget is spent rather than the overall size of the budget. The most contentious item is the expenditure on agricultural subsidies under the CAP. This reached a horrendous level of 80 per cent of the total budget in 1973 but has been steadily reduced (not without rancour) and although now capped at 41 per cent is still considered far too high. Several nations are urging that the CAP requirements be reduced, but that the next largest segment of the budget, the structural funds for the regions, should be increased. However, these issues and the size of the budget will again come into prominence as the experience of enlargement grows.

The nations who joined the EU in May 2004: Bulgaria, Cyprus, Czech Republic, Estonia, Hungary, Latvia, Lithuania, Malta, Poland and Slovenia are likely to be a drain rather than a net contributor to the budget. In other words the EU will require an increased budget. This concerns Germany, by far the largest net contributor, and the six other net contributors including Britain. This factor alone highlights the desperate need to eliminate the CAP and to constrain the growing ambition of the Commission to expand its control over taxation in order to provide new direct revenue streams.

Faith in Britain's economy

The Europhiles have mounted a continuous jeremiad about the economic prospects for Britain if she did not join the euro and wholly commit to the new Europe. They are being proved wrong. Now six years after the launch of the euro, whatever President Chirac might say, Britain is in the economic fast lane while France and Germany are the economic sluggards. Foreign investors are flocking to Britain and investment year by year surpasses record levels. In 2000 the UK attracted more than 700 inward investment projects that at the same time created over 150,000 new jobs. The UK now attracts more than half of all inward investment from America and Japan into Europe, more than half as much again as goes into France and double the level put into Germany. More to the point, a large proportion of the new investment is into hi-tech and e-commerce opportunities, the business generators of the future. Certainly foreign financiers and businesses are showing their faith in the future strength of the British economy outside the euro. British companies are now among the most profitable in the world, according to the British government survey. They enjoy an average rate of return of 12.9 per cent on their capital investments which compares with 9.9 per cent in the USA and just 3.4 per cent in Germany, once considered the centre of wealth creation. British productivity in retailing and commerce were among the highest in the world and contributed to the 15 per cent return in the service sector. The only nations ahead of Britain were Finland and Norway.

The German exodus

BASF, Europe's largest chemical company, has turned its back on Germany to move the headquarters of its £1.4 billion global drugs business to Britain. 'London is the leading centre of excellence and talent in Europe', said a BASF spokesman. 'By setting up our headquarters in Britain, BASF pharmaceuticals will benefit from becoming better managed, make faster decisions and have more flexibility'. In another example the Japanese firm Sony shut a TV factory in Stuttgart with the loss of 3,000 jobs and switched production to Wales, blaming high wage costs and inflexible German unions. At the end of 1999 a survey of 7,100 medium sized industrial and service sector firms revealed that a fifth had made 'concrete' plans to quit Germany, citing Britain as one of their favoured destinations. More than 1,000 firms have now carried out their threat to pack up and leave. These companies represent the backbone of German industry for the future. Britain is an attractive location for many companies because of the lower costs there in terms of start-ups, tax breaks and labour costs. Executives have pointed out that an average German industrial worker costs his employer around a third more than in the UK. Additionally companies also have to pay 7 per cent of every worker's salary into a welfare fund, plus a further 7 to 15 per cent into pension funds if they earn more than £210 per month. Chancellor Gerhard Schroeder had proclaimed that 'he wanted to make a society that was the most equitable in Europe', but that is not much help if the cost of that society destroys the jobs and revenue on which the welfare depends. Margaret Thatcher taught Britain that lesson back in the 1980s.

Qui, moi?

The French are joining the exodus, but, as one might expect, exhibit some quirks of their own. Air France moved a large part of its operation to London in 1999 because of the 'linguistic abilities of the locals'. This reason was hard enough to swallow for a dedicated Anglophile but how the *Academie Français* reacted has not been reported. The airline, in association with American airlines Delta and TWA, has closed nine reservation centres across Europe and relocated them as a multi-lingual call centre in Wembley. Air France denied a French union charge that the 'real reason for relocating to England was to take advantage of lower labour costs and greater work force flexibility', as several German corporations had already done. Frederic Verdier, head of the new centre, said, 'London is probably the most cosmopolitan city in Europe and is ideal for the recruitment of multi-lingual staff'. London does have some 33 ethnic communities each more than 10,000 strong, and an estimated 275 languages are spoken in the capital. Perhaps we insular British need to be reminded that London is the only truly cosmopolitan city in the EU and that this provides a major advantage to the UK in the global market.

London and the South East are the UK version of Silicon Valley and thus attract workers from other regions of the UK and now from France. Thousands of French highly skilled workers use the freedom of movement and work within the EU to work in southern England. The cross-channel ferries, Eurotunnel and weekend flights between Britain and France are filled with French workers commuting between the two countries. In time this is bound to have an effect on French eating and buying patterns to the advantage of the UK. The power of choice will invade the French supermarket to an extent not yet realised. Another blow to Gallic pride came with the announcement that the British Peugeot factory at Coventry in England was to make the Citroën C3, successor to the famed 2CV. Citroën, the sister of Peugeot, announced that the decision to build in Coventry was a tribute to the efficiency of British workers and the profitability of the UK market.

Conclusion

The more one looks at the current divergence in social and economic strategies between the UK and the inner ring of

EU members the more one asks what do we commonly believe in: why should we come together? And again most nations or empires grow over time into bureaucratic and decadent societies. *Europe seems to want to start that way.*

Chapter Six

A Divisive Single Currency

Up and down the City Road
In and out the Eagle,
That's the way the money goes –
Pop goes the weasel.

W.R. Mandale, nineteenth century

'If the Euro succeeds in its present form, it may render the pan-European ideal unrealisable. If it fails, it will precipitate the mother of all crises.'

Norman Davies, *Europe. A History*

From the outset, a distinction must be drawn between a single currency and a common currency. The former entails a loss of control over monetary policy, the latter does not. Eurosceptics like Sir Richard Body can exclaim, 'Forward with the Euro *and* the Pound'. In the UK we can already use the euro as a parallel currency as with a common currency. The advantages of a single currency to a group of nations with a common economic and political system are fairly obvious. A single currency would:

• Make life simpler and cheaper for businesses, consumers

161

and holidaymakers who will no longer have to pay to change money from currency to currency.

- Allow shoppers to compare prices for the same goods across the whole area. This will make corporate pricing strategies more transparent and will ensure that companies do not charge differently in different countries. In other words it should stimulate price competition.
- Reduce the impact of sudden exchange rate variations on business planning.
- Provide stable interest rates across a much wider area.
- If successful, enable the area to carry greater weight in international currency and financial issues and better fit the economy for the global market place.
- In combination all these benefits should combine to strengthen the overall economy of the area by stability in inflation and other economic measures.

There can be little dispute about the benefits of the stated premise. That is the intention of the euro club and the Commission. However, a principal argument of this book is that, in the EU, premises are too easily accepted so that the ensuing argument is concentrated on the subsidiary elements of the issue. For too long the debate in this country about whether Britain should or should not join the EMU and accept the euro, has concentrated on the convergence criteria or somewhat xenophobic calls to 'save the pound'. The wider issue that is ignored is whether or not the single currency is right for the whole of the community at this stage in the development of the Union.

The root of the problem is that at Maastricht and Amsterdam all the members too readily accepted the premise that the EU was, or at least was close to, being a group of nations with a common economic and political system. Quite clearly they were not and are still not. That is not wicked or even

162

reprehensible; indeed it would be amazing if they were. But what is reprehensible is that these facts were blatantly ignored and as a result the EU may now be launched on a very perilous road. The proponents of the EMU, principally Germany, France and the Commission, were so blinded by their vision of an integrated Europe as to use the EMU as another functional step in their overall strategy.

Basis for a single currency

If the political argument had concentrated on the premise rather than the actions defined in the treaties, it would have been clear to all, let alone Britain, that the EU is not yet ready for a single currency. Once again the EU has put the political cart before the economic horse. It happened with the Common Agricultural Policy, it happened with the Common Fisheries Policy and now it has happened with the single currency. To paraphrase an earlier judgement by Sir Winston Churchill on another issue, 'When all is said and done. Three times is a lot'. Once again the Europhile politicians want to push ahead with their pet project, the European super state, and leave the rest of the community to pick up the pieces.

Strong disagreements were raised at the time but largely ignored. The international banker, Stanislas Yassukovich, said, 'the monetary union in the EU is a political initiative masquerading as an economic one'. Bernard Connolly, author of *The Rotten Heart of Europe*, has gone further and argued that the launch of the euro raises the old spectre of war and ruin in Europe and adds 'bureaucrats will rule once free nations'. Again, David Smith, the *Sunday Times* columnist, argues that in time the single currency is bound to fail because it ignores 'the simple lessons from the success of the dollar economy in the USA'. These are serious arguments

163

by respected commentators and need to be examined before we focus on the relevance of the single currency to Britain.

David Smith notes that nearly 40 years ago the economist Robert Mandell set out the three conditions for an 'optimum currency area', in other words a group of countries that can prosper under a single currency. The conditions were: *first* wage flexibility, needed when countries lost the ability to vary their exchange rates. *Second,* geographical mobility of labour, so that if certain regions became depressed (and lacked the means to do anything about it) people would move elsewhere in search of work. *Finally* 'resource transfers', a big enough central budget to allow government spending to be directed at areas particularly hard hit by economic circumstances. These are almost exactly the conditions present in the United States, which has the largest single currency area that works. The economic environment in Europe in contrast is almost exactly the opposite.

Newt Gingrich, a former Speaker of the US House of Representatives in an article in the *Chicago Sun Times*, pointed out that Europe appears to be approaching this economic change in the reverse order to the American model. The colonies first fought for their political independence, then for their political unity. They did this through the Articles of Confederation, the movement for a Constitution and then a Constitutional Convention. The last step was the emergence of a unified tariff, a unified currency and finally a unified national debt for one national economy.

Since the US has a national economy it has a national labour system. As Gingrich explains, this means that as cotton became less profitable to harvest by hand, black labour could, and did, move to Detroit and New York. As rust belt jobs became less useful, people could move to Houston and Los Angeles, and as the dust bowl drove people out of the Great Plains, they could move to Southern California. Again and again America has been a country of enormous migrations and enormous openness. This openness allows the most entrepreneurial, the most innovative and the most rapidly growing areas to draw people to them. In addition America has had a tradition of mobile housing, transferable mortgages and a population very willing to uproot itself.

Furthermore, North Americans have had a free-market, entrepreneurial model in which companies go bankrupt on a routine basis. The USA may kill 300,000 jobs a week, but it also creates 350,000 jobs a week. The result is a constant dynamic shifting of wealth, opportunity and jobs in a manner that seems very chaotic and hard-hearted to many Europeans. The European model of safeguarding jobs means that in the long run Europe protects more jobs than the USA, but it also creates fewer. For example in just November and December 1997, more jobs were created in the United States than had been created in Europe over the previous 10 years. Since the early 1970s the USA has created more than 30 million net new jobs and more than 12 million in the 1990s alone. This contrasts sharply with Europe's depressing record of fewer than 4 million net new jobs since the 1970s, and even more important a net reduction in private sector employment.

It is worth remembering that during the Industrial Revolution in Britain millions left Scotland, Wales and Ireland to find work in England. Had they been separate states with different languages, England could not have prospered and achieved her economic predominance.

By establishing a European monetary union before they established a mobile flexible labour market, a housing market and an economic system that allows jobs to disappear and entrepreneurs to grow, Gingrich believes that European politicians are taking a great gamble. Europe runs the very great danger of forcing a series of crises that its political system might be incapable of resolving.

Bernard Connolly echoes the theme with an even direr

forecast. He states that the EMU is intended to destroy the individual nation state and to create a European empire. The empire will not be based on freely given assent and allegiance to a set of democratic national political institutions. The euro puts the peoples of the economic colonies entirely at the mercy of the Franco-German political and bureaucratic elites who really run the European Union. The resultant anti-democratic system will foster a set of ugly nationalisms feeding on race, language and religion. The European empire would be a dangerously negative force in the world.

David Smith, in a *Sunday Times* article in January 1999, also highlighted the differences between the European and the American economic systems. Wages are flexible in America because they have to be. On becoming unemployed, Americans initially receive a level of benefit about two-thirds of income, not far below the levels in Europe. But those benefit levels fall off sharply after six to nine months. In many European countries, by contrast, benefits are either not time limited or actually increase the longer that people are out of work. In Sweden and Finland, for example, the initial income replacement rate of 89 per cent rises to 99 per cent. In that environment why ever look for work? The American labour market works on the basis of incentives, in the form of low taxation together with a limited role for the trade unions. Only 18 per cent of Americans are covered by collective bargaining arrangements, compared with more than 90 per cent in several European countries and about 47 per cent in Britain. The Davos world economic forum of businessmen rated 53 countries according to labour market flexibility; in order of flexibility Spain was 47th, Belgium 48th, Germany 51st, France 52nd and Italy 53rd. Britain ranked fifth. A dramatic contrast. Europe clearly fails the flexibility test.

Europe also fails, even more spectacularly, the test of geographical mobility. Labour mobility in Europe has been stagnant or declining since the 1970s, both within and between member states. This is the more interesting, as one of the key objectives of the EU is the free movement of labour. European workers when faced with unemployment tend to stay put. In the case of Germany and France, at the heart of the new Europe, mobility in respect of other EU countries has halved in the past 20 years. Language is overwhelmingly cited as the main restraining reason but also there is no incentive to move because of state subsidies and in any case it is difficult to move. Once again the diversity of cultures is ignored. The third condition set by Robert Mandell was a central budget to divert resources to areas of depression. The American economy does provide substantial movement of federal funding, spending and tax relief programmes to aid crisis areas.

In view of these dire warnings, what evidence is there of this fundamental weakness of the EMU? Certainly the early weak performance of the euro in the world exchange markets came as a surprise to many Europeans, and in particular the Germans. But the general or complacent view to date seems to be that this is a temporary phenomenon, and in fact the euro has stabilised. Even in Britain the assumption underlying the debate about joining the euro is that somehow the single currency will muddle through. Europe is not an optimum currency area now, nor as David Smith makes clear, does it look likely to be so for some years to come. Though it is only fair to note that the recent problems for the dollar still raise the same issues.

If all this were true, we have to ask how on earth did we arrive at this position and what should we now be doing about it to prevent a financial disaster? Once again the plea is for evolution rather than instant revolution, and a mindless rush for ill-considered change. However, it is worth looking at how the EMU and the single currency became a central theme of EU integration. The process is symbolic of

167

much of what is wrong with the direction of the European movement.

The founding fathers of the European movement were talking about a single currency from the outset, but the concept really took root in the late 1950s. At that stage they believed that monetary union would promote cross-border trade and be a symbol of unity in post-war Europe. They also saw it as the final step to a federal Europe. After several false starts Jacques Delors, Helmut Kohl and others intent on economic and political integration revived the plan in the mid-1980s. Helmut Kohl originally believed that a federal European state would have to precede a single currency, until President Mitterrand and Commissioner Delors persuaded him that it could work the other way round.

It was in Luxembourg in December 1985 that Jacques Delors, then President of the European Commission, out manoeuvred the 'troublesome Anglo-Saxons' and began to put Europe on the road to monetary union. At this summit Delors persuaded all the EU leaders, including a deeply sceptical Mrs Thatcher, that a 110-word chapter entitled 'Co-operation in Economic and Monetary Policy' should be enshrined in community law.

Not for the first time, Britain had been duped. Mrs Thatcher, who had been persuaded by the Foreign Office not to veto the crucial chapter, said afterwards that the words were largely meaningless. If they had been anything else, she insisted that she would have vetoed them. This was the moment that the journey towards monetary union could have been stopped in its tracks. But the arch Machiavellian Delors, supported by Kohl and Mitterrand, was able to drive these 'meaningless' words into agreement to the whole concept of the EMU and the single currency through to the treaties at Maastricht and Amsterdam.

Fears about the convergence of disparate economies were allayed at Maastricht by the development of seemingly tough

168

criteria for joining the EMU. Yet in retrospect we can now see that Europe's leaders shamelessly bent the rules laid down at Maastricht. All eleven initial joiners of the EMU managed to get their budget down to three per cent of GDP but most only after highly dubious one-off measures. Italy and Belgium had public debts twice those allowed by the Maastricht Treaty, and later Greece would be allowed a similar latitude.

It is time that the leaders of the individual nation states of the Union understood that almost invariably conflict put off is conflict lost. For all engaged in complex negotiations the adage holds, 'Forget the facts and focus on the truth'. The euro club to date have won their objective time after time by drowning the decision makers in detail and 'dubious facts'. The future of the European Union has been lost in complex references to Chapters, Articles, Acts and segments of Treaties, which EU leaders only partly understand and are thus easily made malleable by the EU apparatchiks. Europe desperately needs a clear purpose or set of principles which all agree should be the measure of success. (See Chapter Ten, *Purpose*.) Though the proposed new European Constitution is far from providing this clarity.

The position of the United Kingdom

On the surface the United Kingdom is in a strong position in that it is not a member of the EMU and has not accepted the euro as its currency. It shares that position with several other members of the European Union. The weakness of the British position is that it has already declared its 'intent' to join when the convergence criteria set by the government can be met. A saving grace, perhaps, is that the government has also agreed that it will not enter the EMU until a referendum of the people decides in favour.

The downside of the UK position is that it has created a

psychological situation that eventually Britain will join the EMU and so the debate has concentrated on the convergence criteria and the timing of the referendum on the proposed Constitution. Much of the argument has been obfuscated by reference to the minutiae of political election dates and party political calendars. Of course there has been discussion of the pros and cons of the UK's accepting the single currency, but again these issues are being obscured by a slogan war of commitment or not to the Constitution and European Union. There has been little or no purposeful debate in Parliament or in the British media on the overall efficacy of a single currency to Europe as a whole.

Convergence criteria

In October 1997 Chancellor Gordon Brown made the UK government's position statement on Economic and Monetary Union. The key parts of this statement were:

- The government was committed in principle to taking the UK into the EMU.
- The UK's membership of the EMU was ruled out during the lifetime of the then parliament. So the UK would not be a member of the first wave of countries entering the EMU.
- The UK would only enter the EMU if this decision would be in the national economic interest, determined by five economic tests.

Brown defined the five economic tests of the UK's convergence criteria as follows:

1. Are business cycles and economic structures comparable so that the UK and others could live comfortably with Euro interest rates on a permanent basis?

2. If problems emerge, is there sufficient flexibility in both labour and product markets to deal with them?
3. Would membership of the EMU create better conditions for firms making long-term investment decisions in the UK?
4. What impact would entry into the EMU have on the competitive situation of the UK's financial services industry, particularly, the City of London?
5. In summary, will joining the EMU promote higher growth, stability and a lasting increase in jobs?

Intriguingly, a Eurosceptic could argue that it would be more apposite for the Euroland states to consider the convergence criteria in reverse. When will the EMU states be ready to converge with the successful economic strategy of the United Kingdom to allow the British to join the EMU?

In June 2003 the Chancellor of the Exchequer, Gordon Brown, delivered the Treasury verdict on the British economy in relation to the five economic tests. Using a mountain of paperwork evidence from the Treasury on each criterion and one-to-one meetings with every member of the largely Europhile Cabinet, Brown was able to force Blair and the Government to accept that the convergence criteria had not been met. Brown had used Monnet concepts to drown the issue and win his case.

However, the price that Brown had to pay was to make a strong statement that the Government was still committed to eventual membership of the EMU. The convergence criteria were now to be reviewed at the next Budget and presumably at each successive Budget until the criteria were met. There was no commitment as to when the Government would call the promised referendum. The reply 'not yet' seemed to sum-up the whole Government position.

The 'not yet' attitude was forced upon the Labour leadership by the internal party conflict between the Europhiles and those who demanded more evidence or were committed anti-Europeans. The *Independent* newspaper summed up the Europhile viewpoint with a banner headline 'Once again, this timid Government has failed the only test that matters: that of political courage'. The Eurosceptics in all parties took solace in the indecision and lived to fight another day.

But linked with the agreements over the EU Constitution and the mounting demand for another referendum the whole European debate appeared to be re-opened after a long period in the doldrums. Could a growing concern over Europe capture debating time from the public services, crime and immigration issues? With a botched restructuring of the Government, division over Iraq and amendments to the Constitution by the elimination of the post of Lord Chancellor without proper debate the Blair Government appeared to be in disarray. Now the demand for a referendum on the European Constitution was coming from Blair's own back-benchers and finally the clamour had to be met. Blair was in retreat to the Eurosceptics. Europe seemed to be moving back to centre stage.

A partial reason for the historic paucity of debate on the euro or any other EU issue in the UK is the typical British apathy to party politics and obscure foreign issues. Despite the massive increase in overseas holidays, the English, in particular, travel in cocoons of national attitudes and cuisine. For many of them sampling 'international' food and drink means pasta, pizza and kebabs liberally laced with tequila or ouzo. It really doesn't matter if the phrase 'the wogs begin at Calais' is or is not politically correct if deep down the average English person still identifies with the sentiment. The common attitude that 'foreigners are funny' is a fact that has to be considered in evaluating national attitudes. Sophisticated readers may abhor such attitudes, but that does not make them go away. Before we admonish our fellow countrymen it is well to remember that similar attitudes are found amongst the French and the Germans.

Manipulative politicians understand this simple truth and know how and when to arouse the deep-seated emotions of their electorates. This approach can be encapsulated as 'highlight a mythical fear and provide a mythical dream'. In the last century the most potent example of this political approach were the Nazi slogans of '*Juden Raus*' and '*Deutschland Erwach*', (Tr: 'Jews Out' and 'Germany Awake') summed up in the song from the film *Cabaret*, 'Tomorrow Belongs to Me'. Playing on the fear of being left behind; 'missing the boat' and the vision of being 'at the heart of Europe' may not be so immoral as the 1930s slogans, but they are playing on the same emotions. Initially discussion about the euro in Britain was focused on the advantages, and in particular the benefit of being able to travel across Europe without continual money changing, while opposition was rather muted and tended to concentrate on issues such as the Queen's head on the coinage. The new currency was launched, but Britain was not yet involved, and in any case the Chancellor provided a safeguard in defining convergence criteria that must be present before entry. If the government had called for a referendum in 1999, there might have been a majority for Britain to join the EMU and accept the single currency. Close scrutiny changed the mood. As the argument continued throughout the early 2000s, support for the euro fell until even the Confederation of British Industry, an early strong supporter of the euro, reported that its membership was evenly divided about British entry. The 'NO' vote in the Danish and Swedish Referendums acted to confirm the overall view in Britain, and provided a sense of security that the United Kingdom was not alone. By the end of 2002 it was clear that a referendum would reject the euro by a decisive majority, and New Labour politicians were clearly moving a possible referendum to some years ahead.

Early in 2000 the clear government viewpoint had been that Britain was committed to entry and it was only a matter of time before the convergence criteria were met. To the chattering classes this appeared to represent the majority opinion in the UK. In a spirit of euphoria, the government launched a pro-euro campaign on an ostensibly cross-party basis. The Prime Minister, Tony Blair, was joined on the pro-European platform by the leader of the Liberal Democrat Party, Charles Kennedy, and two past giants of the Conservative Party, Michael Heseltine and Kenneth Clarke. That was the high point of support, but from then onward the Europhiles were on the back foot. It was not only that the opposition argument was being heard, but, that it was getting organised. More than 30 opposition groups, which at one stage would have been viewed as minor splinter groups, were beginning to cooperate. At the Congress of Democracy meeting in London, a joint statement was issued and focus group research was commissioned. Lord Owen, a formerly pro-EU Foreign Secretary, who became famous as the leader of the gang of four, which left the Labour Party to launch the Social Democratic Party, became a natural leader of the newly organised opposition.

Of the thirty dissident groups, perhaps twelve are properly staffed and funded. They liaise on a regular basis and would be at the forefront of a referendum campaign against joining the EMU. Because Europhiles have dominated British politics for so long this co-ordination of the Eurosceptic opposition was an important change. It is too early to evaluate the long-term impact of the coalition of Eurosceptic support but the composition and source of this group covers a wide spectrum of British politics and business. The multiplicity of groups is seen as an advantage, as long as they continue to co-ordinate their activities, as each group will focus on different target audiences.

The leading groups, now liaising together, who make up

British resistance to the single currency were summarised in the *Daily Telegraph* as follows:

Democracy Movement. This is the successor to the late Sir James Goldsmith's Referendum Party, which fielded hundreds of candidates at the election in 1997. Its main job will be to mobilise the foot soldiers at grassroots level in a referendum campaign. Paul Sykes, the Yorkshire multi-millionaire who funded anti-EMU Conservative candidates in the 1997 election, is the Movement's chairman and has promised to spend up to £20 million to fight the euro.

Global Britain launched by Lord Pearson of Rannoch, a Conservative peer. This is a think tank with a much more aggressive approach to the European Union than most of the other organisations. Global Britain is in favour of complete withdrawal on the grounds that the EU obstructs global free market competition. Its most notable member, the Euro-sceptic journalist Christopher Booker, edits Global Britain's magazine.

Bruges Group. This is the main academic front against the euro. Launched to support the philosophy of Lady Thatcher's anti-Brussels Bruges speech, it is run by Dr Martin Holmes of Oxford University and concentrates on publishing research papers. Lord Lamont, the former Conservative Chancellor of the Exchequer, is the vice-president.

UK Independence Party. This arch-sceptic party made a significant electoral impact in the 2004 European election when it won 12 seats. It caught the mood of the electorate to a much greater extent than the Conservative Party, which had done so well at the previous European election. Robert Kilroy-Silk, the ex MP and TV Show host made a major impact with his mastery of the media and TV in particular.

The spectacular success of the UKIP in knocking the Liberal Democrats into fourth place, leaving the Labour and Conservative Parties with less than 50 per cent of the vote between them raises serious questions about the future shape of British politics. However, the withdrawal of sponsorship funds and the Kilroy-Silk led leadership battles are damaging to the UKIP image.

Business for Sterling. As the name suggests, this is the organisation that will marshal business expertise and potentially millions of pounds of City of London money against the single currency. Although headed by Lord Marsh, a former Labour minister, Business for Sterling is a cross-party organisation. Sir Stanley Kalms, the Thatcherite boss of the giant retailer the Dixon Group, is one of the leading figures on the council. Sir John Craven, the former chairman of the Deutsche Morgan Grenfell finance group is also a key supporter. This group is increasingly heard in the media.

European Foundation. Run by Bill Cash, a Conservative shadow minister, the Foundation's main contribution to the campaign is the publication of a monthly heavyweight magazine called the *European Journal*. When Mr Cash had to refuse donations to the Foundation from Sir James Goldsmith because of the tycoon's decision to run referendum candidates against the Conservatives, Lady Thatcher, controversially, gave Mr Cash a cheque to compensate.

European Research Group. Chaired by Sir Michael Spicer, a leading Conservative backbencher and Chairman of the 1922 Committee, the Group focuses on mobilising political opposition to the euro. Sir Michael also convened the Congress for Democracy that helped develop the umbrella anti-euro organisation.

Campaign against Euro-Federalism. This group operates within the trade union movement and produces a regular publication called the *Democrat*. It has managed to change the previously-held view that the British Trade Union movement is firmly pro-EMU.

Campaign for an Independent Britain. Led by Sir Richard Body, a former Conservative backbencher and a leading writer on Europe, this all party organisation has its roots in the 'No' campaign that was set-up during the Common Market referendum of 1975. It publishes a newsletter called *Independence*, but is a relatively small group.

Labour Euro-Safeguards Campaign. This is the main Labour party anti-EMU organisation. It also has its origins in the 1975 referendum campaign and is dominated by 'Old Labour' figures like Denzil Davies, a former Treasury Minister, and Austin Mitchell a prominent TV contributor and MP.

People's Europe. Another Labour anti-EMU organisation, this group represents the left-wing case against the single currency. Supporters are associated with the arch-socialist Campaign Group and they fear that the EMU would stop Britain ever introducing socialist economic policies.

Others. Dozens of other organisations will play a part in any formal campaign against the single currency. The *Conservative Party* is by far the most significant political party formally opposed to early entry, but the *Green Party*, and, in Northern Ireland, the *Ulster Unionists*, *Democratic Unionists* and *UK Unionists* are all opposed. Major business organisations like the *Institute of Directors* and the *Federation of Small Businesses* will also join the fight against the euro.

The importance of listing these organisations in this book

is that now that they are collaborating it will be impossible to view opposition to the euro as a few disparate and minor sceptics. The breadth of representation and the calibre and reputation of the individuals and organisations noted should make it ludicrous to continue to label Eurosceptics as wild extremists. The Europhiles of Brussels and their associates may have crossed a bridge too far and too soon.

Today the reasons for opposing the single currency have gone far beyond the original emotional argument about the loss of sovereignty or antagonism to Brussels. Reflection and research is now providing solid economic and political evidence of the perilous path on which Europe, and potentially Britain, are embarked. The instinctive reaction of those conversant with the reasons for Britain's long history of independence could be portrayed as emotional and old fashioned by the New Labour modernisers and the Europhiles of all parties. They were dismissed as of little consequence to the new leaders of the UK. Now these instincts were still intact, if not enhanced, and were now being shared by a wider group of an awakened populace. The opposition, now led by the Conservative Party of Michael Howard has reinforced that it opposes the euro with powerful practical evidence without abandoning the emotional appeal of patriotism.

The principal British arguments against joining the EMU and implementing the single currency can be summarised as follows:

- It is unlikely that a single currency implemented across diverse economic systems can succeed.
- The convergence criteria established by the Commission and by the Labour government in the UK do not address the reality of the diverse economic systems in Europe.
- The inability of individual nations (and thus the UK) within the EMU to alter their interest rates, makes it

exceptionally difficult for individual states to react to economic circumstances.

- Individual governments would be restricted to fiscal measures rather than the now proven effectiveness, in the short term, of monetary measures.
- Since the Thatcher revolution, the British economy has moved much closer to the global economy determined by the USA. Dependent on initiative and competition, rather than the semi-socialist ideals of government intervention and protectionist union attitudes, Britain would be walking backwards to embrace the economic systems of Germany and France.
- The only way to solve the issues involved in imposing the single currency over diverse economies demands a further EU drive to remove the diversities. This would require a convergence of taxation and industrial or employee policies to the detriment of Europe's and Britain's position in the global market. Britain would have lost all ability to act independently.
- The preparatory cost to British business of implementing the single currency (estimated to be over £30 billion) far exceeds the financial benefits it will gain from reduced transactional costs.
- Joining the EMU would reduce British influence on the future direction of the EU economy in the sense that it would have accepted the Commissioner's solution before 'starting the argument'. Britain's influence is greater outside the euro.
- Rather than being left behind in the race for economic success, Britain would actually face increased unemployment, higher direct taxes, a massive increase in debilitating restrictions and a general loss of freedom if she joined the EMU. She would also lose her unique position in world markets.
- In conclusion the European Union would lose the last

major obstacle to pursuing Europhile objectives. British acquiescence in the EMU would persuade Euroland government that it can safely keep postponing the much needed structural reforms of continental EU economic strategies.

To quote Sir John Nott, the former Defence Secretary and Chairman of the Commission, set up by former Conservative leader William Hague to consider the issues surrounding Britain's entry to the European Monetary Union: 'Keeping our currency, and with it our economic independence and competitiveness, is in fact the key to Britain's prosperity in a new age'. Perhaps once again Britain, in pursuing its own interests, will prove in retrospect to be also pursuing the interests of Europe.

PART TWO

FUTURE UNCERTAINTIES

Part One made clear that a purposeful fog has surrounded the future direction of the European Union. Part Two deals with the three key issues that need to be brought out in to the open, debated, and resolved, to disperse the fog and provide a firm future for Europe.

Chapter Seven

Widening or Deepening

'Not deep the Poet sees, but wide.'

Matthew Arnold, 1822–1888

Ten more nations from central, eastern and Mediterranean Europe joined the European Union in May 2004. Others are waiting in the wings striving to meet the entry criteria. This recent growth and the likelihood of the EU being further extended over the next decade raises major questions that can be summarised as follows and are the key subject for this Chapter:

- **Preparation:** is the EU and are its individual members sufficiently prepared and ready for this scale of enlargement?
- **Re-organisation:** what changes will be needed in the organisation of the Commission and the decision-making processes of the EU to enable it to operate efficiently when enlarged?
- **New entrants:** what benefits, liabilities and problems will the new nations bring to the Union?
- **Deepening:** will the process of widening the European Union delay or accelerate the possible deepening of political union towards a federal super state?
- **Diversity:** what are the political, economic and cultural

183

implications for both the new entrants and the EU as a whole?

Preparation

The inter-governmental conference at Nice in December 2000 was intended to complete the negotiations for a new Treaty that would modify the management processes of the EU in preparation for the enlargement of the Union. The Nice Treaty was also expected to continue the progress of integration.

Though a Treaty was negotiated and agreed at Nice there was almost unanimous agreement that the conference was a disaster. Most considered that the Treaty itself was a fudge of last-minute compromises and left more questions than answers about the progress of enlargement. Subsequent conferences have been conducted with less acrimony but have provided little further clarity. There was also agreement that France (which was host nation as current holder of the EU presidency) was to blame, and there was strong condemnation of the arrogant behaviour of President Chirac. The London *Times* in its verdict on the Nice Summit, quoted the *Book of Common Prayer*: 'We have left undone those things which we ought to have done; And we have done those things which we ought not to have done.'

The debacle at Nice was primarily the result of poor preparation and little *real* pre-negotiation about critical issues. The Commission, under the direction of its President Romano Prodi, must take some responsibility but President Chirac had made a tour of the major countries to promote his objectives and ostensibly to listen to and to take into account their concerns. On arriving at Nice, the first French draft of the Treaty produced consternation amongst the participants. As leaders, such as Prime Minister Blair of the UK and

184

Chancellor Gerhard Schroeder of Germany, realised that their arguments or positions had simply been ignored, they exploded with fury. The atmosphere of the Summit was set from the outset.

Apart from the specific details of the Treaty that we will discuss later there were some intriguing political results from the Summit. Some were apparent immediately, while others emerged later. These issues can be grouped under the following headings:

- The Commission weakened
- The Franco-German axis fractured
- The apparent end of the European Super State

The Commission weakened

Romano Prodi is no Jacques Delors. The inevitable result of two relatively weak presidents of the Commission in succession began to show at Nice. Most certainly Delors would not have agreed to be excluded from Chirac's 'confessionals' and would have held his own duplicate meetings. He would never have stood for being publicly shouted at and humiliated by President Chirac. Perhaps more to the point Chirac would not have tried.

Few of the Commission's objectives, or new functional steps towards integration survived in entirety in the new Treaty. The overall intentions to streamline the Commission, reduce the number of Members of the European Parliament and eliminate the national vetoes were not achieved. The remorseless march to power of the Commission was partially halted but it would be foolhardy to believe that the danger has passed.

Other dissensions that arose at Nice may still enable the Commission to divide and conquer and appear as the protector of the small nations and resume its acquisition of power.

185

However, there is a great opportunity for people of vision to create a new purpose for Europe. A real partnership free of the clinging tentacles of bureaucracy could just be possible.

Fracture of the Franco-German Axis

A real surprise at the Nice Summit was the obvious fracture of the Franco-German Axis that has survived every vicissitude since the Treaty of the Elysee in 1963. The Germans were demanding more votes in the formula for quality majority voting to represent the substantial population difference between themselves (80 million) and the other leaders, Italy, France and Great Britain (around 60 million each). The United Kingdom and Italy were prepared to accept a minor increase in the German allocation but the French were adamantly against the proposal.

It was the manner of the French dismissal of the German case that did more damage than the issue itself. President Chirac reportedly told an angry Gerhard Schroeder that France deserved as many votes as his country because it had nuclear weapons and was on the right side in two world wars. This deeply wounding insult will not be forgotten. The German Chancellor is a warm, tactile individual and his body language later in the conference made his own attitude clear. He left a photo-call of ministers by placing his arm around Tony Blair and pointedly ignored the then French Prime Minister, Lionel Jospin, leaving him alone and isolated to the obvious interest of observers.

The Nice Summit made clear that the future interests of Germany and France are not necessarily in tune. Many of the new entrants will naturally look to Germany rather than France as their natural partner. German investment in Eastern Europe will develop that relationship, giving Germany much more self confidence and generally reducing French influence in the expanded Europe. Issues over the European army and a general reaction to French intransigence could lead to a working Anglo-German alliance in the future of Europe. But of course the discord between France and Germany may soon be overcome, as it has in the past. The stance taken by both over the Iraq war is some indication that the alliance is still strong.

End of the European super state?

The naked pursuit of national agendas and the weakness of the Commission at Nice were heralded as the end of the dangerous remorseless march to the European super state, by political commentators and the media alike. Following the Summit a *Sunday Times* headline proclaimed 'Death to the European super state' while its sister paper *The Times* carried the headline 'Eurosceptics face death by a thousand cuddles'. In the debate following his statement on the Treaty of Nice to the House of Commons, Prime Minister Tony Blair unusually trounced the then Leader of the Opposition, William Hague, over the issues of loss of veto power and the threat of a super state.

All the warnings of the Eurosceptics were once again falling on deaf ears. So does this mean that all the concerns expressed in this book were unfounded? Should the authors, as discredited Eurosceptics, halt their labours and throw away their manuscript? To the contrary: Nice supported a major theme of this book. The diversity of the nation states involved, would, in the end, make it impossible for a European super state to long endure. For a moment of time the truth was clear for all to see. This book is not opposed to an alliance of European nations, as Part Three will make clear. It is opposed to those who are committed to a federal state, who continually initiate measures to achieve their ends and are doing irreparable damage to the real purpose of a new *Grand Alliance*.

There has been no evidence since Nice that the euro club and its supporters have changed their objectives. Nice may have represented a stumble on the road but the destination remains intact. Indeed it has now become clear that some of the decisions made at Nice, which appeared innocuous at the time, were really another *functional* step along the road. Two of those were the EU's new Charter of Fundamental Rights and the proposed European Constitution that are both becoming a fractious issue that is likely to last for years to come.

Re-organisation

The decision-making processes of the EU are already under strain. Clearly the enlargement of the EU over the next decade will demand substantial changes. Since Maastricht, key areas have emerged as the principal targets for reform. The Treaty of Nice was designed to address these organisational issues which can be summarised as:

- Elimination or reduction of national vetoes
- Introduction of qualified majority voting (QMV)
- Agreement on individual nation voting power for QMV
- National representation on the Commission and the European Parliament

All of these issues are contentious. Some exist in terms of national pride and comparison with others, but elements of all the issues went directly to the heart of the kind of Europe that was envisaged. Perhaps in charity it was not surprising that the really contentious issues were not solved at the first attempt at Nice. The Germans and the British demanded another inter-governmental conference to attempt to resolve the remaining problems. But as Blair said after

Nice, 'We cannot do business in this way again'. So the preparation for 2004 was exacting. In fact the conference held in 2004 was conducted in a more gentlemanly manner but did little to advance the key issues and has not resulted in a new treaty.

National veto

The national veto has become a black and white issue between the federalists and the Eurosceptics. On the one hand, the retention of a national veto is a surrender to the 'forces of conservatism', whilst on the other hand any reduction in Britain's power of veto is a surrender of 'our sovereignty'. In a meaningful alliance of nations both arguments, taken to the extreme, are patently unreasonable.

The concept of a national veto being available to every nation on every issue would make an alliance of a possible twenty-eight nations totally unworkable. Equally, the concept of no national veto on any issue would be a complete abdication of any right to survive as an independent nation. This is the crunch decision for every nation involved in the European Union. From the British perspective one can only echo Winston Churchill's question after Pearl Harbor, 'What kind of people do they think we are?'

The decision for every nation at Nice was a matter of principle and the exercise of that old dictum of common law 'what would the reasonable man expect'. From the wider British point of view, Prime Minister Blair made what in all fairness could be called 'reasonable' decisions at Nice. He held firm on the retention of the veto on vital issues such as the control of taxation and social security policy, defence and foreign policy. He accepted the end of the British veto on some 39 issues on a few of which the UK has an opt-out position including border security.

There was a mixed reception from the Eurosceptics to

the number of veto areas that Britain (and the other states) had surrendered at Nice. Most seemed happy that Tony Blair had successfully retained the veto in sensitive areas including defence, taxation and social security. Some, like Edward Heathcoat Amory, the Eurosceptic journalist, looked at the areas of lost vetoes in detail and warned that there were many signs of danger to Britain.

In an article in the *Daily Mail* in December 2000 Amory highlighted 'what we lost in the "Battle of Nice"' in a series of areas.

Foreign policy: By surrendering the right of veto over the appointment of the Common Foreign and Security Policy Special Representative the UK has lost its ability to ensure that the man or woman who will be running the EU's joint foreign and security policy recognises Britain's unique position. Europe can also sign some binding international treaties without Britain's agreement.

Mutual aid: Britain has lost the right to veto community financial assistance to member states in severe difficulties. If Italy or Ireland were to go broke and endanger the euro then Britain might have to help pay for the bail out. Similarly the clause on products could feasibly allow the EU to take control of Britain's North Sea oil supplies. The latter issue became more concrete in April 2001 with the Commission's draft proposals for legislation to deal with times of international energy shortage. The plan states 'reserves held by member states must be brought into the community framework'. The draft says that there should be a plan 'which will enable petroleum stocks to be "communitarised" within a short space of time'. Heath gave away our fish; is Blair now about to give away our oil? Francis Maude, the then shadow foreign secretary, accused the EU of attempting a 'smash and grab raid' against Britain's assets. He said, 'This measure is a naked power grab to utilise Britain's oil reserves and sends a powerful signal that the EU's ambitions to transform itself into a super state are alive and well'.

Cohesion: Europe spends large sums encouraging economic 'cohesion' between member states. In other words transferring funds from the richer regions, such as Britain, to poorer countries such as Greece. At Nice, the UK gave up its veto on how the system works and could lose out in the process.

Politics: The UK gave up its veto on the way that MEPs conduct their business and political parties are regulated. We would be unable to prevent huge pay rises and lay ourselves open to interference from Brussels as happened to Austria, after the electoral success of the right-wing Freedom Party.

Immigration and Asylum: Though Britain retained the opt-out position it is used as a last resort so this is another area that the Commission might influence. Recent evidence of the UK's Home Office confusion and incompetence in this area, leading to a Ministerial resignation, only serves to heighten this concern.

There were some further examples, but in the main moderate Eurosceptics recognise that there must be some give and take in an enlarged EU, and considers that Britain achieved a reasonable result in the area of the national veto.

Voting power and representation

With the influx of mostly small nations, it was clear that the EU needed a radical overhaul of the representation and voting power of member states. Before Nice the system was, to quote the German Chancellor Gerhard Schroeder, 'scandalously undemocratic'. Little Luxembourg had 2 votes for 400,000 people; Belgium had 5 votes for 10 million people. Germany had 10 votes (the same as Britain, France and Italy) for 82 million. In other words the minnows held a block vote out of all proportion to their size. Each new enlargement had weighted down the scale in favour of the smaller nations and unless that situation was changed, the 'big four', or most certainly France and Germany, would veto any enlargement. The *re-weighting* of votes was the major issue of contention at Nice, with the *existing* small nations determined to retain most of their advantage.

Prior to Nice, the declared strategic intention was to streamline both the Commission and the European Parliament but both these objectives fell victim of the 'horse trading' battle on the conference floor. Blair and Schroeder insisted on revisiting all of these areas at the inter-governmental conference in 2004. Following the two conferences the revised figures, rather than reducing the current 20 Commissioners, the number will rise to a maximum of 27 Commissioners when the two countries negotiating entry are accepted. The European Parliament had 626 MEPs prior to Nice. At the 2004 European Parliament elections it had risen to 732 MEPs. These ludicrous compromises were the price of settling the 'revolt of the small nations' over the weighted voting issue.

At Nice, the result of the sometimes bitter negotiations was that the number of votes each nation has in the EU's policy settling councils were rebalanced. To an extent, some of the fears expressed by nations such as Britain over QMV were alleviated by the agreement that a passing majority would need 255 votes out of 342 and that the nations in the majority accounted for 62 per cent of the EU population.

Germany was the biggest winner in the sense that it negotiated more power over decision making than Britain and France. It also argues that in justice on the basis of population, it should also have had more votes. The other surprise winner was Poland in that as a new entrant, it achieved voting parity with Spain. Poland may have reaped the reward for its strong and positive diplomatic offensive on the EU front over a number of years.

The reform of the Commission has been an objective of both France and Britain for some years because both felt it was already unwieldy. Their intention was to bring down the number of Commissioners from 20 to a workable 12 members. In the horse trading at Nice this objective was abandoned and the new Commission will not reach a ceiling until 27 members, thus making it even more cumbersome.

The President of the Commission, Romano Prodi, who felt defeated by the continuation of the national veto in key areas, and insulted by the crude behaviour of President Chirac, was nevertheless able to win new powers to organise the Commission his way. The Commission President will be able to control portfolios, appoint new vice-presidents, and initiate the sacking of any Commissioner. This is likely to lead to an executive team for the EU in which there are clear senior and junior Commissioners and more relevant direction of resources. Though undoubtedly giving the President of the Commission more power, it would appear to be a wise step towards overcoming some of the weaknesses of the Commission we noted in Chapter Three. However, on the other hand, with the increase of Commissioners and MEPs, the Brussels gravy train will just get longer.

The new entrants

The background of the entrant nations will bring a new dimension to the EU. The diversity of cultures will become more obvious and could change the very nature of Europe. The aspects of the new dimension that will challenge the future progress of the EU include ethnicity, political heritage, industrial and business development and the fact that the new entrants are with the exception of Poland, relatively small nations.

From the beginning as the EEC and then the EU, the development of the European alliance has been involved with establishing a balance between the contrasting cultures of the Germanic and Latin nations. That balance will be upset by the absorption of many nations of Slavic origin. Probably, in the early stages of the new Union, more immediate economic issues will dominate cultural diversity. However, over time, these ethnic differences may emerge to form new groupings of nations within the EU. In considering one great European state, it is worthwhile remembering that the issue of race dominated much of the last century. In those terms Europe is really composed of three great races that, from time to time, have a magnetic pull to their peoples. The Slav nation is a new issue for the EU.

The political heritage of the new entrants adds yet another dimension to the widening of the European Union. In the longer perspective of the future of Europe there are intriguing aspects to the motivation of these countries. Ten of these nations have decided (or in fairness are now free to decide) to change their allegiance from one free trade area, Concom and the Warsaw Pact, to another because of the fall of the Soviet empire and the demise of Yugoslavia. This type of volte-face has happened before in European history, and is just another example of the transitory nature of converging interests. (Did someone mention the balance of power?) But what will happen if Russia, also freed from the suffocating yoke of socialism, should overcome its present difficulties and once again emerge as a major power, but this time with democratic credibility? Russia certainly has all the natural resources, geographical position and skilled people (if their potential was released) to achieve such a renaissance. Would the ex-communist new nations be tempted to realign their allegiance to meet their new perceived interest?

Another issue that compounds the situation is the fact that *all* the new entrants are well behind the existing member states in their industrial, commercial and agricultural development. From the author's recent visits and teaching in some of these countries the enthusiasm of the young is exhilarating, but they have three generations of bureaucratic management styles to overcome. Their leaders of academia and business talk the new language of the market but their internal practices are archaic in the extreme and will not be changed easily. What will happen if they are unable or do not intend to change?

The EU has already paid a crippling price for the Common Agricultural Policy in central subsidies and costly food because of the inherent slowness of the French and Bavarian farmer to adapt to the market economy. Is this cancer at the heart of Europe to be intensified rather than treated with the accession of these new states?

The summits at Nice, and subsequently Thessalonica in June 2003, provided no answers and this 'sin of omission' may have serious long-term consequences. Certain policy reforms are vital to enlargement, but the most important of these issues, the CAP, was not discussed at all. The 'structural' and 'cohesion' funds intended for poorer states and regions should in all logic be largely diverted to the new nations. But these decisions were put off and some of those nations such as Spain and Ireland, who already have their snouts deep in this trough, have managed to use the six year budget terms to extend their allocation of these funds until 2013; long after the entry of most of the applicants. Where are the funds coming from to support the new nations, as so many of the existing nations were helped when they joined the EU?

In Chapter Two we noted that small nations tend to ally

themselves in a parasitic relationship with a larger nation or form clusters for their mutual strength and protection. Eleven of the new entrants are small nations and the possible scenarios of relationships within the future EU is intriguing and almost impossible to forecast. The only certainty is that the EU will be different and probably much more difficult to direct or manage. Initially they will be easily categorised as members of the 'dependent circle,' but the numbers then in that circle are likely to initiate the historic trends. Our simple circle system becomes more complex as more floating circles are introduced. For example, a number of small nations could see Germany as their natural pole, particularly as Germany is the most powerful single state in Europe. Poland is joining the EU on an equal basis with Spain and so is likely to find its place in the 'independent circle'. In turn that strong position could act as a centre for the Balkan states and even Belarus and Hungary. This cluster of states would represent a new Warsaw Pact but this time within the EU.

Clearly the multiplicity of small nations that will form the new European Union will add to the diversity of sovereign states and cultures that has made a real union of Europe into a single nation impossible in the past. What this means to Europe in the near future is one of the key issues in the next chapter.

Old quarrels; new opportunities

Since the Nice Treaty it has been natural to consider those nations involved, as part of the EU, but it must not be forgotten that, with the exception of East Germany, no single 'old communist' nation has joined the EU since the collapse of communism more than a decade ago. A large number of nations have been left in a vacuum without guaranteed open markets and with minimal support. Old enmities have been allowed to fester, and new attitudes have developed. A few have been encouraged to focus on future membership of the European Union.

In 1992, François Mitterrand, the then president of France, said that it would take 10 or 20 years for the countries of the former Warsaw Pact to be admitted to the European Union. His remark shocked those who had romantically assumed that those countries' courage in throwing off the communist yoke gave western Europe a moral obligation to integrate them rapidly. Now, more than a decade after the liberation, Mitterrand's judgement seems to have been correct. The blame lies not with the candidate countries but with EU member states, especially Germany.

The suspicions of EU foot dragging began in 1998 when Austria suggested that there should be a transitional period of between 10 and 20 years before Polish, Hungarian and Czech workers would be granted the same right of free circulation within the EU as other existing members.

A more ominous revival of the old enmities came with the proposal by Erika Steinback, a Christian Democrat deputy of the German Bundestag to make Polish and Czech entry conditional on Germans being given the right to resettle the areas from which they were expelled in 1945 (principally Silesia and the Sudetenland). And upon compensation being paid by Poland and the Czech Republic for their expropriation. This could not be dismissed as just the reaction of a pressure group when the then Chancellor Kohl confirmed that there were still open questions about property rights of expelled Germans. The Bavarian and other *Länder* demanding the return of 'cultural goods' taken from Germany after the Second World War exacerbated the situation. One item at issue was the Prussian Library now in the Polish city of Cracow.

Jerzy Buzek, the Polish Prime Minister reacted with fury

197

to these suggestions. When one considers the callous German rape of Poland and destruction of its cultural history during the War, it raises the spectre of new German demands for *Lebensraum.*

The Czech Republic experienced similar problems with Germany. Late in 1998, Milos Zeman, the Czech Prime Minister, criticised the presence of representatives of the German Sudeten Association in the steering committee of the German-Czech Forum for dialogue and called them 'right-wing radicals'. The German reaction was redolent of Adolf Hitler in the late 1930s. 'The Czechs must understand', thundered Theo Waigel, the German finance minister, 'that we and the Sudeten Germans will not allow ourselves to be treated in this manner'. Other German officials said that Zeman's remarks disqualified the Czech Republic from EU membership. The German ambassador to Prague said that the new Czech government had to learn how to speak as a representative of the state!

But both the Poles and the Czechs were also angry at being told by Brussels to end rules that prevent foreigners from purchasing land. They believe that their neighbours, the Germans in particular, will purchase great swathes of their countries. The Estonians, Hungarians and Slovenians have expressed similar fears. On a lower level the Czechs have reacted angrily to the threat to their specialist sausage, and national delicacy called the *utopence,* that Brussels considers unhygienic.

These are not isolated or trivial matters, but very little of this is reported in the UK press. It is almost as if we were back to the attitude of Neville Chamberlain's 'far away countries of which we know nothing'. Though the relations between these central European nations are nothing like as intensive or aggressive as they were in the 1930s it is worrying to hear the same sort of language being used.

The Helsinki summit decision to allow Turkey to begin

negotiations for entry to the EU, though not advanced at Nice, does open other new issues for the future of Europe. The discussion about Turkish entry has centred around her human rights record with her Kurdish minorities, and the occupation of territory in Cyprus, a country already accepted. Clearly the Turkish entry date will depend on progress in these areas, but should the Turks be admitted a new serious issue would emerge for the EU.

The enmity between Greece and Turkey over Cyprus will probably continue for a period, but the real issue is: does her admittance open the possibility of a major widening of the EU concept? The combination of Turkey and Cyprus turns the eastern corner of the Mediterranean. Turkey would be the first Moslem state to join the EU, and raises the question, of how long before the North African states are knocking on the door? As we noted earlier, most North African nations are orientated towards Europe rather than their southern African neighbours.

In other words the concept of widening is now widening far beyond the EU concept of even a few years ago.

Deepening

Wherever one stands in the spectrum of opinion on the EU, there can be little doubt that in recent years the opinion of the peoples in Europe has been steadily moving against any moves to further integration and deepening of the Union. It is easy to forget the close shaves national governments – even France – faced in ratifying the Maastricht Treaty. Since then opinion polls in every EU member state and most of the new entry countries have consistently provided clear evidence of a growing cynicism over the progress of the EU. The European parliamentary elections in Britain in 1999, and 2004, and then with even greater impact, national referenda in Denmark, Sweden and Ireland confirmed the trend.

In Britain there has always been a general apathy towards Europe, and the ideal of a European super state seemed remote to most people. In general they were content for the politicians to get on with it and argue the issues out amongst themselves. Then Brussels and British bureaucrats changed the mood. A series of annoying and often nonsensical 'interferences' from Commission directives such as the prosecution of a trader for daring to sell bananas by the pound rather than the kilo, gave credence to the sovereignty arguments. Continual strikes in the Channel ports and demonstrations on the roads of France, together with the French ban on British beef, added to growing anti-European sentiments in the United Kingdom.

Across the rest of Europe other issues took precedence. Some were born of old enmities and power struggles. In Austria, support for the EU fell from 75 per cent in 1994 to less than 30 per cent in 2000. A campaign, launched to pull Austria out of the European Union to 'save the country's sovereignty and money', achieved more than 200,000 signatures – more than double the number required to force a government debate and a possible referendum. One of the campaign leaders, Gabriele Waldyka of Action EU Exit, said 'We believe in the outlook of one Margaret Thatcher, who was sceptical of Europe. We share that view'.

In Germany the Chancellor Gerhard Schroeder may not wholly share the extreme Europhile arguments of his foreign minister Joschka Fischer. Schroeder is under considerable pressure from the *Länder*, his powerful regional governments, which are getting increasingly angry over what they see as power grabs from Brussels. The German bid for increased power, her increasing political confidence and the weakening of the Franco-German alliance are changing German opinion.

200

The summit at Nice made clear the burgeoning relationship between Schroeder and Blair and perhaps a new resistance to the euro club. That relationship was not overly damaged by the divergence of opinion over the Iraq war; Blair tends to blame Chirac wholly.

The Nice Conference, of course, emphasised how easily the states in the EU return to national interests when the kitchen heats up. The Dutch were rude about Belgians: Portuguese bad-mouthed the Spanish: Danes grumbled about Finns: Italians rubbished Greeks and everybody was nasty about the French. The concept of a United Europe, let alone a deepening union, is beginning to crumble.

In their present mood the British electorate would almost certainly vote No in a referendum to join the euro or ratify the new EU Constitution. They would also be against any other overt move towards greater integration or deepening of the Union. The politicians have taken note and have begun to hedge their bets or take strong Eurosceptic positions. This is not the environment for Europhile leadership and it is unlikely that any will be forthcoming.

It would be very unwise to see these trends as victory for the Eurosceptics or long-term defeat for the Europhiles. The public mood could change dramatically and relatively quickly in reaction to events. A serious rise in unemployment in the UK, blamed on the discrepancy between the value of the pound and the euro could totally reverse the attitude towards the referendum on the euro. A serious threat to investment in public services could reverse the whole trend towards the free market economy and make the more regulated economies of France and Germany seem attractive to Britain. The possibility of deeper integration has not disappeared.

There are a number of other areas that relate to the enlargement of the EU but they are also integral to the arguments over 'Community or Super State' and so will be

201

discussed in the next chapter. They include the Common Agricultural Policy reforms and the Charter of Fundamental Rights.

Chapter Eight

Community or Federation?

'No man has a right to fix the boundary of the march of a nation; no man has a right to say to his country – thus far shalt thou go and no further.'

Charles Stewart Parnell, 1846–1891

'The nations which have put mankind and posterity most in their debt have been small states – Israel, Athens, Florence, Elizabethan England.'

Dean Inge, 1860–1954

The reader will be in no doubt that this book is not in favour of Britain being part of a federal super state of Europe. That does not mean that it is wicked for Europhiles or even the euro club to believe that the people of Britain would be better served in the new world order by becoming a subsidiary part of a much larger new super state. Indeed it could be argued that it is a natural progression of political entity to meet the challenge of the global economy. After all, Britain, France and much more recently Germany and Italy are themselves the product of political mergers of what were once small but no less proud countries.

Equally this book is not making an extreme Eurosceptic argument that Britain must not surrender *any* sovereignty or should leave the Union. Every alliance is by definition a constriction on some national freedom of action. It would be only reasonable to expect that a large number of nations entering into a grand alliance for their collective security and economic advantage should make mutual reductions in their national sovereignty over many issues. The question is: when does that mutual sharing of power cross the line between being a sovereign nation or a subsidiary state?

In other words, a reasonable case can be made for either the federal super state or a community of sovereign independent nations. The crucial issue is that there should be a clear and democratic *choice* between the two objectives for each of the countries involved. It is of interest that in those nations that have given their people that clear and democratic choice, the people have voted against the Union. The people of Denmark, Sweden, Norway and Switzerland have different motivations, but have all rejected either the euro or membership of the EU in national referenda. However, the issue is not so much how they voted but that they had the choice.

The most dangerous elements of the European issue are that great nations are moving to irrevocable decisions on the future of their countries and of Europe as a whole without open debate and democratic choice. Even worse, since the Treaty of Rome and even more directly since the Treaty of Maastricht, Europe has been set on a course to federalism by subterfuge and often downright deceit. The purpose of this chapter is to examine the principal arguments of choice and to expose the subterfuge. We will also highlight some of the current issues that bring this debate to the fore.

The super state

The founders of the European movement were committed

to a European super state from the outset. They were all either elite functionaries or civil servants or frustrated politicians. They were frustrated by the pettiness and parochialism of the national politicians of their period. They made little or no allowance for the trauma of two World Wars. The politicians were anxious to put their 'utopia' into effect. However, they soon recognised that the 'narrow' politicians would find the concept of a federal Europe difficult to accept at that early stage. In this mood they eagerly accepted Monnet's concept of functional steps or gradualism to attain their ultimate objective.

From the Treaty of Rome until the Treaty of Maastricht, almost without demur (Margaret Thatcher excepted!) they relentlessly pursued their objective. In time the wider elite of the euro club and the Commission succeeded the original leaders of the European movement. As each functional step or directive seemed to encroach on the sovereign rights of individual nations, the idea of the super state was played down or denied. The Eurosceptics, who were becoming increasingly alarmed, were easily dismissed as antiquated traditionalists or nationalists and condemned to the periphery.

Then the creeping influence on the outpouring of Brussels' directives began to change public opinion in the member states. As the clamour increased, so national governments began to deny that there was any intention between the member countries to move towards a federal state. In Britain, the duplicity of the Heath and Wilson governments is now clear. The people of Britain and other member states were being consistently misled and deceived by their leaders.

The concept of the United States of Europe is reasonable, and, at first sight, would seem to mirror the development of the United States of America, the most powerful nation in the world. Earlier, in Chapter Three, we discussed some essential difference between these concepts, but it is not surprising that many in Europe would hanker after that vision. Most certainly, Joschka Fischer, Foreign Minister of Germany, the most powerful nation in the EU, and his Chancellor Gerhard Schroeder have publicly made clear that they envisage a Federal Europe.

In his inaugural address to the German parliament Schroeder spelled out his own attitude to Europe. 'Only through the future development of a political union, as well as a social and environmental union, will we succeed in forming a Europe that is close to its citizens'. Later he went on to say 'we do not want to replace or do away with national identities. However, or just because of this, a federal order in Europe seems the best guarantee for solidarity and progress', and 'with us in Germany the federal system has proven itself'. Since then Schroeder has openly called for a European Government.

Schroeder's Foreign Minister, Herr Fischer is the leader of the Green Party in the German coalition. He has a colourful past as a left-wing militant but has now developed into a leading figure on the European scene. The writer Stephen Shakespear relates an intriguing incident. 'I asked one of the German journalists how to spell Mr Fischer's name. He grinned: 'JOSCHKA – it's time you learned it, my friend'. Fischer has never made a secret out of the fact that he is a strong proponent of the federal super state.

In the American quarterly journal *New Perspectives* in 1997 an article by Herr Fischer entitled 'Europe's Choice: Full Unity or Old Balance of Power Wars' explained his views. In arguing for the euro and the transfer of sovereignty from the participating states to the European Central Bank, he stated 'For the first time ever, individual states will delegate a central piece of national sovereignty to a European institution'. He added 'This is where opponents and advocates of an integrated Europe will grow apart. *Anyone who refuses to accept the European Union as politically sovereign over member states cannot but refuse and decidedly fight this*

206

step into the common economic and monetary union'. And to make sure no one misunderstood his position he concluded: *'Once this has been achieved, the complete political integration of Europe, and thus the abolition of the sovereign states, can hardly be stopped. This is precisely what I consider to be an absolute necessity'*. (my italics)

Fischer is the modern inheritor of the mantle of Stresemann and Monnet. He argues the case for a federal Europe cogently and on every possible occasion. He writes that European integration is the result of the great European Wars between 1914 and 1945 and notes, 'that more accurately this war only ended with the end of the Cold War in 1989'. This European project of integration is thus 'the peaceful reaction of the most important Western European nations to the self-destruction of the continental balance of powers in the first half of the 20th century'. Fischer sees the challenge of the EU as *'either return to the European balance of powers system or European integration'*. Those with a sense of history might accept the choice and come down in favour of the former.

In a speech to the Belgian Parliament, Joschka Fischer repeated his approach to organising the EU he first raised in his USA article. 'The future political structure of a unified Europe will be based on a division of sovereignty between Europe and the individual nation states. This implies the necessity for closer institutional ties between the European national government and parliament'. He added that the *'Council of Ministers* consisting of delegates from the national governments and *not the Commission will become the permanent European government* which will take on the competencies of a sovereign executive. It will be controlled by a European legislature consisting of two chambers: a first chamber whose delegates will be directly elected by member states, the present European Parliament and a second chamber consisting of representatives of the national parliaments. The

207

latter will also be members of their national parliaments who would elect them'. (my italics)

Fischer is not alone amongst European politicians in arguing for more integration and the super state. Hans Tietmeyer, when governor of the German Bundesbank said of the EMU project: 'A European currency will lead to member states transferring their sovereignty over their financial and wages policy. It is an illusion to think that states can hold on to their autonomy over taxation'. Romano Prodi, then President of the Commission, has made clear his support for the integrated Europe and has argued vehemently against national vetoes. An earlier President of the Commission, Jacques Delors had his own European dreams and was the architect of the Maastricht Treaty, which provided the directives that made the greatest advances towards the super state. However, the national French situation is a little more complicated. Presidents François Mitterrand and Jacques Chirac at varying times argued strongly for greater integration. Of course Chirac in his address to the German Parliament called for the 'fast lane to greater integration' and made references to federalism. Yet it seems that the instant Chirac realised at Nice that the French might not be running the new super state he became a nationalist!

We have reached a stage in 2004 that whilst all the arguments about federalism and sovereignty have gone on, the step-by-step functional process of treaties has taken the EEC and the Common Market toward European Union. The EU has a Parliament, an executive, tax revenue, a common currency, an anthem, a flag, passports, a written constitution and possibly an army. As Edward Heathcoat Amory said 'It may not be so super, but if it is not now a state, it soon will be'.

Subterfuge

To envisage the establishment of a European super state

because of a history of disastrous conflict and so enable a unified Europe to meet the challenge of the global economy is a reasonable proposition. To believe that the same objectives are more likely to be achieved by an alliance of free nations retaining their independence and sovereignty is also a reasonable argument. One may agree or disagree with either proposition, but that is no reason to prevent the advocacy of the case. Indeed, open debate is more likely in the long term to find a workable solution that will receive democratic support.

The long debate over the future of Europe has unfortunately been neither open nor reasonable. From the outset the argument has been characterised by hyperbole, calumny and downright subterfuge. The Eurosceptics are often guilty of hyperbole over each new directive from Brussels. However, the Europhiles are the main offenders. To some extent this is because they are the proponents of a substantive change to the status quo and they recognise the inbuilt fear of change. Yet we should remember that subterfuge was the policy of Jean Monnet, the founder of the European movement. He devised the drip-by-drip approach of *functionalism* and declared, 'The destination will only reveal itself little by little'. We should also remember that the majority of the early leaders were functionaries or mandarins of the civil service who had never been subjected to democratic election. To many of them democracy was a nuisance, necessary or not. For these reasons the ultimate objective of the European super state had to be hidden from the democrats and electors. It has to be said that until recently their strategy of obfuscation and subterfuge has been successful.

In the light of the evidence it is hardly credible that most British Europhiles can still deny that there is any danger of the EU becoming a federal super state. Robin Cook (who as Foreign Secretary at the time knew what Fischer and other European politicians were saying) can cynically dismiss the fears of a super state as 'Eurosceptic myths that are betraying Britain's integrity'.

Since Britain joined the EEC in 1972 a succession of British politicians have misled Parliament and the people over the true purpose and destination of decisions and treaties over Europe. Sir Edward Heath (perhaps the most culpable), Sir Leon Brittan, Kenneth Clarke, Michael Heseltine, Neil Kinnock, Chris Patten, Tony Blair, Peter Mandelson and Robin Cook have all continuously treated Eurosceptics as scaremongers on this issue. If they really believe that the federal super state is not a viable result of recent treaties, why are they not making speeches denouncing the arguments of Fischer, Schroeder, Prodi and their like as totally unacceptable?

Earlier chapters have provided many examples of the Commission's acts of subterfuge in increasing its power and/or ensuring support for the pro-integration arguments. Another example of their pernicious agenda is the EU scheme to indoctrinate children. In 2000 the bureaucrats of Brussels put out a multi-million pound tender to recruit expert groups to study the EU's educational needs. The tender documents make clear that the Commission plans to introduce pro-European 'information' or as the then shadow foreign secretary Francis Maude called it, 'propaganda'. He also claimed that the Brussels move was 'the first step in the creation of a single EU curriculum'. Certainly the tender documents include a specific request to evaluate the 'European dimension in education, including analysis of the cultural, or socio-economic/political elements appropriate for inclusion in the curricula in both primary and secondary schools'.

This approach is not a new issue for Brussels. Since the Adonnio report, *A People's Europe*, set up under the Solemn Declaration on European Union signed at Stuttgart in June 1983, member states were expected to use schools to promote the benefits of EU membership. Since then British schools have been exposed to a relentless barrage of 'information' supplied by the Education Department, the Foreign Office and the Commission. In 1998 the Office for European Education (OFEE) supplied every school with a glossy information pack, *Partners in Europe*, including detailed guidance for teachers on how to build 'a European dimension into almost every subject and stage of the curriculum'. A glossy booklet, *Euroquest*, produced by the Commission told younger children how 'the EU continues to work to maintain peace and relieve suffering'. It showed them a 'EU passport that made it easier for you to go on holiday' and invited them to 'hum the European anthem'.

As the European media has reacted to public opinion it has tended to become much more critical of Brussels. This is particularly so of the British media which has a strong tradition of *lese-majeste* towards politicians. The European Commission is not used to and doesn't like this sort of criticism. In late 2000 Neil Kinnock, vice-President of the Commission attacked the British media for 'continually pumping out bilge which doesn't have a basis in fact in order to discredit the EU'. This followed press comment on a Brussels proposal to introduce the European passport as a replacement for national passports, which would entail the removal of the Royal crest that adorns the current British passport.

Admittedly the British press are no strangers to hyperbole but Neil Kinnock is not really in a position to be so sensitive, or to use media Euroscepticism as a whipping boy. The European Commission, in a way that is not possible under the British system, is a bureaucracy with the right to initiate legislation. Although un-elected it is therefore very powerful and funded by the taxpayer. As the *Daily Telegraph* pointed out: 'it should surely couch its public statement in the tones of careful sobriety, not with squeals of pain and bellows of rage'.

In a subsequent debate with Neil Kinnock about the anti-Europe bias in the media Charles Moore, the then editor of the *Daily Telegraph*, amusingly described the new important figure in all EU propaganda who is called Nobody. As in 'Nobody is suggesting...', we are told, and then the appropriate words are added. Usually Nobody is suggesting that we have a European super state or identical taxes or more power for Brussels. Mr Moore went on to observe that Nobody is a remarkably influential figure in Brussels, and that most of his suggestions, though not fully in place, are moving to fruition. A few months ago Nobody was suggesting that the Charter of Fundamental Rights would form the basis of an EU constitution. Nobody seems to get what he wants!

Charles Moore continued, 'Put simply, successive British governments have lied to the voters'. Both parties have again and again told the British public that what is at stake is not the creation of a European super state, or even a federal Europe, not the giving up of sovereignty or the dilution of the rights of the British parliament. The Single European Act (which too late now sticks in Margaret Thatcher's craw) was presented as the completion of the single market without explaining the very wide powers it took away from member states. The supporters of the two say again and again that entry will not affect our rights to set our own taxes and economic policy, when almost everyone on the continent believes that it will and, in most cases, should.

The fact that the press has changed its mind may annoy Mr Kinnock, but it is recognition of the growth of public discontent, which was not adequately reflected earlier. It is intriguing that it is the Commission's actions rather than the political debate that is awakening public opinion across Europe. All this stems from the peculiar position of the EU. In the Union there isn't exactly a government and there certainly isn't exactly an opposition. The process of making rules and laws in the EU is notoriously complicated and obscure, and it takes a great deal of journalistic digging to find out what has happened. In those circumstances most commentators depend heavily upon official sources.

Moore makes a powerful point in commenting on the lack of openness in the conduct of EU affairs when he says 'Incredibly, the proceedings of the Council of Europe, probably the most important in the whole set-up, takes place in private, and no one ever has a full, open account of what happens in them. The methods of 19th century diplomacy are being used to produce 21st century laws'.

Sovereign state

It is in the nature of things that arguments defending the existing system appear negative. At times in history when 'change is all about' resistance to mindless change is easy to categorise as old-fashioned, ignoring the obvious or demonstrating the 'evil forces of conservatism'. That is the low level of debate, which allows people or arguments to be labelled as fascist, racist or even Eurosceptic. In reality, political conservatism has never meant opposition to all change. In desiring to conserve what is good in the existing system, conservatives only oppose mindless or ill-considered change – or change for the sake of fashion. But the present generation hardly needs to be reminded that in Britain the need for radical change was first recognised and then implemented by the 'forces of conservatism'. Changes that are now in principle recognised and accepted by the opponents of conservatism.

Defence of the continuance of the sovereign state and the concept of a *Grand Alliance* of European nations is not a negative idea. It is a concept that recognises and welcomes, rather than wanting to eliminate, the unique and exciting diversity of attributes and cultures of the nations of Europe.

It is an idea that wants to keep alive and use these diversities for the greater good of the whole, an idea that rejects the functionalism of 'one shape fits all', and an idea that will have no truck with ignoring or subduing the initiative of its people. In short, a vision of the togetherness of free and equal peoples, in charge of their own destinies but in liberty committed to a 'Greater Europe'.

Increasingly the people of Europe are becoming aware of what is being done in their name. The democratic heart of Europe is stirring and beginning to influence political leaders. The much-maligned forces of conservatism are regaining their confidence. Francis Maude, former Conservative Shadow Foreign Secretary, while echoing the general call after the Treaty of Nice that 'integration has gone far enough', made a strong positive plea for a new Europe. 'We want a great move forward, with an enlarged EU at last embracing the whole family of European nations. That means a more flexible EU. Failed centralised policies, such as the common agricultural and fisheries policies, and the appalling EU aid programme, must be returned more and more to the nation states. For Britain, it means an end to the endless reinterpretation of the treaties to extend the EU's scope'.

He labelled the current arguments for greater integration as 'this outdated dogma' and he went on to say, 'In the era of globalisation, a modern Europe needs flexibility, democratic accountability and legitimacy. We need the nation today more than ever'. This is what the mainstream majority wants and, as we argued in Chapter Three it is what Europe and the world needs. Maude went on 'When a turning point in history is reached (he was referring to the Danish referendum) one never knows it at the time. But there is a real chance that, if Britain were to make the case for this modern multi-system EU, it could succeed'.

This is a forthright call for action in contrast to the slithering weasel-like contortions of the Europhiles and a

Commission acting by stealth to do what it knows the public would reject. As Mr Maude concluded 'Conservatives are the genuine Europeans – because they understand that, without serious reform the EU will fracture and die'.

Choice

Little Denmark has become the catalyst. The Danish rejection of the euro has forced every good European to stop and take stock. As Josef Joffe, the Danish politician quoted in *Time* magazine, explained, 'We don't know where we are going on this journey, but we have reached the end of a 50 year old road along which European integration was practised on the sly. The classic Monnet method was to Europeanise this or that economic sector on the half-hidden premise that each step would set up irresistible force toward ever more integration – all the way to the political realm. *And we don't like it*'.

That Dane has put succinctly much of the argument of this book. But if it were just Denmark, the EU could just shrug it off. But the Danes have articulated a malaise that stretches from Barcelona to Berlin. Where are we going and why? Having lost much of our autonomy, do we want to give up our sovereignty as well? Are we in this merely for the 'goodies', such as the freedom to trade and travel, or do we want to switch our national loyalty to Brussels?

The British and the other people of Europe, through their nations have three choices, namely:

- Continue on the present path and muddle through allowing a Europe of 'differing speeds'.
- Abandon the journey and withdraw from the European Union.
- Stop, take stock and really answer the question 'where

215

do we want to go and why?' Then have the courage to reform the EU and all its structures to meet the new purpose.

The first choice 'muddling through' is really the story of this book so far and the third choice 'a new purpose' is the main theme of Part Three – *A New Vision*. Withdrawal from the EU has never been the preferred option of the authors, though it has been tempting from time to time.

A particularly forceful proponent of withdrawal from the EU is Andrew Alexander, the former City Editor of the *Daily Mail*. He expressed the Eurosceptic view cogently in a stream of beautifully written articles that deserve careful consideration. He wrote that everything that happened at Nice merely served to underline our incompatibility with the structure and aims of the Union. He states, 'I say that our departure has become inevitable with some regret. Being against joining the Common Market in the first place is not the same thing as looking forward to our leaving, since the process will be drawn out and is sure to produce much ill-tempered bother here and abroad'.

Alexander dismissed the popular belief fed by EU enthusiasts with confusing statistics, that Britain is massively dependent economically on continental Europe and that leaving would risk millions of jobs. It simply isn't true. Sales of British exports to Europe comprise just 40 per cent of our total worldwide export of goods and services. But exports make up but a minor part of our total production on which jobs depend. Those to the EU account for little more than 10 per cent of our annual national output. Conversely the EU nations sell more to us than we do to them. We are the EU's biggest single export market, bigger even than the USA. The Continental nations cannot afford to lose their trade with Britain. In other words they need Britain perhaps more than Britain needs them.

Alexander argues that in any case there is no danger of our trade being 'cut off' as Europhiles claim. When we joined the Common Market tariffs between nations were very high. These days they are very low, averaging around 4 per cent and the World Trade Organisation is aiming to get them down to zero. With our trade balance we could insist on a free trade agreement such as Norway and Switzerland have with the EU.

By leaving the EU Britain would immediately free its industry (and much of its social life) from the creeping, cramping rules and regulations flowing from Brussels, a flow about to increase with new Brussels amendments to produce a uniform legal system. Furthermore, we would no longer be paying a net £5.5 billion a year to Brussels, most of which goes to finance the monstrous Common Agricultural Policy.

Andrew Alexander has developed in his articles the positive advantages to Britain of once again being free to make its own economic and political decision to its own advantage. He makes the case that the UK is now well placed to take advantage of the global economy because it has a larger network of diplomatic and trade relationships than any other independent nation within the EU.

He concluded that the fierce national debate about Europe would continue. But it will shift gradually and remorselessly from the terms on which we stay, to the terms on which we leave. In his view, hard facts will prevail over political nonsense.

For the undecided there are a number of other issues to be debated or resolved that could influence the final choice between the three options, namely:

- A unified legal system.
- The Human Rights Act.
- The Charter of Fundamental Rights.
- Budgeting

Unified Legal System

Until relatively recently the contentious legal issues in the EU were conflicts between national courts and the European Court of Justice (ECJ) in Luxembourg. The ECJ is often confused with the European Court of Human Rights in Strasbourg. However, the Court of Human Rights is an adjunct of the Council of Europe and has nothing to do with the EU. The ECJ is the highest court of the EU. Where community law conflicts with national law it outranks the domestic supreme court, for example superseding Parliament and the House of Lords as the ultimate legal authority in England and Scotland. There is no appeal against its rulings. It effectively makes law, through the constructive interpretation of the European Treaties, and, as a result, it increasingly challenges or strikes down national law. The ECJ is, therefore, central to any discussion of sovereignty.

Rodney Leach points out that those who value the principle of sovereignty are troubled less by the supremacy of Community Law, where it conflicts with national law, than by its continuous encroachment. It operates outside its principal function as the advancement of European integration, and is at odds with the British concept of the law as the last bastion of individual protection against over-mighty authority. He raises some powerful questions, which should be at the forefront in reforming the EU. Where would be the checks and balances if the ECJ were to exceed its lawful powers? Could it deprive a member state of its independence by setting aside an Act to repeal the terms of its accession to the EU? Given the reliance of English courts on precedent, the concern of British Eurosceptics is that the House of Lords might one day accept that Parliament's authority had ebbed away and become subordinate to that of the EU.

Concern over the powers of the European Court of Justice pales into insignificance compared with the plans of Brussels for a unified system of laws and jurisprudence across Europe. If successful, all the Europhile/Eurosceptic arguments over sovereignty will be obsolete. The single European nation-the super state would be in being.

What is proposed is the establishment of a EU criminal code, complete with a European Public Prosecutor. As a first step, national prosecution services will be combined into a unit known as 'Euroquest'. In due course a separate EU jurisdiction will be created covering such areas as drug trafficking, terrorism, money laundering and fraud. This is not a matter of national cooperation but a system in which petty crimes would be tried under national state laws, but serious offences would be dealt with under federal law.

The European Commission is also considering '*Corpus Juris*' proposals for a Continental-style 'inquisitorial' system, rather than the British 'accusatorial' system, for all member states. Of course at this stage the proposals are disguised as an approach to tackle large-scale international crime. Yet the document says 'For the purposes of investigation, prosecution, trial and execution of sentences the territory of Member States of the Union consists of a single legal area.'

Suspects could be held for up to nine months and transferred to the country where the crime took place without extradition proceedings. At the trial stage courts would consist of 'professional judges' who would be experts in certain fields and not ordinary jurors or lay magistrates as in Britain.

These new proposals would mark an end to the historic British courts system, which is envied and imitated across the world. It includes the principles of Habeas Corpus, which prevents defendants being held in jail without trial for long periods and the concept of trial by jury. *Corpus Juris* is still subject to veto but how much would survive in the usual compromises of EU summits?

Human Rights Act

The Human Rights Act of 1998 brought the European Convention on Human Rights into operation at the end of 2000 and enshrined its terms in English law: it had already been adopted in Scotland. Many senior judges and other lawyers are forecasting a flood of litigation as lawyers become more familiar with the Act. We can already see evidence of that trend. According to Lord McLusky, a senior Scottish judge, we are facing 'a field day for crackpots and a gold mine for lawyers'.

That may well be, but the Act has also provided a false field day for the Eurosceptics. A rash of headlines and inflammatory articles appeared in the press as for example, 'How Euro Law Will Change Your Life' in the *Sunday Times*, 'Euro Rights Panic' in the *Daily Telegraph* and 'Euro Law Time Bomb' in the *Daily Mail*. In other words 'those wicked men from Brussels are up to their tricks again'. This book is critical of the Commission and its usurpation of power but many of these stories are a travesty of truth.

First of all the entire Act itself is an initiative of the British government and was passed by the British Parliament. One might suggest that it was prepared in a rush to prove that the new government was 'properly European' but that is another argument. The second point, conveniently over-looked, is that the European Convention of Human Rights is a product of the Council of Europe and has nothing whatsoever to do with the Commission or the EU. Finally the European Convention was not drawn up by 'tricky foreigners', but by Sir Winston Churchill and the initial legal drafting was by Sir David Maxwell Fyfe, the chief British war crimes prosecutor at Nuremberg. Much of the Eurosceptic comment on the Act could be described as a spectacular own goal.

220

European Charter of Fundamental Rights

The Charter is a different matter to the Human Rights Act. To begin with, it is a child of the Commission and includes 52 individual citizens' rights. It has now become a major issue of contention between Europhiles and Eurosceptics.

At the initial launch, the British government at the summit in Biarritz in October 2000 endorsed the Charter. However, it was intended to include the Charter in the Treaty of Nice as legally binding text but this was rigorously resisted by the United Kingdom and Ireland. At Biarritz, Mr Blair's spokesman, Alastair Campbell, insisted that it was merely a 'non-contentious restatement of existing entitlement with no legal force'.

However, Brussels issued a document called 'Legal Nature of the Charter of Fundamental Rights', which said the European Court is 'highly unlikely to seek inspiration in the charter' – in other words to make legal judgments on its provisions. Other EU spokesmen have reiterated that it is intended that the Charter should 'in time' become mandatory. The Charter has become another 'functionary nibble' at the sovereignty of the British legal system.

Confusingly, the Charter runs parallel to the non-EU European Convention on Human Rights, but goes much further. It covers a host of new social and economic rights that fit uneasily with England's common law tradition. The European Commission describes the Charter as marking 'a turning point in the integration of Europe'. The French minister for Europe said 'it does not merely reaffirm existing rights, it enshrines many new ones'. Clearly our colleagues in Europe see the Charter in a different light to critics in Britain.

Eurosceptic commentators in the British press and parliament have indicated more than 20 articles out of the 52 that could prove contentious in the British legal system. Perhaps about 7 have serious issues for UK business and citizens. They are summarised below:

Article 3 includes *'the prohibition of the reproductive cloning of humans'*.
This issue has nothing to do with Europe, but now any decision taken by the UK government to permit cloning could be challenged in the European court.

Article 9 promises *'the right to marry and right to found a family'*.
This could be used by gay couples to insist on their right to marry and adopt children.

Article 11 provides *'a right to freedom of expression'*.
Under these rules it may be impossible for the British Board of Film Censors to operate. The same article also states that *'the freedom and pluralism of the media shall be respected'*. In the original draft this article was *'guaranteed'* but it has been changed to *'respected'*. Many senior Brussels politicians would like to limit the right of the media to criticise the EU and its officials.

Article 15 states that *'nationals of third countries who are authorised to work in Member States are entitled to working conditions equivalent to those of citizens of the European Union'*.
This could prevent Britain treating migrant workers differently from British nationals. It is feared that asylum seekers could take the Government to the European Court if they were not given the same social security benefits as everyone else, potentially undermining Britain's asylum policies. Britain has already experienced asylum seekers arguing for better homes.

Article 19 includes the statement *'no one may be extradited to a state where there is a serious risk that he would be subjected to the death penalty'*.

Extradition to the USA, where many states have the death penalty, would be illegal.

Article 21 prohibits '*discrimination on grounds of sex, race, culture, ethnic or social origin, religion or belief, political or other opinion, membership of a national minority, property, birth, disability, age or sexual orientation*'.
This allows any one of these minorities to go above UK law and apply to the European Court for a judgment.

Article 27 states '*workers must be guaranteed information and consultation*'.
Lawyers believe that the European Court could interpret this to mean that workers must be given seats on company boards and a say in management as is now the case in Germany.

Article 28 includes '*the right to take collective action, including strike action*'.
There is no limitation to this right, so the police, armed forces and others who are prohibited from going on strike could apply to the European Court to have the UK law overturned.

Article 31 states that '*every worker has the right to working conditions that respect his health, safety, dignity and a right to daily and weekly rest periods and to an annual period of paid leave*'.
The Charter article ignores the Working Time Directive that Britain has signed with two agreed caveats which are not repeated in the Charter – the right of the workers to work longer hours if they choose to so do and several other occupations which are excluded from the scope.

Article 32 states that '*the employment of children is prohibited. The minimum age of admission to employment may not be lower than the school leaving age*'.

This could end the traditional British teenage paper round and 'Saturday' jobs.

Article 34 promises *'a right to social security'*.
This could open a back door route for directives in areas that have been fiercely rejected by Britain.

Article 38 states that *'Union policies shall ensure a high level of consumer protection'*.
Again, this would open the door for the Commission to consider that it had a duty to interfere in anything that involved consumer protection.

Article 51 allows all these rights to be *'limited'* if necessary to *'meet objectives of general interest by the Union'*.
This is the great EU Catch 22. All of these rights are inviolate unless considered necessary by some EU bureaucrat. It sounds like a recipe for benevolent fascism by the euro club!

Budgeting

Each of the issues that we have discussed in this chapter are going to play a part in influencing the people of Britain in their attitude to the EU and the choice between community or super state. Experience over time will either strengthen or dissipate the innate fear that the UK is being taken over by Brussels. But there is one further issue that will make all the others pale into insignificance – the future budget of the EU.

The budget issue could bring the whole edifice crashing down like a pack of cards. For more than three decades the EU has put off reforming the Common Agricultural Policy and the whole budgetary process. At Nice, the member nations aimed to establish the rules for and the reforms of the EU in preparation for widening the EU by up to thirteen more states. Not one single hour was devoted to budget issues at Nice other than France, Portugal, Spain, Greece and Ireland ensuring that revision of their receipts from the EU was safe for another twelve years. Then again at Thessalonica it appeared at first sight that the CAP had been radically amended but closer scrutiny showed that the French and Bavarian farmers could again relax at the local bistro or beer hall.

Without radical reform of the CAP, other subsidies and the whole budgetary process, the existing nations of the EU will have great difficulty in surviving united. As the EU expands eastwards and into the Mediterranean the pressures will intensify and could split the EU.

Britain and now Germany have no intention of financing the expansion to the degree that the 'needy' nations may expect. Though Britain is still hanging on to her 'handbag' rebate, the real sticking point for her is a matter of principle about the efficacy of high subsidies. Germany, already the highest contributor to the EU, just cannot afford to increase its burden. The former East Germany has mammoth economic and social problems to the extent that the Bundestag President Wolfsons Thierse has said: 'The economic and social situation of eastern Germany is balanced precariously on the brink'. So far the west and primarily Germany has paid over £200 billion more to achieve parity. Germany cannot finance its Eastern *Länder* and the new entrants to the EU.

The detailed elements of the budgetary issue have been noted earlier and do not need repetition here. At this stage the Commission leaders may proclaim the importance of widening the EU in social and political terms as 'either the West stabilises the East or the East will destabilise the West'. There is some truth in that assertion but unless the EU members face up to reality and accept that the 'gravy train' is over, such statements are mere platitudes.

Europe has no hope of an independent role in the global economy unless she first puts her own house in order.

Chapter Nine

Global Role for Europe

'Forward, forward let us range,
Let the great world spin for ever
Down the ringing grooves of change.'

Alfred, Lord Tennyson, 1809–1892

'No nation was ever ruined by trade.'

Benjamin Franklin, 1706–1790

A supranational European state would clearly have a fundamentally different global role from that of a European Union or community of independent states. The federal super state would act as one nation on the giant chessboard of world power. On the other hand the community would seek consensus amongst the independent countries to achieve influence rather than power on the world stage. It is very difficult to see how a compromise can be engineered between these two visions of Europe.

The vision of the European super power competing directly with the United States of America for world leadership seems to be what spurs on so many Europhiles. It is clearly what motivates the French, but others in Europe share the same feelings, though perhaps not to the same obsessive level. Europhiles seem to hanker after European foreign ministers,

227

European ministers for trade, the environment, and every other trapping of the great power. Naturally they also want European armed forces (an army will never be enough, they will also need a navy and an airforce, in other words a complete '*Wehrmacht*'). In a paradoxical sense the Europhiles are the great reactionaries. Convinced that the smaller nation has little or no power in the present world, they can only achieve their old imperial dreams by forming a new superpower.

The Eurosceptic cannot accept the Europhile's view of the world or their nation's part in it for two main reasons. First, they see it as a profoundly defeatist attitude and consider the Europhile as incapable of facing the truth. The Eurosceptics have confidence in their nation and its people and are proud of the hard won independence it has achieved. They believe that their nation's sovereignty is worth defending. They may even recognise that in the new global economy, flexibility and speed of reaction are key elements at risk in the larger entity. Second, they are not convinced of the alternative. They intuitively recognise that the diversity of cultures implicit in 20 languages and many more dialects, and more than 100 political parties within the individual 15 nations, make it highly unlikely that a European super state would long endure.

Clearly these two widely-divergent concepts of the EU and its role in the wider world do not mix; there are no simple compromises to bridge the gap. Unfortunately that is precisely what the EU is trying to achieve and the results are there for all to see. A security alliance with the United States of America (NATO) that Europe is incapable of replacing, but tries to pretend does not exist. A projected army that is not really an army. A dubious foreign policy that was unable to prevent another European conflict from breaking out in Yugoslavia and a series of other overseas aid and world-wide initiatives that have supported corruption and chaos. Europe is not a nation (and should never be) and the EU should stop pretending that it is.

A new world

As Europe looks outward at the technology-driven global economy it is presented with a world that bears little relationship to the world existing at the time Britain joined the EEC in 1972. In less than thirty years the relative stability of a world managed by competition between two superpowers has been replaced by a much more dynamic, dangerous and changing world. Quite apart from the normal economic and political competition, other issues such as global terrorism, world debt, human and animal rights and the environment have taken on a political significance that crosses all boundaries.

This new world offers a mixture of real hope, frustration and fear for its citizens. Rapid economic growth in China, India and South East Asia has opened the door to prosperity for hundreds of millions of people. There will be political and economic setbacks, but generally the prospect for those people is one of hope. A slower but similar pattern is beginning to emerge in Latin America. Russia and her associates immediately to the east of Europe are still a frustrating conundrum with a massive potential. Africa is a continent in turmoil with little sign of joining the new world in any political or economic sense in the near future.

Relations with the United States

In surveying this new world the most pertinent fact for Europe is that there is only one actor on the world stage that can play a strategic role in all this confusion and that is the United States of America. The aftermath of the September 11 horrors has brought this fact into focus and at the forefront of strategic thinking for most nations. So, quite apart from historical associations, it behoves Europe to maintain good working relationships, if not partnership, with the USA. Yet attitudes to the USA are now another example of the diversity rather than the unity of Europe.

There is a strong undercurrent of anti-Americanism within the EU that has prevented a wholehearted relationship between the USA and the EU. Throughout the 20th century and most noticeably since the end of the Second World War, there has been a major shift of power from the European nations to the United States. Even today, despite the growing prosperity and influence of Europe, it still plays a subordinate role to the USA in world affairs. This has created a natural jealousy over the reversal of power roles, which is easily stirred by politicians and agitators. Added to this potent mixture is the cultural chauvinism so often evident in General de Gaulle. The hostile French attitude towards the vulgar Anglo-Saxons has been transferred from the English to the Americans along with the change in power status. In the late 18th and early 19th centuries France and the United States were great friends and allies united against the English. In those days there were also strong cultural ties based on the shared concept of '*liberté, égalité* and *fraternité*' as evidenced by the Statue of Liberty, a gift from the French people to the American people.

French dominance of the EU until very recently has resulted in her native attitudes being adopted by the EU in many areas. To some extent the establishment of a single European currency was based on the dream of the French 'elite functionaries' for a currency that could usurp the power of the dollar. Marginalisation of NATO and the development of the European Army are other examples of this French influence. In fairness, France has made little attempt to hide this contempt for an Atlantic alliance, as have others in Europe.

This EU attitude has created a dilemma for Britain. Of course there are elements of anti-American feeling in the UK, but Britain has remained a mid-Atlantic nation. More than the EU, Britain is intricately bound in alliance with the United States through shared defence and intelligence, and massive financial and business cross investment. Unlike the French, the British feel a cultural and political affinity with Americans only partly based on a shared language. This is sometimes paraphrased as the 'special relationship'. At times in the war against terrorism Tony Blair, has taken this relationship or alliance to an extraordinary level. This has clearly disconcerted other European leaders, and President Chirac in particular.

Tony Blair's vigorous support of President Bush over Iraq created political problems within his own Labour Party. However, that was tame compared with his battle with President Chirac and to a lesser extent Chancellor Schroeder. At the same time, the division at the centre of the EU caused reactions that support many of the arguments in this book. Spain and most of the new entrants to the EU strongly supported Blair and the USA though this support was reversed after the 2004 Spanish general election. Poland sent military forces to Iraq to join the coalition. This enraged Chirac, who thought that the new boys should sit quietly in the corner until spoken to. Overall it was difficult to avoid the conclusion that France and Germany were motivated by their own economic interests. But that is the issue: Europe is still a set of individual nations working in their own interests.

As Britain under successive governments has made cautious steps towards the 'centre of Europe', these attitudes have created a dichotomy of choice. There is a false choice between Europe and America that bedevils internal politics and our relations with our European colleagues. This is the reason why so many in the EU can label the British as 'not really European'. But as we are drawn closer to the core of Europe the choice becomes harder. But there is another choice. As Newt Gingrich pointed out in the article, quoted earlier, the US Congress would look favourably on a British application to associate with the North American Free Trade Agreement (NAFTA), the richest and most dynamic trading bloc in the world. This option does not entail the total loss of sovereignty implicit in full membership of the EU. There is no danger of Britain becoming the 51st State of the USA. Britain would be in a similar relationship to that which exists between the USA and Canada or Mexico.

The authors are not arguing that Britain must make that choice now and withdraw from the EU but to recognise that it can present its argument with enthusiasm within the EU councils, secure in the knowledge that it has another viable option. In this environment Britain would not only be supporting its own objectives but also fighting for a European Union that can face the world in *partnership* with the United States.

NATO and the European Army

Most EU members and aspirant nations are already partners in the North Atlantic Treaty Organisation. Even former members of its previous enemy the Warsaw Pact, have joined NATO. Despite her attitudes to America, France is a member of NATO, though with her own 'opt outs' that survive from the days of General de Gaulle. NATO is effectively driven by and militarily commanded by Americans, yet it has worked effectively and mostly without rancour for more than fifty years. It is a military alliance without parallel in the history of the world. Its success is based on the fact that all member nations retain their sovereignty and their armed forces retain

232

their identity. Above all, its members are united in its clearly defined purpose 'an attack against any signatory in Europe or North America shall be considered an attack against them all' which was invoked at the start of the anti-terrorist campaign. That is a focus on collective security for every European nation.

The NATO alliance is still vital to the external security of Europe. However much the EU plays with the idea of the 'rapid reaction force', or the European Army, there is no way that Europe alone can match the capability of NATO. Certainly the EU could develop a picturesque European Army that could parade up the Champs Elysees with tanks and big guns to take the salute of President Chirac and the applause of the French people. But it would not be an army that could defeat determined foes any more than a similar French army did in 1940. Even if the EU was prepared to match the USA's contribution to NATO, which it shows no inclination to do, with similar resources for a European Defence Force it still could not match NATO. It would take the EU decades and billions of euros to duplicate the industrial military complex and catch up with the technological experience and lead of the Americans. NATO should remain in being and be enthusiastically supported as a cornerstone of the European Union and its security. This British government should see this issue as the most important of their 'red lines' that they are not prepared to cross.

Putting aside the phobias of the French, there are reasons for the EU to consider the development of a 'rapid reaction force'. One can envisage many incidents around the borders of the EU and in the protection of its spheres of interest, fishing and oil rights that would not be perceived as a sufficient threat to involve the whole might of NATO. Indeed, for Europe to have this ability to react in its own interests could be considered as a strengthening of the NATO alliance in that it provides an easy possibility for limited response.

Understanding this situation would allow the EU to develop its own rapid reaction force as highly efficient armed forces with no temptations to *'folie des grandeurs'* in creating a global strategic force. Acceptance of this stance would enable the discussions between EU member nations to arrive at reasonable conclusions without some of the ridiculous hype that surrounds the decisions on the EU contribution to European and world security. The alternative could be an American return to isolation.

Finally, one test for Britain in the arguments over the rapid reaction force: would the UK still have the sovereign ability to launch a Falklands campaign? Britain was able to do that without fracturing its NATO alliance despite the fact that some members of NATO were against the British aims.

Foreign policy

Since the launch of the single currency within eleven of the EU member states, the euro club and the Commission have returned to political integration as the driving strategy towards the super state. Once again they employed a Machiavellian diversion in the centre while quietly rolling up the Eurosceptic flanks. The arguments over the European Army and the issues of enlargement were the bones thrown to the Eurosceptics to squabble over.

First, Chris Patten was appointed Commissioner for External Affairs. Patten was a British politician with relations with the two main political parties and a reputation as a reasonable Europhile. Then the respected Javier Solana, the former NATO Secretary General who led the alliance during the Kosovo war, was appointed as the EU High Representative to work closely with Patten. The Commission then began the drive to give Europe an effective military and defence policy. Meanwhile the European Parliament approved plans to create a fully-fledged foreign service with the intention of having its own embassies around the world and the establishment of an elite training academy.

The European Parliament also voted for a system of 'co-ordinated representation' in international bodies. If it eventually becomes EU policy that harmless-sounding phrase would mean that Britain would lose its individual seat on the United Nations Security Council as well as its vote on the boards of the International Monetary Fund and the World Bank. 'It's another building block in the construction of a European state,' said Geoffrey van Orden, the Conservative Party spokesman for foreign affairs in the European Parliament. He continued, 'What they are really advocating is a European Foreign Office run by a single European Foreign Minister'. Chris Patten diplomatically noted 'that the European Commission would pay close attention to the proposals in drawing up its own plans for reform of the EU diplomatic staff'.

Brussels has also drawn up plans for a 5,000-strong paramilitary police force able to carry out 'preventative and repressive actions' in support of global peacekeeping missions. This new body, which would be called The European Security and Intelligence Force, would be in addition to the 60,000 Rapid Reaction Force. Eurosceptics have said that is a deliberate challenge to the United Nations. In other words the European Union is working hard to become a leading player alongside the United States in policing the world. The new police force, like the 'European Army', will be under the control of a political and security committee, composed of ambassadors from each EU country. But the effective operational command will be in the hands of Javier Solana. A spokesman for Solana said that the police units would be modelled on such paramilitary forces as Spain's *Guardia Civil*, the Italian *Carabinieres*, and the French *Gendarmerie*. Critics noted that the description would fit

235

units that may eventually be used to suppress order within EU states. The Commission replied that 'detailed rules of engagement' have not yet been drawn up.

The impetus for the creation of the force was the perception of Britain, France and Germany that the UN failed to act effectively in preventing bloodshed in the Balkans. But the present plan is considerably more ambitious, calling on the EU to intervene on the world stage in co-operation with or instead of the UN or the USA. In other words, another source of potential conflict has been created.

All the declared plans to date envisage foreign policy being determined by the Council of Ministers with Britain retaining its veto. However, when the foreign service, the rapid reaction force and the police force are effectively controlled by the Commission the line between EU and individual nations becomes blurred; a major step toward the super state.

Foreign aid

The principle activity of the EU in a global role has been in aid to 'third world countries'. It has hardly covered itself in glory, and its aid programme has become a byword for bureaucratic delay, mixed objectives and inefficient implementation and auditing.

In June 2000 the British government persuaded the Council of Foreign Ministers to intervene and delay a Commission intention to begin payment of a £35 million aid package to Liberia despite strong opposition from the Development Commissioner Raoul Nielson. 'It can't be "business as usual with Liberia" when the President of Liberia is actively supporting rebels in the neighbouring state of Sierra Leone' said Keith Vaz, then Britain's Minister for Europe. This was a reasonably typical example of the insensitivity to international politics in administering the aid programme.

In many cases the EU was wrecking its own aid programme by creating competition between differing objectives of the EU. In an attempt to assist the poor farmers of the South West African state of Namibia, the EU promised a £2.5 million grant to build abattoirs there that would supply meat to the lucrative market of South Africa. By the time the money arrived more than a year late, Namibia's meat industry was being devastated by the competition from subsidised European beef that had been 'dumped' on the South African market at half the price of local beef.

The EU has also undermined its aid programme by demanding that recipient countries must practise free trade and open their markets to EU imports, and, of course, many of them will be heavily subsidised EU farm products. This was a particular facet of the negotiations in 1998 with the African, Caribbean and Pacific group of 71 countries. That could have disastrous consequences on the indigenous farmers. The only way to help those countries is with preferential aid to enable them to help themselves. Total free trade is inappropriate for vulnerable countries.

The EU's development policy has also been criticised for its inefficiency. The programme is understaffed and hidebound by procedures and paperwork that can delay projects for months or even years. The *Sunday Times* in May 1998 noted that one project required the applicants to go through 28 bureaucratic stages to qualify for aid. It also noted that, in Cameroon, £680 million worth of work on a dam and river-bridge was destroyed because the EU balked at spending £15,000 on a consultant's report to check whether the swampy ground was solid enough to support the scheme. When it was half-way built the dam broke and disappeared into the swamp together with a number of trucks.

While other international donors have long since shifted the emphasis of aid to health, education and training, the EU remains wedded to road building and other infrastructure

237

projects, often under heavy pressure from companies in member states pushing for a share of lucrative EU aid projects. It's curious how all the roads in eastern and southern Africa seem to be built by the Italians.

Chris Patten, the EU Commissioner for External Affairs, is addressing the problems associated with EU aid. But as Mr Graham Kelly, Head of the European Commission Overseas Inspectorate between 1995 and 1999, pointed out in a letter to *The Times* in May 2000, that while accepting the delays, over-centralisation and the sheer weight of bureaucracy, these faults of the Commission should be viewed in balance against two principal causes. 'The first has been the abject failure on the part of the member states (including Britain) to give the Commission the human resources necessary to implement its aid responsibilities efficiently. This has led to the centralisation in Brussels'. The second reason for the bureaucracy is the 'obligation of the Commission to balance the urgency for aid with the need to safeguard European tax payer's money'.

While accepting that the EU should take an interest in, and promote aid to, Third World countries it does not need to implement the process through the Commission-managed agencies of the EU. The aid programmes would be better administered by individual member nations who are experienced in delivering flexible, time conscious and politically or socially sensitive projects.

Immigration

The most crucial global issue facing the European Union and the majority of its member countries is immigration. Despite the fact that immigration is a very live and emotive issue in Britain and across Europe, few seem to understand the scale of the problem. If the EU nations continue their relatively modest present growth over the next 20 to 30 years they will face a tide of would-be immigrants that could exceed *120 million* people. To provide a sense of scale, that is twice the existing population of Great Britain.

Current social and political attitudes in most EU countries would consider such a vast human flood as a massive disaster to be resisted at any price. So the focus is on collaboration to prevent illegal immigration and a concern over porous borders as the EU is enlarged. On present classification, the vast majority of these immigrants would be illegal. Their motivation is to better the standard of living for themselves and their families. They are escaping poverty rather than persecution. The general reaction, particularly in Germany and Britain, is: Yes, we understand that, but we cannot afford the social turmoil involved in welcoming more immigrants, so we need policies to control immigration.

There also seems to be a view that this mass immigration of people is unique and partly a result of easy global travel. There may be a small element of increased mobility, but, to provide a sense of perspective, this movement of people is not unique. It is broadly similar to the influx of immigrants to the United States at the turn of the 19th and 20th centuries. The riposte of Europeans would be that there is no similarity between our present problem and those faced in the USA. America was a vast empty continent that desperately needed people, whilst Europe is already overcrowded.

But again that is an over simplification. Europe as a whole is not so overcrowded as we think, but more importantly, if the European economy is to grow it will desperately need a major influx of immigrants. Indeed, opening Europe's borders could be an act of self-interest. Europe's industries and services are in dire need of more manpower. A UN report in 2000 found that because of a bulge in the aged population and declining birth-rates, the EU by 2025 will require an influx of 35 million new adults to offset labour shortages and to support the failing pension systems of Europe. Those 35 million will not be found from the current classification of legal immigrants.

Yet the other side of the argument cannot be easily dismissed as racist, fascist or middle-class greed. A vast influx of immigrants from totally different cultures *does* create social tension and a pressure point on the provision of benefits, housing, transport and every service of our modern complex civilisation. It is not wicked to be concerned over this issue.

It is of interest that the French government prepared a report issued in July 2000 that argued that the EU states as whole should accept an influx of 75 million immigrants over the coming decades. The French government claimed that Europe must become a racially-hybrid society, absorbing the newcomers to rejuvenate the shrinking population. Again, based on a UN survey, it is claimed that the population of the EU will fall over the next half century from 730 million to 638 million – a drop of nearly 100 million. The then French Interior Minister Jean-Pierre Chevenement said 'a sensible and limited opening of borders would bring in 50–75 million immigrants'. Chevenement has issued a challenge to the political will and imagination of all the politicians involved in the European Union. Community or super state, the problem is essentially the same.

Economic prosperity

The primary role of the EU in the global market is to promote and support the efforts of its people and enterprises to achieve economic prosperity. Putting aside the economic issues discussed in Chapter Three, is there any area in the global economy in which Europe has the greatest opportunity for market leadership?

The answer to that question is a simple application of business analysis. Clearly the broad arena for success in the next few decades is the application of technology. So the questions to be asked are: First, does Europe have a unique or leading position in any of the key technologies? Secondly, do any specific corporations have an opportunity to take that advantage worldwide? Finally, what does the EU need to do to maximise that opportunity to win the global market?

There is a tendency in Europe to believe that the United States dominates most modern business technology. That is not the case, if only because the USA is so often the pioneer that she ends up with the wrong long-term answer. In recent decades the choice of lineage for TVs, the selection of operating codes for videos (PAL versus NTSC) and mobile phones cells for transmission prove the point. In contrast, the European weakness in supporting its original inventions often hands the technology leadership to America and sometimes Japan. But coming second and getting it right can sometimes provide the right long-term answer.

Advanced research in wireless technology, nano-technology, bio-technology, communications infrastructure, practical implementation and security software give Europe a vital edge in the booming medical, mobile and internet markets. In a dramatic reversal of fortunes, Europe is the leader in the mobile phone sector and the United States is playing catch-up. The EU must concentrate on removing national barriers, regulations and other impediments to the mergers and alliances that would allow Europe to dominate this market.

PART THREE

A NEW VISION

The authors present their own vision of the future. They are convinced that the present state of the Union is far from that vision, and fear that it is drifting onto the rocks. These chapters explain their commitment to evolution rather than revolution. Many of the issues that have bedevilled Europe for a thousand years are still present. They cannot be resolved in a few decades. These chapters therefore represent a pause for thought.

Chapter Ten

Purpose

'Wither is fled the visionary gleam?
Where is it now, the glory and the dream?'

William Wordsworth, 1770–1850

'Great minds have purposes; others have wishes.'

Washington Irving, 1783–1859

A new vision for Europe is of little purpose if it merely provides an alternative utopia that will still need to be implemented by stealth and subterfuge. Rather it should be a set of guiding practical principles for an evolving Europe. A vision that recognises that the nations and peoples of Europe are themselves evolving as the concept of a unified Europe grows.

This evolving Europe could be likened to a great orchestra preparing to produce that special sound that we all recognise as excellence. The leaders are orchestrating or conducting all the instrumental activities needed to ensure that unity, and make certain that all the players are not rushing madly off in all directions. But there is a complication. It is in the nature of politics (and indeed of life itself) that there is no *precise* score for the conductor to follow, because the score itself is evolving. This could be a recipe for bedlam.

As we observed in Part One, bedlam is too often the result of trying to come to terms with these disparate activities by providing an artificially precise score. We have compared the Platonic answer, or the scientific approach, to a carefully-prescribed score based on the principle of designing systems that minimise the variable effects of human behaviour. This book argues an alternative Aristotelian approach that recognises the organic and evolving nature of both people and nations. Clear principles are needed that complement and encourage the positive aspects of human behaviour in the environment. Rather than a prescribed score (for example the highly detailed European Constitution) the political orchestra requires a framework that can be shared by conductors and players alike, a framework of values, a clear focus on the essential, and an *overall sense of purpose*.

Vision exercises

Over recent decades it has become fashionable for company executives and leaders of other organisations to spend weekends at a country retreat to develop a vision or purpose statement. In the political environment of Britain there have been several examples of such deliberations. These include the Conservative Party vision of Selsdon Man and the New Labour conferences to eliminate the core values of the old Labour Party such as the public ownership of the commanding heights of the economy, and the control by the state of the means of distribution, exchange and production. In the European Union, what are defined as Treaties are similar exercises. The EU Convention and the new European Constitution appear to be a repetition of this emotive activity. There is an implied promise behind all the hectic activity that publication of the latest vision, or even directives, sets the Commission and the EU along the right road.

Unfortunately, for the majority of organisations including the EU, this activity has made little or no difference at all to their subsequent performance. Further, in the case of the EU, rather than providing a sense of unity, it is steadily developing an atmosphere of conflict. The proceedings of the Nice Treaty meeting and the silly 'I can stay awake longer than you – yahoo' overnight meeting were perfect examples of these exercises in mindless change.

There is ample evidence; much of it noted in this book, that *continuously* successful nations have strong value systems and a clear sense of purpose – or at least a sense of purpose that becomes clear at moments of crisis. The point is that these countries did not involve themselves in mechanistic exercises to create their modern vision and values. It would suit the theme of this book if their values evolved simply, but that's not true either. In most cases their values were forged in the white heat of continuous conflict. As a result, these value systems are not identical; they have evolved in different circumstances. In the case of the British, this evolutionary process has created an innate sense of what kind of country *they want to be.* We believe that this must be true of many other nations now within the EU or other applicant nations. Far from being wrong, extremist or old fashioned, these aspirations are real and their recognition is key to a successful collaborative union of European nations.

The argument poses the question as to whether it is possible to establish a set of binding values acceptable to all the peoples of Europe. The authors' reply is that, at this stage of the evolution of the EU, it is probably not, but that is not a negative rejection of the concept of European Union. It is recognition of the present reality.

To proceed with a massive widening of the Union, to continue projects and directives that ignore that reality, is the real negation of union. In other words the Europhiles could be on a course that could destroy the long-term

247

opportunity for a lasting European Union. The future values of the Union have thus become a priority for the immediate future.

In developing the values for the future of the Union none of the existing treaties should be considered as a constraint. Rather, the evidence outlined in this book would indicate that open lasting values would almost certainly entail modification and clarification of the previous treaties that have established the current status. The euro club functionalists are always looking for, and preparing, the next treaty on their path to a European super state. Those nations that are prepared to recognise the need for reflection and a new beginning should look to new treaties to put the Union on a new course, and remove the stumbling blocks to a real collaboration and union between the European states and their peoples.

The purpose of the EU

The long-drawn-out arguments over sovereignity and the real meaning of various treaties since the Treaty of Rome underline the need for a clear definition of the purpose of the Union. It could stop the endless debate over exactly what each treaty really meant over the issue of sovereignty.

Eurosceptics continually claim that the hidden purpose of the euro club and the Commission is to create a European super state. This concern is not surprising when the effect of each treaty is experienced, and when the foreign minister of the most powerful nation in the Union, Joschka Fischer, repeatedly calls for a speedier route to the super state. The Europhiles and successive British prime ministers have strongly denied that Britain is continually ceding fundamental sovereignty to the Union. They claim that there is no risk of Britain being absorbed into a European super state.

The agreement to a clear definition of purpose could refute Eurosceptic claims, support the contention of the Europhiles and release so much energy to the alliance that the Union could become a vision for all of its peoples.

To support the vision, the agreed definition could be proclaimed annually by the leaders of each member state to their peoples. This would maintain a continuous national focus on the purpose of the Union. A national day of 'Affirmation' to the purpose and values of the Union would, over time, develop a real sense of being citizens of Europe.

If it proves impossible to get agreement from the other members of Union to such a statement of purpose then all the fears of the 'extremist' Eurosceptics will be proven to have been valid. But at least Britain would then have a clear choice.

Definition of purpose

The proposed purpose is simple and unambiguous and is supported by operating principles and values.

The European Union is an alliance of sovereign nations collaborating to ensure their collective security and economic prosperity.

Fundamental operating principle: In all its operations the Union shall uphold the rule of law, liberty and democracy.

The meaning of the key words is spelled out below and expresses the proposed values of the Union.

Collective security

The original motivation of the founders of the European movement was to prevent a repetition of the First and Second

World Wars. As so many of the founders were French, it was more specifically motivated by a fear of Germany who had invaded France three times in seventy years. The aim of the founders was to integrate Germany with her neighbours thus making it impossible for another Reich to threaten European peace. This political objective was most easily progressed through the economic route. Additionally, economic collaboration was attractive to most European nations recovering from the devastating economic results of the Second World War. This mixed motivation lies at the root of the ambivalence on the paths to integration.

The nature of the EU alliance is an agreement not to wage war upon one another, and, in reality, a level of integration that would make it very difficult for war to break out between the member states. However, there is a dichotomy amongst the nations over collective security against external threats. Until relatively recently, the external threat came from the USSR and European security could only be achieved with the support of the USA. To co-ordinate and plan military defensive activities between the armed forces of the United States and the nations of Western Europe, including those committed to the Union, the North Atlantic Treaty Organisation (NATO) was established. This highly-successful alliance became the Western bulwark against the territorial ambitions of the Soviet Union.

NATO has proven to be the most successful and lasting military alliance between a wide diversity of nations that history has seen. The NATO nations were prepared to give up substantial control of their armed forces, involved in NATO activities, to American command for the common good. However, these armies always maintained their disparate identities and national sovereignty. France became irritated by the natural dominance of the Americans. Influenced perhaps by General de Gaulle's hatred of the Anglo-Saxons and a national inferiority complex, it withdrew from NATO.

Britain has been the strongest supporter of NATO amongst the Europeans, and is firmly against any diminution of its military influence in Europe.

Other European nations and substantial elements of the Commission want to see the establishment of a European armed force free from American involvement. France, as one might expect from her attitude to NATO, is the leader in this movement but she does have support from other nations and the euro club that see such a policy as another step to integration. There is a case for a European Rapid Reaction Force to handle situations outside the ambit of NATO, but it is vital for British interests that this Force is not allowed to become the European army.

To protect this situation the Rapid Reaction Force should be closely ring fenced and principles stated that clarify the situation and the rights of individual nations as follows:

The European Union recognises that:

- **The foreign and defence policies of the member states are inviolate and remain in their own sovereign domain.**
- **The alliance with the United States expressed through the North Atlantic Treaty Organisation is essential to the external security of the Union.**
- **The European Union will not develop an alternative grouping of armed forces without the agreement of NATO.**
- **The executive of the European Union shall not initiate diplomatic or military actions without the unanimous support of the Council for Foreign Affairs and Defence of the Union.**

Economic prosperity

Since the collapse of communism, the principal concern of the Union has been economic prosperity. This is even more true of the new and aspirant members of the EU. All these countries are united in accepting the concept that a vastly increased market, open to all members and freed from the restraints and barriers that inhibit free trading, must be to the benefit of all. Most reasonable people would also accept that to remove the disparate national restrictions to free trade would entail some diminution of sovereignty but would still enthuse about European union based on that concept.

To a large extent the richer nations within the EU have accepted that for the common good they should also contribute to a central fund to support depressed regions or industries within member states. Reluctantly some have agreed to share or sacrifice their natural geographical and historical advantages for the future of Europe as a whole. The Common Fisheries Policy is the best example of this difficult facet of Union. However, the extent or future boundaries of these areas are becoming an increasing source of conflict between member states. If the present course of the Union towards integration is continued this conflict between states will grow.

But within the Union there is a much more important and deeper conflict about its economic purpose. The core states of France and Germany, to some extent supported by Italy, believed that they were on course to creating a new Pan-European economy, which would rival the USA. Egged on by the euro club and the Commission, they are demanding the integration of national economies to achieve the Single European Economy. This core group has become increasingly frustrated with the 'delaying tactics' of those member states who want to retain control of their own economies. Their attitude is epitomised by their demand for a 'fast track for the *leading nations*'.

All the evidence discussed in Chapter Three should make it clear that the verdict is far from clear on the choice between a single European economy and a co-operative alliance between nations conducting their own economies. The argument between the long-term efficacy of the UK and US approach to managing an economy and the Franco-German approach has a long way to go. Though the authors believe that the UK approach is the most likely to succeed in the global economy, they accept that the case is not yet finally proven. Nevertheless, in the face of all this evidence it would be ludicrous for the Union at this stage to pursue a single European economy. By all means let France and Germany rush along the 'fast track' but EU principles must support the majority, even if it is 'wait and see'. The cost of taking the wrong route is too high.

To meet the arguments of this book the principles become clear.

The European Union recognises that:

- **All member states have the right to join the European Monetary Union with its own currency.**
- **All member states have the right to leave or not to join the European Monetary Union and under no circumstances are they to be penalised for remaining outside the EMU.**
- **All member states have the right to manage their own monetary and fiscal policies to the benefit of their own economies subject to specific agreements with the Union.**

The rule of law

The Union has a legal entity and has the right to enact laws

253

and directives under due process and subject to International Law. The European Court of Justice shall be the Supreme Court of the Union in respect to Union Laws. It shall not have power to alter or overrule the Laws and Courts of the individual Sovereign Nations unless those laws can be specifically shown to contradict EU Law.

- **All powers or responsibilities not specifically designated to the Union are to be exclusively reserved to the sovereign state.**

Liberty

The European Union recognises:

- **Citizens of the member states and provides dual citizenship of the Union.**
- **The liberty of all citizens to move freely and to reside and work within the territory of all member states.**
- **The right of free passage of all goods and services (subject to specific regulations) within the territory of all member states.**
- **That each member state has the right to exercise its own immigration laws for non-European citizens.**
- **That all citizens are equal under the law and that their fundamental human rights should be respected and protected.**
- **That member nations are sovereign states and shall be free to enter into Treaties and/or other alliances that do not conflict with their agreements with the Union.**
- **That it has no power to levy or control rates of taxation in member states.**

Democracy

The European Union is an alliance of democratic nations, but, as one might expect from the diversity of cultures, democracy in Europe takes many forms. There are substantial differences across Europe in the level of devolved power from the centre. For example the strength of the *Länder* in Germany makes it a truly federal state. In contrast, though Britain has made some major steps in devolving power in Wales and Scotland, most real power is still centred at Westminster. There are also substantial differences in the power of parliaments in relation to the executive, and the British electoral system is dramatically different from the system of proportional representation practised in most continental countries. Again, the French president exercises real power and is a direct head of state, whilst in many countries the president or monarch are only titular heads of state.

This is not the place to argue the merits or demerits of these different systems but simply to recognise that it would not be surprising if the democratic processes of the Union were to differ from the UK model. Indeed, there is no reason why they should, but if there is a reason (if Britain is to remain in the Union as an enthusiastic partner) then some principles of democracy should be stated and recognised by the Union as a framework for the future. The practical application of these principles should have a major impact on the organisation of the governance of the Union and will be developed in Chapter Eleven – *Structure*.

To ensure that the democratic ideal is strengthened the European Union recognises that:

- **The powers of the people shall be exercised through the parliamentary or democratic restraints on** national ministerial representatives and the nationally elected European Parliament.

- The powers of the Union are derived from and subject to the peoples of the sovereign states of the Union.
- The legislature and executive of the Union operate ONLY through the constitutional bodies of the member states.
- The executive (Commission) of the Union shall be accountable to the Council of Ministers and to the audit bodies and select committees of the European Parliament.

Conclusion

The principles and values noted are designed to establish a framework of guidelines for the political structure and decision-making processes of the Union. Their purpose is to ensure:

- The sovereign rights of member nations.
- The rights of citizens.
- That democratic processes are strengthened and protected.
- The accountability of the executive and the bureaucracy.
- The sense of ownership and commitment to the concept of the Union by the citizens of the Union.

All the statements and principles will need to be ratified by the Union as a whole. Many will clearly require some modification of earlier treaties, directives or laws previously enacted or agreed.

Chapter Eleven

Structure

'The houses that he makes last
Till doomsday.'

William Shakespeare, *Hamlet*

The political structure of a nation can shape its destiny.
Many nations, notably the United States and the United
Kingdom, but also Spain, Italy and France have fought civil
wars to establish or to defend aspects of their national culture.
In most cases these structures either evolved or were imposed
upon them by strong and charismatic leaders or 'movements'
that were really a coalition of strong individuals. The European
Union is no exception to this pattern.

The founders naturally determined the present structure
of the Union. Its present shape has not evolved smoothly
and it is not an accident. Monnet, Schuman and their associates
were powerful 'mandarins' or functionaries who had developed
a basic contempt for 'democratic interference'. They were
also French, which meant that at the moment of their greatest
influence they were supported by those politicians who had
become frustrated by the nihilism and internecine squabbles
of the democratic Fourth Republic. In other words the present
structure of the Union was designed by a powerful group
of idealists with a vision of a super state unrestrained by
democracy – a Europe run by an elite intelligentsia who do

not want to be constrained from their grand visions by an unthinking and generally uncaring majority.

It follows from our declaration of purpose that the present structure needs reforming to provide a much-enhanced democratic accountability. However, we have not fallen into the trap of chasing some Platonic utopia and devising a totally different structure to best suit our purpose. Rather, we propose major modifications to the current processes to enable free and democratic principles and values to survive and prosper. In that spirit we have not been seduced into exporting a Westminster model or any other 'perfect' system.

The proposed reforms are not designed to fit some Eurosceptic ideal of emasculating the Commission, or to create artificial barriers to the continued evolution of the European peoples as a whole. We have concentrated on the legislature and the executive, though we have noted some possibilities about the judiciary. In other words our proposals relate to the Council of Ministers, the Commission and the European Parliament. The strategic objectives of our proposals can be summarised as:

- **To emphasise the supremacy of the European Council and the Council of Ministers on strategic direction.**
- **To make the Commission more efficient and more accountable to democratic processes.**
- **To enhance the status and limitations to the power of the European Parliament.**
- **To ensure that the conduct of all three bodies conforms to ethical standards.**
- **To clarify the relationship between the European Parliament and national Parliaments.**
- **To ensure that the executive, the legislature and the judiciary are in balance.**

The Council of Ministers

The Council of Ministers is ostensibly the most powerful body of the EU, representing the interests of the member states and responsible for the major decisions of the Union. In reality the actual processes of the Council have had the effect of abdicating much of their power to the Commission and to the European Council.

With 25 member states the organisation of the Council of Ministers has become massive and unwieldy and the mind boggles at the impact of further enlargement. The Council is really a combination of 'specialist committees' relating to different subjects, including foreign affairs, economic affairs (Ecofin), agricultural affairs, education and the environment. Relevant ministers on each subject from each member state can attend Council Meetings. The Council is supported by three bureaucratic organisations: the Committee of Permanent Representatives (Coreper), the Council Secretariat and the Commission.

The Permanent Representatives or national representatives are intended to support their national negotiating positions, resolve differences with other states, and provide a constant flow of information back to their country's policy makers. The original intention was to provide a counterweight to the integrationist tendencies of the Commission. But as they get bogged down in hundreds of meetings, infrequently attended by Ministers, the result has been that controversial issues are either put aside for the twice yearly Summits of the European Council of leaders or disappear at earlier stages into the hands of the Commissioners, who are better operators than Coreper. The Commission representatives also attend every meeting.

The issues are confused by the presidency system. Each member state takes over Presidency of the Union for a period of six months. This encourages short-term thinking and adds to the bureaucratic log-jam.

The objectives of our proposed reforms are to bring a greater openness to the deliberations of the Council of Ministers and to reduce the load so that the Council can concentrate on the strategic issues, reduce bureaucracy and extend democratic accountability. We propose reform in the following areas:

- Openness
- Presidency of the Union
- Permanent Representatives
- Accountability

Openness

The Council of Ministers is too secretive and one of the few law-making bodies in the democratic arena that takes decisions behind closed doors. This creates an environment of mistrust and the manipulation of news. At the same time it keeps the electorate in member states in ignorance of what is supposed to be happening on their behalf:

- **That all Council Meetings shall be held in the open, minutes are to be taken and published. Consideration should be given to televising proceedings.**

Presidency of the Union

The Presidency of the Union rotates between member states on a six-monthly basis, and in so doing creates administrative problems of short-term thinking and lack of real continuity. This was intended as another sop to national sensibilities. From that point of view it was meaningless with 15 member states. With 28 states it would become laughable.

The palpable nonsense of this is recognised and has led to several proposals for change. These include restricting the rotation to the four major nations and electing a President of the Union for set electoral terms.

The European Union is a community of sovereign nations and not a nation in its own right. There is therefore no role for a President or Head of State. This is of course equally true of a national Presidency. We propose:

- **To eliminate the rotating Presidency. At the twice-yearly summit meeting of the European Council a Chairman of the Union could be elected to serve for a period of one year. There would be no rotational basis but a limitation of two successive years on the Chairman would eliminate pointless national competition. Council of Ministers' meetings would be held in Brussels.**
- **To eliminate the rotation of European Council Summits the Council could remain in Brussels, or it could decide venues elsewhere as desired.**

Permanent Representatives

The Council of Ministers is drowned in detail and rarely attended by senior national ministers. Sometimes a minister will attend a meeting and leave a mass of instructions and papers prepared by their national civil servants and then delegate action to the permanent representatives. The Council meetings are supposed to commit national governments but in most cases they will not leave themselves exposed. Either a false unanimity is organised (often by the Commission representative) or issues are referred to the Foreign Affairs Council or the European Council. In a majority of cases the Commission takes over the task of making decisions, regulations and directives.

It also must be said that the Permanent Representatives (and national appointees as Commissioners) have shown a tendency to 'go native' rather than acting as national representatives. Though the tendency was never expected to be so 'instant' as demonstrated by Commissioner Mandelson. This is understandable and rather than pretend it doesn't exist, we should accept for practical purposes that it does. On that basis, many of the 'fairness protocols' have little point and national pride does not have to be assuaged by false structures that could well have the opposite effect to the one intended.

The substantial increase in Qualified Majority Voting will provide the opportunity for more decisions in the various Councils of Ministers, but it doesn't really eliminate the current problems. An increasing amount of legislation is effectively handled by the Commission with little or no democratic accountability. That can be rationalised by specifically transferring more to the Commission but will require other reforms that make the Commission accountable.

The following proposals should ensure that the Council of Ministers concentrates its mind on strategic direction; that the bureaucracy is dramatically reduced, and that the democratic process is strengthened:

- **No meeting of the Council of Ministers will be valid unless a quorum of at least 75 per cent of the relevant Ministers of member states are in attendance.**
- **Two elected members of member state Parliaments shall be entitled to attend sessions of the Council, though not entitled to vote. One of the British members shall be a Chairman of an appropriate select committee.**

Accountability

There have been many suggestions to increase the democratic accountability of the Union. Some, including the British, favour ways for national government to increase their control of the Council, whilst others would integrate the Council of Ministers with the European Parliament, effectively becoming a second chamber.

Our proposals entail a much greater role for the European Parliament and in certain areas the Commission, and at the same time ensure a much greater democratic involvement in all bodies.

- **A representative of an appropriate Select Committee of the European Parliament will be entitled to take part in sessions of the Council of Ministers, though not to vote.**
- **A Senator of the European Parliament will be entitled to take part in sessions of the Council of Ministers, though not to vote.**
- **An elected member of a state Parliament other than a Minister will be entitled to attend sessions of the Council of Ministers, though not take part or vote. Britain should send as its member a Chairman of the appropriate select committee from either House of Parliament.**

The European Commission

The Commission is immensely powerful, acting as the supreme civil service and part government, a role its shares with the Council of Ministers. The Treaty of Rome gave it 'its own power of decision' and 'participation in the shaping of decisions and measures taken by the Council of Ministers and the European Parliament'. It initiates legislation, enforces areas such as the Common Agricultural and Common Fisheries Policies, and draws up the Community's budget. It also manages and dispenses the Community's external aid and internal structural funds.

As a bureaucracy it is much more effective than the Permanent Representatives of the Council of Ministers and has thus absorbed increasing power from the Council. Hiding behind the 'everything or nothing at all power of the Parliament – *en bloc*' it has almost created a situation where it can safely ignore much Parliamentary criticism. As a result the danger of the Commission's power is that it assumes a psychological supremacy within the Union.

It is not our intention to restrict the extent of the Commission's power. Indeed, in our desire to increase the strategic element of the Council of Ministers, new proposals will tend to increase that power. However, it is our intention to reduce the unnecessary trappings of power, reduce excessive national interference and vastly increase the Commission's accountability to the European Parliament.

We also believe that the Commission needs to increase its operational effectiveness as an organisation in its own right. This will tend to give more power to the Head of the Commission, improve and widen recruitment and allow more dynamic control of resources and the development of people.

Some of the reform proposals designed to impact the Commission are by their nature included under the reforms of the European Parliament.

Commissioners

Too much power has been accrued and misused by nationally appointed Commissioners. To add to the difficulties, the enlargement of the Union has created a national conflict over the entitlement to appoint Commissioners. In a sense the appointment of Commissioners is another 'functionary ploy' to create a 'national candy box' to divert focus from the real issues. Meanwhile the Commissioners act as a powerful and unaccountable mafia. This has to end. Our proposals are designed to that purpose:

- The system of the national appointment of Commissioners shall be eliminated.
- The Head of the Commission shall henceforward be entitled Director General of the Commission.
- The Director General of the Commission has the responsibility for the organisation. He/she will control the portfolio of departments to meet the needs of the Commission.
- Departmental heads will be appointed by the Director General of the Commission and will in turn be entitled 'Director General of...' as appropriate.
- The administrative head or Human Resources Director of the Commission will continue to be known as the Secretary General of the Commission. The Secretary General will be expected to give a much greater emphasis on the quality of the DGs and their development in a career path based on merit.

Commission Operations

The European Commission acts as both a civil service and an executive arm of the Union. In that role it must be free to operate most effectively under its own direction. At the same time it must never lose sight of the fact that its power and influence derives from the community of sovereign nations that make up the Union. The dilemma is how to enhance the democratic control of the bureaucracy of the Union without shackling it with an equally burdensome bureaucracy of democratic checks and balances. A very British method is to increase the democratic critique and control by national parliament. But in all practicability is it really reasonable when 28 parliaments of a myriad of structures and traditions are involved? In our view the member nations would be better served by concentrating their attention on the active democratic pressures of the

European Parliament acting as representatives of the sovereign national states.

For that reason the proposals to increase the democratic critique and control of the Commission are included in the reforms of the European Parliament. However, two proposals in this section will emphasise the pivotal position of the Commission:

- **The Director General of the Commission shall have full participatory involvement, short of voting, in the European Council.**
- **The appropriate Directors General of the relevant Commission responsibilities will have full participatory involvement, short of voting, in the sessions of the Council of Ministers.**
- **All directives, decisions or regulations of the Commission are subject to ratification by the European Parliament.**

The last proposal is intended to act as a brake on the outpouring of directives and regulations, and by definition will require the support of specialist staff to guide Parliamentary Committees.

European Parliament

The original purpose of the European Parliament was to provide democratic accountability and thus legitimacy to the processes of the EU. In other words the Parliament should have 'watched over and monitored' the natural transfer of agreed powers from the national elected governments to the executive power of Brussels. To a large extent it has failed in that purpose.

Currently the parliament is limited by the fact that it is

266

competing for authority with the Council of Ministers, national Parliaments and the Commission. In recent years it has gained ground but that is mainly due to a growing scepticism about the lack of democratic control of the Council and particularly of the Commission.

Despite this growth in influence, the European Parliament has always suffered by the minimal impact it has had on the electorates of member states. The turnouts at the national member elections for Members of the European Parliament (MEP) are laughably low and reflect the minimal respect of the average European citizens for the efficacy of its 'Parliament'.

This overall lack of respect for the Parliament derives in our view from three factors: its structure, its defined authority, and the way in which it conducts its affairs. Our proposed reforms are directed at those areas:

Structure

- **The European Parliament should consist of two chambers; an appointed Senate and an elected House of Members of Parliament.**
- **The government of each member state shall appoint four, three or two Senators, determined by population size. All appointed Senators are to be ratified by the relevant national parliament.**
- **The Members of the European Parliament shall be free to organise into political or national groupings as they may wish. However, no political or national grouping or their leaders will enjoy special privileges within the Parliament.**
- **The House of Members will elect a leader and a deputy leader of the European Parliament for the Parliamentary Term.**
- **The Deputy will chair a Committee of Selection.**

267

This committee will appoint all members of the Select Committees, who in turn will elect a Chairman. Committee membership shall be ratified by Parliament.

Authority

The influence of the European Parliament as the representatives of the people of the member states of the Union will be enhanced by the authority given to it by the Union to represent the democratic will and in general by the way its Members and the Parliament conducts itself. These proposals are directed at the delegated authority of the Union to the Parliament:

- **All directives, regulations and decisions of the Council of Ministers, the Commission and other agencies of the Union are to be ratified by both Houses of the European Parliament.**
- **The Senate is a delaying chamber only and can only reject directives, regulations and decisions once, but they cannot be re-tabled in less than six months.**
- **The Senate is empowered to ratify or reject the appointment of Judges to the European Court of Justice and Directors General of the Commission. In the case of rejection they can be over-ruled only by a Special Session of the House of Members of Parliament.**
- **Any member of the Commission and any other EU body can be directed by the Chairman of Joint Select Committees to give evidence to the appropriate Select Committees of the European Parliament.**
- **All reports of the Joint Select Committees are to be published and their recommendations must be replied to within a set period by the relevant Ministers of the Council or Directors General of the Commission.**

Operations

The operations of the European Parliament are grossly hindered by its seasonal locations shared between Strasbourg, Brussels and Luxembourg. This is another palpable nonsense stemming from national pride and French dominance in the early stages of the Union.

The image of the European Parliament is continuously diminished by the behaviour of some of its Members and the general conduct of its operations. Some are just inefficient; others are grossly unethical.

Our reform proposals are directed to improve both areas:

- **The Members of the European Parliament by a simple majority shall select the single permanent location of the European Parliament and its Secretariat.**
- **All votes of the Parliament shall be recorded individually and published in the proceedings.**
- **No decision of the Parliament shall be valid unless a quorum of ten per cent of the House of Members is present within the Parliament and voted in division.**
- **A Joint Select Committee of the European Parliament will prepare a Code of Conduct for all members in declaring interests and ethical behaviour. Their report will be ratified and/or amended by a majority of the House of Members. The Court of Auditors will be responsible to the Select Committee to monitor Members' behaviour in relation to the code.**

Conclusion

These proposals for the reform of the European Union are not presented as a definitive structure or a solution to all the ills of Europe. Rather they are proffered to provoke thought about the present condition of the Union and possible directions for reform. The argument of this book has been to demonstrate that the European Union is currently embarked on a route that will eventually destroy all its dreams and lead to ruin. But we also provide a message of hope. It is not too late, and we want the Union to succeed, but we do not believe that can happen without fundamental reform.

The Bilderberg Group

'The French and Italian statesmen seemed interested in the prospect of the encirclement of England on all seas and all countries facing her shores which, they were assured, would lead to British collapse if the (European Community) of which the Fuhrer had spoken was achieved.'

Gordon A. Craig, *Germany 1866 to 1945*

In researching this book we have found many references to the Bilderberg Group. At one extreme, commentators see the Group as a secret elite with connections to the occult conspiring to overthrow democracy to establish a 'new world order'. There are many degrees of opinion about the Bilderberg Group, but generally most outside commentators feel uncomfortable about the secrecy surrounding it and its apparent influence on the euro club and the road to a European super state.

A vociferous critic of the Bilderberg Group is the political economist Rodney Atkinson whose book, *Europe's Full Circle – Corporate Elites and the new Fascism*, identifies Bilderberg and other corporatist elites as the principal enemies of democracy and national sovereignty. In this book he draws many analogies between the objectives and statements of the Nazi ideologists of the 1930s and their aims of creating

271

a European State under German dominance. The authors, whilst not agreeing with Atkinson's whole thesis, consider that he has raised many questions about the activities of the Bilderberg Group that need answering.

The Bilderberg Group was founded by Dr Joseph Retinger, a Polish émigré to Britain, after the German invasion in 1939. He was active with the representatives of the émigré governments in the UK during the Second World War and seemed to enjoy 'behind the scenes' organisation of opinion. After the War he helped found the European movement and, financed by the CIA, set up the 'American Committee on a United Europe'. In 1954 he approached Prince Bernhard of the Netherlands to take the lead in forming the Group and issuing the first invitations. The Group was named after the hotel in the town of Oosterbeek in the Netherlands that was the site of their first meeting in May 1954.

Retinger was helped and financed by Paul Rykens, then the Chairman of Unilever. Senior executives of Unilever have since been regular attendees at the annual Bilderberg Conferences. Each of these meetings takes over a major hotel where up to 150 guests are surrounded by security guards to ensure privacy and secrecy. This raises the question: who finances the Bilderberg Group? The annual conference alone must be a very expensive operation, as we assume that most of all those invited have their travelling and living expenses paid for by the Group.

The choice of Prince Bernhard was of particular interest. Before marrying the future Queen Beatrix of the Netherlands, he was the German 'Prinz zur Lippe Bresterfield'. He was a member of the Nazi Party and an honorary member of the SS from 1933 to 1937. He only resigned from the Party the day after his marriage. He later resigned from the Bilderberg Group in 1976 after it was revealed by a Dutch Government Commission that he had accepted a bribe of $1 million from the Lockheed Corporation.

In more recent years Lord Carrington (former British Foreign Secretary, former Secretary General of NATO and Chairman of Christies International PLC) has chaired the Bilderberg Conferences. Other regular attendees have included Denis Healey, Labour Chancellor of the Exchequer 1974–79; Eric Roll, Chairman of the Warburg Group; Martin Taylor, former chief executive of Courtaulds Textiles and chief executive of Barclays Bank; and Edward Heath, former British Prime Minister. Rodney Atkinson noted that not one of them mention the Bilderberg Group in their *Who's Who* biographies.

It would be invidious to cast any aspersions on those attending Bilderberg Conferences or to implicate them in any form of deliberate conspiracy. Elected politicians and political leaders rarely comprise as much as 20 per cent of the attendees. The majority are corporate leaders, elite functionaries (known in Britain as the Mandarins of the Civil Service) or financiers. Many of those invited have never returned for a second conference, including Margaret Thatcher, who later noted 'It is an honour to be criticised by the Bilderberg Group'. Nevertheless, the leaders of the Group are networkers and hope to influence leaders to support their objectives.

But is the Bilderberg Group a conspiracy? It certainly has influence and is a powerful lobby group, but that is not necessarily a conspiracy. The problem with the Bilderberg Group is twofold:

- It operates at the very highest level of major corporations, financiers, EU functionaries and political leaders.
- It is surrounded by obsessive secrecy.

The authors believe that these two facts alone are a matter for concern. The history of Europe has been bedevilled by the activities and machinations of secret organisations organised by some form of elite who believe that they have the right to determine events. They range from extreme elements of the Roman Catholic Church to Freemasonry. In Britain the latter is fairly harmless but still raises some concern over its secrecy. At times on the continent it has certainly exercised conspiratorial power.

It really is not good enough to explain away the secrecy as a means of ensuring privacy from constant demands from the media for access. Many press barons and other media leaders have attended Bilderberg meetings but very few working journalists. Despite the high level meetings there has been minimal press comment over the years. Some journalists have endured harsh treatment from the security personnel at conferences. Even more strangely, the Bilderberg security staff seem to be supported by national security and local police. This does not easily fit in too well with an open democratic society.

Retinger's friend and biographer, John Pomian, quotes the Hungarian diplomat Paul de Auer as saying, 'Monsieur, in politics those are important which important people think are important'. By this simple rule the Bilderberg Group is certainly important.

Eurosceptics are naturally concerned about a group of influential corporate leaders and EU functionaries who are meeting in secret to discuss a future 'New Order' for Europe. It is also a natural concern for reasonable men and women who are dedicated to democracy.

Bibliography

Thousands of books have been written about European Union. The following selection includes books that have references in our text and others that the authors have found interesting, and sometimes helpful.

Atkinson, Rodney, *Europe's Full Circle*, Compuprint Publishing, Newcastle upon Tyne, 1996.

Bagehot, Walter, *The English Constitution*, Fontana, London, 1966.

Barham, Kevin and Rassam, Clive, *Shaping the Corporate Future*, Unwin Hyman, London, 1989.

Body, Sir Richard, *Europe of Many Circles*, New European Publications, London, 1990.

Booker, Christopher and North, Richard, *The Castle of Lies – Why Britain Must Get Out of Europe*, Gerald Duckworth Ltd., London, 1996.

Borkin, Joseph, *The Crime and Punishment of I. G. Farben*, Barnes and Noble, New York, 1978.

Bower, Tom, *Blind Eye to Murder*, Andre Deutsch Limited, London, 1981.

Brittan, Leon, *A Diet of Brussels*, Little Brown & Company, London, 2000.

Carrington, Lord, *Reflect on Things Past*, William Collins Sons & Co., London, 1998.

Clutterbuck, David and Cranier, Stuart, *The Decline and*

Rise of British Industry, Mercury Books, London, 1988.

Condel, Bill and Robins, Lynton, *Contemporary British Politics*, Macmillan Education Ltd., 1980.

Connolly, Bernard, *The Rotten Heart of Europe*, Faber and Faber Limited, London, 1995.

Conservative Central Office, *Campaign Guides*, 1989, 1994 and 1997.

Couteaux, Paul-Marie, *Europe's Road to War*, June Press, London, 1997.

Covey, John, *The Faber Book of Utopias*, Faber and Faber Limited, London, 1999.

Cromwell, John, *Hitler's Pope*, Penguin, London, 1999.

Davies, Norman, *Europe – A History*, Oxford University Press, Oxford, 1996.

Drake, Norman, *New Europe*, Hodder & Stoughton, London, 1994.

Dudley, James W., *Strategies for the Single Market*, Guild Publishing, London, 1989.

Duff, Andrew, *Understanding the Euro*, Federal Trust, London, 1998.

Economist, The, Various issues from 2000 to 2004.

Freedland, Jonathan, *Bring Home the Revolution*, Fourth Estate Limited, London, 1998.

Galbraith, John Kenneth, *The Anatomy of Power*, Houghton Mifflin Company, Boston, 1989.

Gibbs, Phillip, *Doing Business in the European Community*, Kogan Page Ltd., London, 1990.

Goldhagen, Daniel Jonah, *Hitler's Willing Executioners*, Little, Brown and Company, London, 1989.

Healey, Denis, *The Time of My Life*, Penguin, London, 1990.

Heseltine, Michael, *The Challenge of Europe*, Weidenfeld & Nicolson, London, 1989.

Hutchinson, *Directory of World History*, Helicon Publishing Ltd., London, 1997.

Johnson, Paul, *A History of the American People*, Weidenfeld & Nicolson, London, 1997.

Jones, Alun and Budd, Stanley, *The European Community*, Kogan Page Ltd., London, 1987.

Kavanagh, Dennis and Seldon, Anthony, *The Thatcher Effect – a decade of change*, Oxford University Press, Oxford, 1989.

Kay, F. George, *The British*, Gordon City Press, London, 1969.

Kennedy, Paul, *The Rise and Fall of the Great Powers*, Vintage Books, London, 1989.

Killanin, Lord Michael, *Four Days*, William Heinemann, London, 1998.

Klemperer, Victor, *I Shall Bear Witness*, Weidenfeld & Nicolson, London, 1998.

Lamont, Norman, *Sovereign Britain*, Duckworth, London, 1995.

Laughland, John, *The Tainted Source – the undemocratic origins of the European Idea*, Warner Books, London, 1998.

Leach, Rodney, *Europe – a concise encyclopedia*, Profile Books Ltd., London, 1998.

Macdonald, John, *Calling a Halt to Mindless Change*, Amacom, New York, 1998.

Macmillan, Harold, *Winds of Change*, Macmillan & Co. Ltd., 1966.

Major, John, *The Autobiography*, HarperCollins, London, 1999.

McRae, Hamish, *The World in 2020*, HarperCollins, London, 1995.

Neil, Andrew, *Full Disclosure*, Macmillan, London, 1996.

Norton, Philip, *The Constitution in Flux*, Basil Blackwell Ltd., London, 1989.

Newhouse, John, *Europe Adrift*, Pantheon Books, New York, 1997.

Owen, Geoffrey, *From Empire to Europe*, HarperCollins, London, 1999.

P.M.S. Publications, *Parliamentary Companions*, Padnell, London, 2000–2002.

Pond, Elizabeth, *The Rebirth of Europe*, Brooking Institute Press, Washington, 1999.

Rawlinson, Peter, *A Price Too High*, Weidenfeld & Nicolson Ltd, London, 1989.

Redwood, John, *The Death of Britain*, Macmillan Press Ltd., London, 1999.

Reitzel, William, *United States Foreign Policy 1945–1955*, The Brookings Institute, Washington, 1956.

Roney, Alex and Budd, Stanley, *The European Union*, Kogan Page Limited, London, 1987.

Roney, Alex, *EC/EU Fact Book*, Kogan Page Limited, London, 1990.

Roth, Andrew, *Can Parliament Decide About Europe or Anything*, Macdonald, London, 1971.

Schaetzel, J. Robert, *The Unhinged Alliance – America and the European Community*, Harper & Row, New York, 1975.

Seldon, Anthony, *Major*, Orion Publishing Group Ltd., 1997.

Servan-Schreiber, J.J., *The American Challenge*, Avon Books, New York, 1968.

Smith, David, *Will Europe Work?*, Profile Books, London, 1999.

Smith, Gordon, *Politics in Western Europe*, Heinemann Educational Books, London, 1972.

Stevens, Robert, *About Europe*, The Bluebell Press, London, 1997.

Thatcher, Margaret, *The Downing Street Years*, HarperCollins, London, 2002.

Thatcher, Margaret, *Statecraft*, HarperCollins, London, 2002.

Theiner and Campbell, *Encylopedia of World Politics*, Faber and Faber, London, 1950.

The Times, Guide to the European Parliament, 1984.

Urwin, D.W., *Western Europe Since 1945*, Longman, London, 1984.

Weidenfeld, Werner and Wessels, Wolfgang, *Europe from A–Z*, European Commission, Brussels, 1996.

Williams, Maria and Pearce, Dave, *European Studies*, Hodder & Stoughton, London, 1998.

Young, Hugo, *This Blessed Plot*, Macmillan, London, 1998.

Index

282

283

287

289

290

291

293

World Trade Organisation 217
World War I 10
World War II 10, 19
  French collaboration with the
    Gestapo 81